GULF WOMEN'S LIVES

GULF WOMEN'S LIVES

Voice, Space, Place

**edited by Emanuela Buscemi,
Shahd Alshammari and Ildiko Kaposi**

UNIVERSITY
of
EXETER
PRESS

First published in 2024 by
University of Exeter Press
Reed Hall, Streatham Drive
Exeter EX4 4QR, UK

www.exeterpress.co.uk

Copyright © 2024 selection and editorial matter, Emanuela Buscemi, Shahd Alshammari and Ildiko Kaposi; individual chapters, the contributors.

The right of all contributors to be identified as authors of this work has been asserted by them in accordance with the Copyright, Designs and Patents Act 1988.

With the exceptions of Chapters 5 and 9, all rights reserved. Apart from short excerpts for use in research or for reviews, no part of this document may be printed or reproduced, stored in a retrieval system, or transmitted in any form or by any means, electronic, mechanical, photocopying, recording, now known or hereafter invented or otherwise without prior permission from the publisher.

Chapters 5 and 9 are licensed under the terms of the Creative Commons Attribution 4.0 International (CC BY-NC-ND 4.0) licence (http://creativecommons.org/licenses/by/4.0/), which permits use, sharing, adaptation, distribution, and reproduction in any medium or format, provided you give appropriate credit to the original author(s) and source, link to the Creative Commons licence, and indicate any modifications.

Any third-party material in Chapters 5 and 9 is not covered by the Creative Commons licence. Details of the copyright ownership and permitted use of third-party material are given in the image (or extract) captions. If you would like to reuse any third-party material, you will need to obtain permission directly from the copyright holder.

British Library Cataloguing in Publication Data
A catalogue record for this book is available from the British Library

https://doi.org/10.47788/OIJE8138

ISBN 978-1-80413-108-4 Hardback
ISBN 978-1-80413-109-1 ePub
ISBN 978-1-80413-107-7 PDF

Cover image: Thuraya Al Baqsami, *Waiting*, 1987. Courtesy of the Barjeel Art Foundation.

Typeset in Adobe Caslon Pro by S4Carlisle Publishing Services, Chennai, India

Contents

Contributor biographies	vii
Editors' acknowledgements	x

Introduction: Revisiting Women in the Gulf	1
Emanuela Buscemi, Shahd Alshammari, and Ildiko Kaposi	

PART I: VOICES   19

1   From Stigma to Speech: An Autoethnography of Bedouin
Culture, Writing and Illness   21
Shahd Alshammari

2   Women Talking Back: In Conversation with *Sekka* Magazine's
'Managing Storyteller' Sharifah Alhinai   38
Ildiko Kaposi

3   Bodies on the Margins: Nonconforming Subjectivities in Gulf
Women's Literature   54
Emanuela Buscemi

GULF WOMEN'S LIVES

PART II: SPACES   73

4   Unmasking Patriarchy: Emirati Women Journalists Challenging
     Newsroom Norms in Pursuit of Equality   75
     Noura Al Obeidli

5   A Critical Analysis of Women's Petitions and Gender Reform
     in Saudi Arabia   95
     Nora Jaber

6   Divorce: The Narratives of Qatari Women   114
     Maryam Al-Muhanadi

PART III: PLACES   131

7   Female Socialization in the Omani Oases and the Impacts
     of Modernization on Women's Identity after 1970   133
     Aminah Khan

8   Women's Narratives and (Im)mobilities in English:
     Modern Literature from the Arab Gulf   154
     Alice Königstetter

9   Palestinian Women in the Gulf: Gender, Sexuality
     and Alienation in Selma Dabbagh's Fiction   172
     Nadeen Dakkak

     Index   190

Editors and contributors

Editors

Emanuela Buscemi is an interdisciplinary scholar in the social sciences based at Zayed University (UAE). Her research focuses on social movements and resistance, gender politics, performance, memory, and belonging in the Arabian Gulf and Latin America. She is currently completing the manuscript for a book on Mexican youth feminist activism against gender-based violence to be published by Brill.

Dr Shahd Alshammari teaches literature at Gulf University for Science and Technology. Her research areas include illness narratives, disability studies, and autoethnography. She is the author of *Head Above Water: Reflections on Illness* (Neem Tree Press, London; Feminist Press, New York).

Ildiko Kaposi is a social scientist whose work focuses on issues of democracy from the perspective of media and communication. She holds a PhD in political science from Central European University, Budapest, and has studied the roles of the press and internet in fostering participation in emerging or transitioning democracies in post-communist Europe and the Middle East. Employing mainly qualitative methods, she specialises in in-depth explorations of the intersections of democratic principles and their interpretations in specific social, legal, political, and cultural contexts. She is currently affiliated with the Department of Communication at Budapest Business University (BGE).

Contributors

Maryam Al-Muhanadi holds an MA in Women, Society and Development from Hamad Bin Khalifa University and a BA in English Literature and Linguistics from Qatar University. Her research interests include Qatari Law, domestic/intimate-partner violence, divorce, and guardianship/custody. Maryam is dedicated to bringing about social justice through her research and writing, which is grounded on feminist methodology—most notably, the lived experiences of women.

Noura Al Obeidli is a Research Fellow at the Humanities Fellowship Program for the Study of the Arab World at New York University Abu Dhabi (NYUAD). Her work in the field of feminist media studies began at the University of Westminster, where she defended her doctoral dissertation in April 2020. As a fellow at NYUAD, she will expand her research by focusing primarily on the impact of tribalism on Emirati women's quest to develop identity through self-expression.

Nadeen Dakkak is Lecturer in World and Postcolonial Literatures at the University of Exeter. She was IASH-Alwaleed Postdoctoral Fellow at the University of Edinburgh in 2021–2022 and completed her PhD in English and Comparative Literary Studies at the University of Warwick. Her research examines literary and cultural works on migration in the Gulf.

Nora Jaber is a socio-legal scholar. Her research lies at the intersection of Public International Law and Middle East Studies. It mainly focuses on the role and limitations of international human rights law in promoting gender justice in non-Western contexts, with a focus on Arab and Islamic contexts. Nora's research captures and centres non-Western and non-liberal rights frameworks and epistemologies that are largely overlooked in legal scholarship and practice. She is a Lecturer in law and an affiliate of the Institute of Arab and Islamic Studies at the University of Exeter.

Aminah Khan is an affiliate postgraduate student at the University of Nizwa. She has studied and conducted research in Oman, based at the UNESCO

EDITORS AND CONTRIBUTORS

Chair for Aflaj Studies – Archaeohydrology at the University of Nizwa. Her specialties include Oman and its people before 1970, and *aflaj*-oasis environments in Oman. Aminah holds a bachelor's degree with honours: BA (Hons) TESOL and Arabic and Master's by research degree (both from the University of Central Lancashire, Preston, UK).

Alice Königstetter is a PhD candidate at the Institute for Near Eastern Studies at the University of Vienna, Austria. Her dissertation project deals with contemporary women's fiction from Kuwait, which analyses depictions of marginalization at the intersections of language, nationality, and gender. She is currently a Visiting Fellow at the Vrije Universiteit Brussel, Belgium, where she is affiliated with the Department of Linguistics and Literary Studies. Her research interests include cultural production of the Arab Gulf region, gender studies, and postcolonial literature.

Editors' acknowledgements

We are indebted to Kuwaiti artist Thuraya al Baqsami for generously agreeing to let us use her powerful artwork for our book cover, as well as her daughter Monira al-Qadiri for her assistance. We are equally grateful to Sultan Sooud Al-Qassemi and the Barjeel Art Foundation, including Suheyla Tekesh, for their mediation and assistance on the matter, as well as for providing the high-resolution image of the artwork.

At Exeter University Press we wish to thank Anna Henderson for believing in our project, as well as Nigel Massen and David Hawkins for overseeing its publication. We are also thankful to the Exeter University Press design team for their great work on the cover.

We appreciate the effort and insights of the blind reviewers, whose suggestions helped us strengthen our arguments and make a tighter case for this book project.

We are also indebted to the scholars who agreed to write the book's endorsements for their engagement with our volume and for showing up for us.

Most of all, we value the friendship and connections that our book has contributed to shape and strengthen so far, the community of likeminded people, inside and outside of academia, and the rich dialogue and exchange that took place during the writing and revisions.

Introduction: Revisiting Women in the Gulf

Emanuela Buscemi (0000-0003-2126-7858), *Shahd Alshammari* (0000-0002-2364-3231), *and Ildiko Kaposi* (0000-0003-1365-8939)

'When I walk, I swagger with pride'

Wallada Bint al-Mustakfi (1091)

In 2012 Sophia Al-Maria and Fatima Al Qadiri, both intellectuals and creative minds, coined the term *Gulf futurism* as a cultural feature 'marked by a deranged optimism about the sustainability of both oil reserves and late capitalism' (Dazed 2012b). Drawing on their insiders' grasp of the area, these young Khaleeji women highlighted the discourse over the future as a driving force in the political, economic and cultural spheres at the local level, but also the problematic relationship with the past and its revised official narratives, the at times complicated connections between the local and the global, the over-reliance on hydrocarbons, the demographic imbalance between natives and expatriates, and the differential in generalized gender conditions. Gulf futurism, thus, in the minds of its creators, consists of a 'subversive new aesthetic, which draws on the region's hypermodern infrastructure, globalized cultural kitsch and repressive societal norms to form a critique of a dystopian future-turned-reality' (Dazed 2012a).

By reflecting on alternative temporalities, Sophia Al-Maria and Fatima Al Qadiri recuperate an artistic and cultural avant-garde rooted in the Italian aesthetic and intellectual scene at the beginning of the twentieth century

Emanuela Buscemi, Shahd Alshammari, and Ildiko Kaposi, 'Introduction: Revisiting Women in the Gulf' in: *Gulf Women's Lives: Voice, Space, Place.* University of Exeter Press (2024). © Emanuela Buscemi, Shahd Alshammari, and Ildiko Kaposi. DOI: 10.47788/UIJR2942

(Powers 2020). Futurism was inspired by its deep confidence and belief in the transformative potential of technology, the ideas of dynamism and speed, the cult of youth and violence as the end result of vitality and a palpitation for life. The connections between the Italian cultural movement and the current situation in Gulf countries lie in the disturbance and contestation that these artistic practices operate against official narratives, the appropriation of the margin between imagined temporalities and imagined communities, the problematic interrelation between the urban, the ecological and the human (Parikka 2018), as well as the reclamation of 'the right to the future' (Parikka 2022: 4).

Gulf futurism(s) and the overarching narratives of permanent wealth and abundance built on othering and difference not only serve power discourses and national political constructions, but also contribute to problematizing the complex nexus between the local and global dimensions, the modern and the traditional *topoi*, as well as the tensions between homogenization and authenticity. With technoscapes, mediascapes and ethnoscapes projected onto idealizations of nation-states, the future becomes the metaphor for a present that is never quite as imagined, or not exactly as envisaged. In this sense, the politicization of the future is a powerful tool to ensure stability while perpetuating sameness through divergence (Appadurai 1990). But it is also an equally powerful instrument of defiance and agency at the hands of those subjects who are not fully included or contemplated in the masculine, local and affluent imagined communities, albeit as vehicles and transmitters of dominant cultural narratives (Kandiyoti 1996a). Paraphrasing Arjun Appadurai (1990), one woman's imagined community is another woman's political prison.

As part of the new generations of Gulf youth (Buscemi & Kaposi 2021), and especially women, who inhabit a glocal dimension and whose world is characterized by consumerism, connectivity and immediacy, both Fatima Al Qadiri and Sophia Al-Maria interrogate the current political, cultural, social but also gender landscapes of Gulf countries, as well as the everyday lives of Gulf citizens and residents alike. This is what this volume seeks to posit and question: the relevance of otherness in the voices, spaces and places reclaimed, revisited and reinterpreted by women in the Gulf, and the struggle for the inclusion of legitimate assertions and prerogatives in the official national discourse of the past, present and future.

INTRODUCTION: REVISITING WOMEN IN THE GULF

Margins, liminalities and in-betweenness

The notion of 'Gulf women' employed in this volume aspires to include a wide representation of women living, working and expressing belonging towards the Gulf, beyond mere accidents of nationality. In this approach it follows a tradition from fiction and social scientific research that has tended towards greater inclusivity in explorations of belongings, adding corrective depth and nuance to official narratives. Writing about Gulf feminism, Mai Al-Nakib (2013: 462) observes that it is 'more radically manifest in art and literature' than in scholarship or activism. This observation can be extended to other contentious issues whose exploration is often relegated to fiction as a pre-political, safer space. Among such issues, Gulf writers and novelists have engaged with resident non-citizens' sentiments of feeling connected to their Arabian Gulf host countries. These connections have been scrutinized in relation to nannies and other female domestic worker figures in works like Saud Alsanousi's *The Bamboo Stalk* (2015) and Mia Alvar's collection of short stories *In the Country* (2015). Slaves and forced labourers joined the cast of characters in the historical fictional depictions of Omani life between the *falaj* (canal) and the urban environment in Jokha Alharthi's *Celestial Bodies* (2019), and Bushra Khalfan's *Dilshad* (2021), an intergenerational tale of hardship, slavery and war. In the same vein, social scientists and practitioners have enquired about the layers of ambivalent sentiment towards Gulf countries that are sometimes the only nations to have welcomed migrants and the generations before them. 'I am Gulf!' says an Indian participant in Filippo and Caroline Osella's ethnography on the region of Kerala (2007), highlighting a special relationship with the Gulf, the cosmopolitan outlook of its population, as well as the globalization of the local job market. Similarly, Neha Vora describes the temporariness of long-term residents in Dubai as *impossible citizenship* (2013), Pardis Mahdavi enquires into im/mobilities and intimacy (2016), while Deepak Unnikrishnan's *Temporary People* (2017) investigates, employing a variety of literary genres and perspectives, the impermanence and hybridity of migration to the Arabian Gulf.

What Noor Naga refers to as 'new narratives of ownership by non-citizens' (2021: par. 13) sits at the intersection between nationality, belonging, transience, gender, im/mobilities and im/permanence, rather creating a continuum among binaries and opposites. This notion also applies to Gulf writers, artists and contributors who have been residing in the Gulf, have mixed nationalities or have a strong connection to the area. Among them are Qatari-American artist and writer Sophia Al-Maria, creating a continuum between hyper-consumerism and Khaleeji identity; Kuwaiti-American novelist Layla AlAmmar, whose incursions into the topics of sexual and domestic violence, as well as trauma and societal taboos, scrutinize the double standards of the local gender discourse; Kuwaiti-Palestinian Shahd Alshammari, who connects her dual and hybrid identity with the liminality of illness and the Palestinian diaspora; Mona Kareem, scholar, poet and translator, who interrogates in her literary production the marginalization of Gulf *bidūn* (stateless people); and Singaporean-Bahraini artist and curator Amal Khalaf, who is involved in social-aesthetic projects on migrant intellectual communities to bridge the systemic racism that she experienced as a young person in the Gulf.

For the sake of the present volume, the discourse around nationality, gender, migration, class, dis/ability, race, sexual orientation, dualities and temporalities lies within the boundaries of intersectionality, intended as the sum total of converging forms and factors of oppression that simultaneously concur to marginalize and discriminate subjects (Alcaraz Alonso et al. 2022). A political concept elaborated around the claims of Black Feminism, it was later theorized in academia as a framework of analysis for the sign of difference located primarily in the lives and experiences of women of colour, to acknowledge that 'the major systems of oppression are interlocking [and] the synthesis of these oppressions creates the conditions of our lives' (Combahee River Collective 2014: 271). Intersectionality can operate as a lens for understanding and investigating the margins of national experiences and narratives, emerging voices, subaltern and marginalized subjects. These nonconforming narratives imply 'an exposure of the self and body that goes against traditional norms of hiding the female body [against] a culture that emphasizes the need for concealment and keeping women's bodies outside of the public sphere' (Alshammari 2022: 57). It is precisely in the interstices between official narratives, invented traditions and performed nationalisms that women's narratives become a testimony, 'a site of resistance [through] their voices and bodies to testify, to bear witness [and ultimately] reclaiming agency over one's life' (61).

INTRODUCTION: REVISITING WOMEN IN THE GULF

Intersectionality also aligns with the postcolonial feminist revindication of de-exoticizing and de-orientalizing the Other woman by allowing a scrutinizing look into differences while contrasting the unequal relations of power underlying them. Chandra Talpade Mohanty reclaims a de-essentialization of the 'Third World Woman' operated by the colonial gaze and white feminism alike as 'a relation of structural domination and a discursive and political suppression of the heterogeneity of the subject(s) in question' (1988: 61). The concepts of intersectionality and de-essentialization can, more generally, underscore the lived lives of women who have not been discursively produced as equal by the Eurocentric and neo-imperialist gaze.

To this end, Nadeen Dakkak notes how the voices of second-generation migrants in the Gulf have been absent from the public discourse, breaking the tie between nationality and belonging to reclaim knowledge, attachment, everyday connections and alternative affiliations in contrast to diasporic marginality and rootlessness (2020). On this, Dakkak notes that 'voicelessness' is the norm (2020: par. 1). In a way, she also signals the risk of romanticizing solidarities and affiliations in the margins. In her powerful 'Manifesto Against the Woman', Mona Kareem dismantles hegemonic feminism's attempts at sisterhood by revindicating her own struggle to be unsilenced:

> I write against the *Woman*, this single bothersome entity [...] who thinks brazenly that we are one. She, whose behind perches upon the comfortable chair of citizenship, class, and race. Against the Khaleeji *'kafila'* [female sponsor] who goes to work and becomes a good citizen and liberated woman on the backs of Asian servants in her home [...]. Against the *Woman* who cries foul about having multiple wives (polygyny) but not about having multiple servants. This *Woman* resembles her state and class, not other women.
>
> I write against the *Woman* citizen, the excited participant in the 'democratic process,' searching for an 'equality' that includes only her. (2016)

Mona Kareem warns us against an essentialization of Gulf women and the uniformization of their condition, inviting us to scrutinize the contradictions of liberal brown women oppressing other women in their pursuit for equality and recognition. In a way, Mona Kareem urges scholars and feminists to take off the rose-tinted glasses of a sisterhood and cooperation forged in

5

GULF WOMEN'S LIVES

the Global North and replicated elsewhere, to enquire about the multiple hidden oppressions that operate against othered women whose backs only bridge privilege and exclusion (Moraga & Anzaldúa 1981), women whose embodied symbolic and physical work remains hidden and silenced in its invisibility and pain.

Discourses of marginalities and marginalization are grounded in post-colonial and decolonial theories that posit the duality of the construction of the centre against a multiplicity of peripheries, physically and symbolically relevant in the production of liminality, exclusion and exclusivity: the 'comfort of social belonging' implicated by 'nationness' (Bhabha 1990a: 2). However, it is precisely around those margins that narratives are re-formed and social change is forged: 'A borderland is a vague and undetermined place created by the emotional residue of an unnatural boundary. It is a constant state of transition' (Anzaldúa 2015: 3). Following Homi Bhabha's conceptualization of the nation as 'a social and textual affiliation' (1990a: 2), as well as 'a form of narrative and cultural elaboration' (1990b: 292), we claim women's narratives have a transformative power, a potential for negotiating a more central space as well as reinscribing their cultural elaborations within the official narration of the nation, 'establish[ing] the cultural boundaries of the nation [as] containing thresholds of meaning that must be crossed, erased, and translated in the process of cultural production' (Bhabha 1990a: 4).

For these reasons we revindicate in this volume a notion of the Arabian Gulf that encompasses feelings of loyalty, belonging, duty, and we include a wide range of narratives to bring to light women's voices in literature, Bedouin and oasis culture, petitioning and divorce, and media production, among others.

The current debate on women, their lives and narratives in the Arabian Gulf

In her careful study of Gulf women, Amira El-Azhary Sonbol (2012) points out how, historically, Khaleeji women were incorporated into a patriarchal narrative that was coherent with the foundational myths of the new countries of the region, while the very same narrative also served to support the

INTRODUCTION: REVISITING WOMEN IN THE GULF

nation-building processes and the connected nationalism. Sonbol suggests that this narrative was partly imagined and partly fabricated:

> In this 'imagining', Gulf women were placed under the full custody of male relatives, their movements constrained, and their presence in the public sphere conceptualized as non-existent; their place was always in the home, with other women, with no mixing with males beyond immediate relatives [...]. Over time, this image of Gulf women's history became enframed as a reality (2012: 7–8).

According to Sonbol (2012), then, imagined traditions, foundational myths and nation-building logics have predominantly marginalized women in their national communities, whereby women, as Suad Joseph (2010) maintains, have been closely associated with the very idea of nation, and upheld to embody high moral and social ideals confining them to their domestic, kin and biological occupations. These configurations constitute for women a 'double jeopardy' (Kandiyoti 2000: xiv) consisting, on the one hand, of limited political rights and henceforth limited political participation, and, on the other hand, a legal status somehow restricted to and by issues of kin-based affiliation, social and material reproduction. The resulting gendered participation of women in the perpetuation of the status quo and power maintenance logics, however, does not imply a total submission and silencing. Devising strategies of resistance to patriarchal arrangements or open confrontation, they have become progressively more vocal about and engaged in the expansion of their rights and claiming their rightful presence in the public sphere. Suffrage was extended to women in Kuwait in 2005 after a strenuous and long campaign. UAE citizenship laws for the children of Emirati women married to non-nationals were progressively eased. Bahraini feminist activists campaigned for citizenship equality, and Qatar's women human rights defenders engaged in activism and lobbying. Saudi Arabia's recent laws progressing women's rights may have been introduced as a handout gift from the ruling patriarchy, but the gesture was preceded by waves of vocal campaigning by Saudi women.

We should also acknowledge that women have become active as entrepreneurs, businesswomen and skilled professionals in the private sector. They have served the state as politicians, ministers and government representatives, joined the military and the police force, made inroads into the judiciary.

GULF WOMEN'S LIVES

Away from state feminism, in civil society where artists and writers, instigators of NGOs, lobbyists and intellectuals operate, they have been opening up the discussion on their role in society and claiming revised narratives. Gender can, thus, be employed as an analytic category (Kandiyoti 1996b), as well as a lens through which to examine and investigate the Arabian Gulf, not unveiling but bringing to light, not representing but giving voice, not inviting but sharing journeys, 'challenging established views of culture, society, politics and the literary production in the Middle East' (Kandiyoti 1996a: ix).

Going against the 'trope of the "oppressed Muslim woman"' (Abu-Lughod 1993: xxiv), or the Muslim woman in need of saving (Abu-Lughod 2002), the current debate on Middle Eastern women's lives, voices, spaces and places is complicated by stories of human rights violations, the ongoing debate on citizenship as exclusion (Kareem 2016), migrant labourers' 'enforced transience' (Unnikrishnan 2021), and women's activism following the Arab Spring-inspired protests in Kuwait (Buscemi 2016) and Bahrain, as well as in the streets, schools, houses and open spaces, *diwaniyyas* and *majlis*, around the Arabian Gulf.

Situating women in the Arabian Gulf

Studies surrounding the Arabian Gulf tend to ignore Gulf women's lives while claiming the diversity and interdisciplinarity of the field (Al-Malki 2019). This volume aims to rectify this gap in the literature available. *Gulf Women's Lives* begins with the premise of presenting and exploring, rather than finding results and conclusions surrounding Gulf women's lives. We use the word 'lives' in a general and open sense, an all-inclusive word that emphasizes the colossal impact of lives both lived and unlived, defined by patriarchal, social and religious interactions. These lives are defined by Gulf women who theorize and reconstruct their narratives. By providing a platform for readdressing Gulf women's narratives, the strategies of our volume include 'making space' for these voices to be heard and amplified within research. We look at voice, space and place as a multifold examination of what it is to occupy space in Gulf women's worlds. We consider ways that agency is created, defined and challenged. The narratives in this volume mobilize Gulf women's perceptions,

INTRODUCTION: REVISITING WOMEN IN THE GULF

understandings and reframings of their lives and worlds. The worlds presented here are a mere glimpse into what we hope will become relevant to future scholars and researchers.

It is no coincidence that all the scholars who have made valuable contributions to this volume are women. Knowledge production and consumption is never neutral. Women of colour and marginalized groups are still underrepresented in academia and research. As such, we utilize a transnational and intersectional feminist approach in addressing this inequity in research and knowledge production. Sara Ahmed, feminist critic, reminds us that who we choose to cite, the knowledge we produce and reproduce, is never neutral, and we should consider feminist theory as 'world making' (Ahmed 2017: 14). In this volume, we offer multiple spaces to contest what it means to be living as Gulf women today, what ideologies these spaces can deconstruct, and what new ways of seeing the world their narratives can open up, thus producing 'counter-stories' (Al-Malki 2019).

The emphasis on voice, space and place is essentially about the politics of positionality. Knowledge production within academia is male-dominated, and as feminists doing feminist theory, we must make space, make room in our commitment to 'transcending boundaries' (Kandiyoti 1996b: 1). We consider first our own positionalities and our multiple backgrounds, as well as our diverse disciplines. We (Emanuela, Shahd and Ildiko) are constantly in dialogue, Bakhtinian dialogism in a sense, understanding that life itself is a process of meaning-making and open-ended discussion. As women from different racial backgrounds, we are engaging in Western and Eastern dialogue, and from both non-disabled and disabled bodies. We also worked together through online spaces of collaboration, which meant that we had to become active listeners and engage with each other across different time zones. To inhabit academic space as feminist scholars is to produce knowledge that is invested in listening—to bring women to theorizing. This feminist methodology foregrounds Gulf women's insights, experiences and embodied agency through theorizing their identities in relation to space and place. As such, this volume is meant to provide a platform for ongoing dialogue and questions, and a constant revising of notions of Arab women. We do not position ourselves as editors who offer space to our contributors; rather, we take part in this dialogue, through our own contributions to the volume but also through

9

GULF WOMEN'S LIVES

an awareness that feminist conversations are always about claiming (and reclaiming) space. The conversations in this volume testify to the notion of foregrounding Gulf women's lived experiences and critical reflections, and a commitment to 'talking back' to colonial, patriarchal and neoliberal understandings of Gulf women.

Our initial interest in this feminist conversation comes from a commitment to intersectional feminist politics (Crenshaw 1989). As scholars who work in different fields, we share a vision that constantly interrogates what it means to be a woman, a scholar, and to have a voice that does not exclude those who do not occupy the same space. We began this volume with a question about Gulf women's narratives. First, what are Gulf women's narratives? How are these narratives plural, multifaceted, and how do they diverge from the stereotypical narrative of 'the oppressed Gulf woman'? How do Gulf women author their lives, their selves, and negotiate public and private spaces? What stories are offered space? How are these stories made visible and invisible in various places? Who gets to speak? As Qatari scholar Amal Al-Malki argues, Arab women have 'no voice' (Al Jazeera 2012; Dakkak 2020). To take this statement on board, we envision this volume as a chorus of voices from the Gulf region. There are a handful of works from Gulf women scholars that attempt to situate Gulf feminism and its lived realities (Al-Nakib 2013; Al-Mutawa 2020). To date, there is a gap in the literature from Gulf women scholars about Gulf women.

With this volume, we intend to debunk myths surrounding Gulf women's lives, dig deep into history, and explore oral narratives and ethnography, literature, media studies, migration and family law issues in order to give a truthful account of the complexity, nuance and intersected instances in Gulf women's lives; as well as examining the narratives that they employ and through which they express their agency, resistance, opinions and recuperation of a distant past.

Voices, spaces, places

Gulf Women's Lives tackles orientalizing and orientalized representations, deep-rooted clichés about the Middle East, in three interlinked parts organized around the broader themes of voice, space and place.

INTRODUCTION: REVISITING WOMEN IN THE GULF

Part I, *Voices*, focuses on ways of self-expression through which women in the Gulf give voice to the character and quality of their existence. Speaking in their own voices, women articulate their interests as subordinate groups that demand acknowledgement in the culturally specific institutions constituting Khaleeji public spheres. From Bedouin autoethnography through the creation of a digital media platform to literary breakthroughs, the women featured in Part I are simultaneously constructing and expressing their identity as cultural 'others', carving out unconventional spaces for acknowledgement, participation and dialogue in the process.

Shahd Alshammari's contribution locates lived experiences of disability and storytelling in the researcher/storyteller's narrative. It establishes connections between autoethnography as developed in Western feminist research methodologies and Bedouin *suwalif* (oral storytelling) as a method of enquiry to trace the emergence of her voice as a disabled author, by offering segments of conversations and assumptions around what constitutes a disabled, Bedouin and academic identity. Forging a space for writing an illness narrative becomes necessary and emancipatory, allowing the author to move from stigmatization and shame to writing and healing.

The voice that emerges from the dialogue Alshammari starts with herself and shares with the reading public is amplified, multiplied and projected globally by the UAE-rooted *Sekka* magazine, whose co-founder and storyteller-in-chief Sharifah Alhinai is interviewed by Ildiko Kaposi. The cultural magazine's declared mission is to create a platform for Gulf voices, taking inspiration from Edward Said's observation that the Oriental must speak, otherwise he will be spoken for. The problem, as the interview asserts, is not that the Gulf lacks voices, but rather that the voices often go unheard. The *Sekka* story is a good illustration of the mix of idealism and pragmatism needed to sustain a platform for Gulf women's works on the global media scene. This chapter sheds light on the importance of creative storytelling and journalism as a method of enquiry, while its interview structure affirms the volume's commitment to 'own voices' and stories by Gulf women themselves.

The chapter rounding up Part I shifts the discussion to the literary sphere, where women in the Gulf have been finding an outlet for experimenting with publicly articulated subjectivities. Emanuela Buscemi's sociological reading of

Jokha Alharthi, Shahd Alshammari and Laila Aljohani's works demonstrates how the literary becomes a vocal platform for critically exploring social taboos, challenging dominant narratives, and inviting a dialogue about the Gulf's fundamental political and cultural tenets. Through the introduction of unconventional and uncomfortable characters of slaves, black people and disabled persons, women authors are (re)claiming a de-invisibilization of the conditions of those who do not as a rule take centre stage in the public sphere. Literature, as Buscemi demonstrates, can thus become a vehicle for alternative strategies of garnering support for social reform without issuing an overt political challenge to reigning inequities.

Part II, *Spaces*, explores the mutual transformation of female voices that engage with conventional public institutions of acknowledgement and participation, and the institutions that come to accommodate and channel these voices. Serving as negotiatory spaces, the newsrooms of national media corporations, the courtrooms of family law and the legal channels of petitioning the government see women in the Gulf 'bargaining with patriarchy'. In the process, women construct and reconstruct these spaces of power as a sphere where private and public intersect, entangling the personal with the social structures that continue to regulate their existence.

Noura Al Obeidli's chapter enlists ethnographic methods to expose gender dynamics at work in UAE newsrooms. The government-run Emirati media featured in the chapter operate in a well-established matrix of control. Sociocultural restrictions along gender lines add another, less exposed dimension of subjugation to the institutional operations of media outlets that are tasked with creating and helping maintain social realities in the UAE through daily symbolic representations. Some of the woman journalists speaking to Al Obeidli identify with dominant narratives of their state-enabled empowerment. Others take a more oppositional stance. But most of them end up negotiating with the system to carve out a space for themselves in the professional sphere of work. Al Obeidli's findings also spark a polemic with the chapter on *Sekka* magazine in Part I. Read together, the two chapters create a powerful demonstration of intersectionality and (unacknowledged) positionalities as helpful analytical tools for making sense of Gulf women's lives in media spaces.

Nora Jaber's chapter also engages with the theme of women challenging and negotiating with patriarchal, religious and neoliberal state narratives.

INTRODUCTION: REVISITING WOMEN IN THE GULF

Through her critical discourse analysis of petitions authored by Saudi women, Jaber demonstrates the ways in which women end up reproducing and inevitably legitimizing official discourses when negotiating gender relations. Reproducing state narratives when addressing the state directly is a strategic discursive move dictated by the goal of increasing the likelihood of success. Yet the net effect can suggest adaptation and accommodation rather than subversion, adding reinforcement to non-gender-based hierarchies.

The final chapter in Part II keeps the focus on legal spaces where the fates of women going through divorce are decided. Divorce in Qatar becomes a rupture that reveals the often hidden mechanisms through which the patriarchal state regulates women's bodies and behaviour towards the national order and the perpetuation of the status quo. Maryam Al-Muhanadi situates the lived experience of Qatari women who must contend with the hidden patterns of violence manifested in state laws and the family unit itself. Drawing on qualitative interviews, the chapter employs a feminist methodological approach that values storytelling as data and begins with the premise of the 'personal is political' (Kiguwa 2019). The stories of divorcées foreground Qatari women's voices in retelling their narratives away from the spaces of violence that strive to condition women's everyday existence. The act of centring their voices as important and necessary parts of the conversation on patriarchal attitudes to divorce and divorced women becomes a gesture that points towards the possibility of constructing alternative spaces beyond the confines of legal and sociocultural realities.

Part III, *Places*, expands on the enquiry into the positionality of women in Gulf societies. Aminah Khan relies on oral narratives to initiate a recomposition of histories and traditional notions about the Gulf Arab woman's place in society. Khan's contribution offers a detailed analysis on the status of women in the *aflaj*-oases of Oman before and after the beginning of the Qaboos era (1970–2020). By situating lived experiences of voice and place within a historical timeline, Khan raises important questions of socialization, loneliness, modernization and oral narratives through the voices of elderly Omani women. The chapter argues for an understanding of women's roles as historically more mobile between the interconnected spheres of the private and the public, the home and the economy, than habitually assumed. It also serves as a specifically situated debunking of the foundational myth of the

13

strong patriarchal state stepping in to rescue Omani women from a place of misery.

The remaining two chapters of Part III offer readings of the Gulf through the lens of women's contemporary literary representations, throwing into relief the heterogeneity of the geophysical region where boundaries separating cultures by language or place of origin are increasingly difficult to demarcate, with the resultant questioning of tropes of Gulf exceptionalism and mobility.

Alice Königstetter shifts the discussion to the (im)mobilities of female characters in Gulf women's English-language fiction. Literature written in English is symptomatic of sociocultural developments in the region which the author investigates through the prisms of the new mobilities paradigm (Pearce 2020) and neopatriarchy (Sharabi 1992). The concept of mobility does not only entail the movement of the physical body but also the circulation of ideas and entities in imaginative spaces, and the limitations of heroines' tangible movements stand in conjunction with mental restrictions. Neopatriarchy, a form of patriarchy highly dependent on modernity, is linked to the (im)mobilities of female characters who are kept under legal and social constraints. But, in Königstetter's reading, the heroines and the female authors writing them create intangible spaces as a means of freedom and increased mobility to defy patriarchal order and resist subjugation. In exploring these themes, the chapter adopts intersectional Third World Feminism as proposed by Haneen Shafeeq Ghabra (2015: 3) to add race and class to the discussion about women's place in the Gulf region.

Nadeen Dakkak considers the important role of migration and multigenerational communities in the Gulf. Dakkak calls for a reassessment of the position of Arab non-citizen middle-class women and, more generally, those of middle-class migrant families. Throughout her chapter, she engages with a close reading of Selma Dabbagh's fiction. Dabbagh's texts provide Dakkak's chapter with a foregrounding of the representation of Palestinian migrant experiences in the Gulf. Given the literary tropes and stereotypes often associated with Gulf migrants, the chapter focuses on the complex dynamics of narratives that are under-represented in fiction. Mirroring the complex realities of Arab non-citizen women from middle-class and/or privileged backgrounds in the Gulf, Dakkak's chapter interrogates multiple positionalities: gender, sexuality, citizenship and class.

Conclusions

In the Arabian Gulf the social and cultural norms rooted in the family as primary gatekeeper invest in it, among others, control over women's behaviour, sexuality, conduct, reproductive rights and, more generally, power relations organized along the lines of gender and age (de Bel-Air et al. 2018). Control and stigmatization are closely linked to nation-building processes and power preservation. *Gulf Women's Lives* sees women crafting spaces of agency against this backdrop and symbolically joining forces to create a community of solidarity. The women who write about the experiences of women in the Gulf claim and reclaim their voices in politics, culture and society. This volume constitutes a place of acknowledgement, recognition, rehabilitation and redemption where writing empowers women to relate their stories, bodies, affects and solidarities. The authors give relevance to and account for marginalized subjects and stories, appropriating the narrative from a gender standpoint to highlight intersecting and overlapping stories within the broader sociocultural realities of the region.

This volume contributes to deconstructing and complicating our understanding of the Arabian Gulf, often perceived as the site of excesses in terms of exceptional urban landscapes, unimaginable wealth, opulent and glittery lifestyles, while engulfed in what is commonly regarded as backward mores and overbearing religious requirements, as well as exploitative labour practices and human rights violations. As the chapters here demonstrate, storytelling of the personal, literary or scholarly kind can be powerfully employed as a tool for agency, political in the sense of the personal being political.

The book does not claim an encyclopaedic comprehensiveness across all experiences of all women in the Gulf. Notably absent from the chorus of voices on its platform are those women who understand themselves as beneficiaries and committed supporters of current ways of life in the Gulf. This absence can be accounted for as self-selection bias. We the editors intend the book as an open, inclusive invitation to continue the dialogue about women in the Gulf beyond ahistorical essentialism and exceptionalism. Against the backdrop of Khaleeji urban spaces as geographic and symbolic constructs of modernization, hybridization, loss of authenticity, competing logics and ultimately border crossing, we certainly have a lot to talk about.

References

Abu-Lughod, L. (1993). *Writing Women's Worlds: Bedouin Stories.* University of California Press.

Abu-Lughod, L. (2002). Do Muslim Women Really Need Saving? Anthropological Reflections on Cultural Relativism and Its Others. *American Anthropologist,* 104(3), 783–90. https://doi.org/10.1525/aa.2002.104.3.783

Ahmed, S. (2017). *Living a Feminist Life.* Duke University Press. https://doi.org/10.1515/9780822373377

Al Jazeera (2012). *Why Arab Women Still 'Have No Voice'.* YouTube. https://www.youtube.com/watch?v=GxjKdJ3JNSU

Al-Malki, A. (2019, 21 February). How Women's Studies Could Drive Change in the Arab World. *Al Fanar Media.* https://al-fanarmedia.org/2019/02/how-womens-studies-could-drive-change-in-the-arab-world/

Al-Mutawa, R. (2020). 'I Want to Be a Leader, but Men Are Better than Women in Leadership Positions', *Hawwa,* 18(1), 31–50. https://doi.org/10.1163/15692086-12341369

Al-Nakib, M. (2013). Disjunctive Synthesis: Deleuze and Arab Feminism. *Signs: Journal of Women in Culture and Society,* 38(2), 459–82. https://doi.org/10.1086/667220

Alcaraz Alonso, D.M., Méndez Ortiz, D.V. & Buscemi, E. (2022). Un día sin nosotras: The 2020 Women's Strike Against Gender-based Violence in Mexico Between Intersectionality and Activism. *Culture e Studi del Sociale,* 7(2), 268–76.

Alharthi, J. (2019). *Celestial Bodies* (trans. M. Booth). Sandstone Press.

Alsanousi, S. (2015). *The Bamboo Stalk* (trans J. Wright). Bloomsbury Qatar Foundation.

Alshammari, S. (2022). Life Writing by Kuwaiti Women: Voice and Agency. *IAFOR Journal of Cultural Studies,* 7(1), 53–63. https://doi.org/10.22492/ijcs.7.1.04

Alvar, M. (2015). *In the Country.* Knopf.

Anzaldúa, G. (2015). *Light in the Dark/Luz en lo Oscuro: Rewriting Identity, Spirituality, Reality* (ed. A.L. Keating). Duke University Press. https://doi.org/10.2307/j.ctv1220hmq

Appadurai, A. (1990). Disjuncture and Difference in the Global Cultural Economy. *Theory, Culture and Society,* 7(2–3), 295–310. https://doi.org/10.1177/026327690007002017

Ashour, R., Ghazoul, J.F. & Reda-Mekdashi, H. (eds) (2008). *Arab Women Writers: A Critical Reference Guide 1873–1999* (trans. M. McClure). The American University in Cairo Press.

Bhabha, H.K. (1990a). Introduction: Narrating the Nation. In H.K. Bhabha (ed.), *Nation and Narration* (pp. 1–7). Routledge.

Bhabha, H.K. (1990b). DissemiNation: Time, Narrative, and the Margins of the Modern Nation. In H.K. Bhabha (ed.), *Nation and Narration* (pp. 291–322). Routledge.

Buscemi, E. (2016). Abaya and Yoga Pants: Women's Activism in Kuwait. *AG About Gender—International Journal of Gender Studies,* 5(10), 186–203. https://doi.org/10.15167/2279-5057/ag.2016.5.10.350

INTRODUCTION: REVISITING WOMEN IN THE GULF

Buscemi, E. & Kaposi, I. (2021). *Everyday Youth Cultures in the Arabian Peninsula: Changes and Challenges*. Routledge.

Crenshaw, K. (1989). Demarginalizing the Intersection of Race and Sex: A Black Feminist Critique of Antidiscrimination Doctrine, Feminist Theory and Antiracist Politics. *University of Chicago Legal Forum*, 1989(1), 139–67.

Combahee River Collective (2014). A Black Feminist Statement. *Women's Studies Quarterly*, 42(3/4), 271–280.

Dakkak, N. (2020, 27 June). The Absent Voices of Second-Generation Migrants in the Gulf States. *Migrant-Rights.com*. https://www.migrant-rights.org/2020/06/the-absent-voices-of-second-generation-migrants-in-the-gulf-states/

Dazed (2012a, 9 November). The Desert of the Unreal. https://www.dazeddigital.com/artsandculture/article/15040/1/the-desert-of-the-unreal

Dazed (2012b, 14 November). Al Qadiri & Al-Sophia on Gulf Futurism. https://www.dazeddigital.com/music/article/15037/1/al-qadiri-al-maria-on-gulf-futurism

de Bel-Air, F., Safar, J. & Destremau, B. (2018). Marriage and Family in the Gulf Today: Storms over a Patriarchal Insitution? *Arabian Humanities*, 10. https://doi.org/10.4000/cy.4399

Ghabra, H.S. (2015). Through My Own Gaze: An Arab Feminist Struggling with Patriarchal Arabness Through Western Hegemony. *Liminalities*, 11(5), 1–16.

Joseph, S. (2010). Gendering Citizenship in the Middle East. In S. Joseph (ed.), *Gender and Citizenship in the Middle East* (pp. 3–30). Syracuse University Press.

Khalfan, B. (2021). *Dilshad*. Takween.

Kandiyoti, D. (1996a). Preface. In D. Kandiyoti (ed.), *Gendering the Middle East: Emerging Perspectives* (pp. ix–xii). I.B.Tauris.

Kandiyoti, D. (1996b). Contemporary Feminist Scholarship and Middle East Studies. In D. Kandiyoti (ed.), *Gendering the Middle East: Emerging Perspectives* (pp. 1–27). I.B.Tauris.

Kandiyoti, D. (2000). Foreword. In S. Joseph (ed.), *Gender and Citizenship in the Middle East* (pp. xiii–xv). Syracuse University Press.

Kareem, M. (2016, 14 January). Manifesto Against the Woman. *Jadaliyya*. https://www.jadaliyya.com/Details/32849

Kiguwa, P. (2019). Feminist Approaches: An Exploration of Women's Gendered Experiences. In S. Laher, A. Fynn & S. Kramer (eds), *Transforming Research Methods in the Social Sciences: Case Studies from South Africa* (pp. 220–35). Wits University Press.

Mahdavi, P. (2016). *Crossing the Gulf: Love and Family in Migrant Lives*. Stanford University Press.

Mohanty, C.T. (1988). Under Western Eyes: Feminist Scholarship and Colonial Discourse. *Feminist Review*, 30(1), 61–88.

Moraga, C. & Anzaldúa, G. (eds) (1981). *This Bridge Called My Back: Writings by Radical Women of Color*. State University of New York Press.

Naga, N. (2021, 25 October). Who Writes the Arabian Gulf? *The Common*. https://www.thecommononline.org/who-writes-the-arabian-gulf/

Osella, F. & Osella, C. (2007). 'I Am Gulf': The Production of Cosmopolitanism among the Koyas of Kozhikode, Kerala. In E. Simpson & K. Kress (eds), *Struggling with History: Islam and Cosmopolitanism in the Western Indian Ocean* (pp. 323–55). C. Hurst & Co. Publishers.

Parikka, J. (2018). Middle East and Other Futurisms: Imaginary Temporalities in Contemporary Art and Visual Culture. *Culture, Theory, and Critique*, 59(1), 40–58. https://doi.org/10.1080/14735784.2017.1410439

Parikka, J. (2022). Counter-futuring. *counter-n*, 1–10. https://doi.org/10.18452/24451

Pearce, L. (2020). 'Text-as-Means' versus 'Text-as-End-in-Itself'. *Transfers*, 10(1), 76–84. https://doi.org/10.3167/TRANS.2020.100109

Powers, D. (2020). Towards a Futurist Cultural Studies. *International Journal of Cultural Studies*, 23(4), 451–57. https://doi.org/10.1177/1367877920913569

Sharabi, H. (1992). *Neopatriarchy: A Theory of Distorted Change in Arab Society*. Oxford University Press. https://doi.org/10.1093/oso/9780195079135.001.0001

Sonbol A.E. (2012). Introduction: Researching the Gulf. In A. El-Azhary Sonbol (ed.), *Gulf Women* (pp. 1–24). Syracuse University Press.

Unnikrishnan, D. (2017). *Temporary People*. Restless Books.

Unnikrishnan, D. (2021, 25 October). Introduction: Portfolio of Writing from the Arabian Gulf. *The Common*, 22. https://www.thecommononline.org/introduction-portfolio-of-writing-from-the-arabian-gulf/

Vora, N. (2013). *Impossible Citizens: Dubai's Indian Diaspora*. Duke University Press. https://doi.org/10.1515/9780822397533

PART I

Voices

From Stigma to Speech: An Autoethnography of Bedouin Culture, Writing and Illness

Shahd Alshammari (0000-0002-2364-3231)

Introduction

As a disabled Bedouin researcher, I have searched for Bedouin women's narratives and found a jarring absence—a deafening silence and cloak of invisibility covering Bedouin women's everyday lives, histories and experiences. Historians have paid particular attention to Bedouin culture over the past two decades as more marginalized voices have entered the field, 'adopt[ing] approaches such as micro-history, historical ethnography and oral history as a corrective to dominant narratives' (Franz et al. 2015: 2). Whilst there is a rising interest in Bedouin culture, certain dominant narratives remain in historical, sociological and anthropological disciplines. Most approaches to ethnography and oral history tend to focus on larger collective groups, such as Bedouin communities in Negev (a large desert region in southern Israel), excluding Bedouin autoethnographies (Chatty 2020). In order to counteract the scarcity of Bedouin autoethnographies, this chapter draws on my lived experience as a Bedouin woman writer and academic living with a disability. I uncover my experiences growing up with a disability and subsequently write about the disabled body, attempting to break the silence. First, I relay conversations that capture negative connotations of disability, reflecting on how Bedouin disabled women are perceived. Second, I consider my role as 'aunty' and 'academic mentor' as a form of embodied feminism. Finally, I explore my commitment to telling

---

Shahd Alshammari, 'From Stigma to Speech: An Autoethnography of Bedouin Culture, Writing and Illness' in: *Gulf Women's Lives: Voice, Space, Place*. University of Exeter Press (2024). © Shahd Alshammari.
DOI: 10.47788/MKWD4340

GULF WOMEN'S LIVES

stories and, later, writing two illness narratives: *Notes on the Flesh* (Alshammari 2017a) and *Head Above Water: Reflections on Illness* (Alshammari 2022), the only illness narratives from the Gulf, and specifically Kuwait.

Autoethnography and *suwalif*

The Arabic language has a variety of terms for Bedouins, regarded as a social group which developed until the Middle Ages, 'among them aʻrāb, ʻarab, ʻurbān (roughly 'nomadic Arabs'), ahl al-bādiya, and badw' (Franz et al. 2015: 4). Al-Nakib discusses the Badu in Kuwait as a sociological category; although there are no longer Bedouins in Kuwait who practise a nomadic or pastoral lifestyle, 'the term badū remains in popular use in Kuwait today to designate a group considered sociologically and culturally distinct from the *hadar* (city dwellers) (Al-Nakib 2014). As a Kuwaiti Bedouin, I embrace the term and its roots as a collective group that stands in contrast with the *hadar*. Today, the term Bedouin is an identity marker (Cole 2003). A Bedouin identity is strongly associated with certain values that reflect the sanctity of the tribe and the family. Growing up as part of a well-connected tribe, I place myself as a Bedouin academic, one who recognizes heritage and cultural values, and questions the influence of Bedouin ideologies on my sense of self. I use 'Bedouin' throughout this chapter for consistency. The significance of Bedouin oral narratives speaks to my choice of methodology: autoethnography and narrative enquiry. Bedouin oral narrative is referred to as *salfah*, which is:

> derived from the root *salaf* 'to go before, to happen previously' and in that dialectal area is associated also with the verb *solaf* 'to speak'. These *suwalif* (plural of *salfah*) are viewed as narrations of events historically important to the society, and are felt to embody its values and more. (Ingham 1993: 6)

These *suwalif* (literally, 'oral stories') narrate personal disputes, tales of warfare and historical events dating as far back as the seventh century (Ingham 1993). Because *suwalif* are an integral part of Bedouin culture, groups of men and women exchange them for entertainment, to tell narratives of loss and grief, and to connect with others. *Suwalif* allow the individual to express emotion through narrative whilst simultaneously connecting to the tribe. Although *suwalif* emphasize the role of the tribe, they also help to build strong bonds of empathy and friendship among the tribe's members. As Maisel (2018) suggests, tribal values do not necessarily constitute an 'elimination' or negation of the self. *Suwalif* place the speaker as the story-teller, the narrator, the centre of attention; they emphasize the significance of a well-rounded storyteller who can narrate and situate themselves within a grander narrative. The speaker is able to comment and reflect on many themes, such as grief, loss, love, war and other human experiences, by placing themselves within the narrative. By considering *suwalif* as a method of narrative enquiry, I position them as an oral method within autoethnography. I invoke conversations based on my memory and reflect on their influence on my positionality as a disabled academic and author. Based on the significance of *suwalif*, I later turn to my experience of writing a memoir on disability and loss. *Suwalif* are part of my Bedouin culture, and as such, I have followed the process of telling lives, even when these are lives that remain hidden and marginalized.

Autoethnography relies heavily on Western notions of self-reflexivity, narration and agency. It is used by scholars to emphasize the role of the self in understanding social and cultural aspects; thus, it is an autobiographical research tool that enables researchers to reflect critically on experiences and social interactions. Many influential scholars have contributed to this field and called for its integration into feminist research, ethnography, social sciences and other fields of enquiry (Ellis & Bochner 2000). The researcher is able to use different forms of narrative enquiry, including conversations and memories, to reflect on social settings and study their environment. In terms of drawing on one's memories and situating the researcher within the research, this is particularly emancipatory when discussing Bedouin culture and Bedouin women's lives. As Sarah Wall (2006) argues,

> taking the question of voice and representation a step further [...] an individual is best situated to describe his or her own experience more accurately than anyone else (148).

Because knowledge production reflects a power imbalance between who is speaking and who is spoken for, I offer my personal account of Bedouin experiences as a disabled woman, situating my voice in different cultural settings that have allowed me to reflect critically on disability and gender, shame and the body, and finding a voice as a method of writing against the dominant narrative of disabled women as failing the collective. Through feminist ethics of care and writing about the body, I reclaim my voice and consider the ways that writing has provided a place to expand on *suwalif*, all the way to writing my memoir, a text that offers to heal, moving away from stigma and shame. By considering cultural practices and norms concerning my lived experience of disability (multiple sclerosis or MS), the understanding of *suwalif* and writing is further complicated. I invoke episodic scenes from my memory that have shaped my understanding of female 'aunty' figures and my own process of coming to terms with disability and, later, writing about the shamed body. Situating lived experiences allows me to reflect on power dynamics between able-bodied women ('aunties' from the tribe) and disabled women. For ease of comprehension and to enable a shift to academic reflection afterwards, snippets of conversation and the context in which they occur are italicized in the following sections.

On being a tribal woman and disability

'You have to make sure you marry within the tribe. Make sure you maintain your long hair—it is a marker of Bedouin beauty. Make sure henna is the only thing you ever place on your hair—apart from olive oil, coconut, eggs, and that mix I used to grow my hair this long,' my aunt says, listing the ingredients for a successful life. I am only seventeen years old, and I hate my long hair, but there is no way out of it. All Bedouin men love long hair, my aunt reminds me. She had married and had her share of sons to strengthen the tribe. A woman who has given birth to sons will always be better than a spinster, she says.

The Bedouin sexual code dictates this manifesto. The gender discrimination afflicting Bedouin women's lives is perpetuated by two governing cultural codes: the sexual code and the collective code. In the words of Abu-Rabia-Queder, a Bedouin academic who aims to centre voices of Bedouin communities in Negev, the sexual code 'affects every aspect of a girl's upbringing, from childhood to marriage', with perceptions of honour and shame dictating behaviour (Abu-Rabia-Queder 2006). Here I am, a Bedouin disabled spinster, unable to marry and give birth. Disabled women in Arab societies are often overlooked in scholarly research, but some sociological studies conclude that Arab disabled women are less likely to marry (Alshammari 2019). Bedouin aunties serve as the gatekeepers of the tribe's morals, strength and reproductivity. Hearing about my disability from my father, who has divulged the secret, causes a chain of anxious reactions. Disability is almost unheard of within the tribe.

> *'What disability? There aren't any women in this family who are disabled. No one in the tribe is! This is a healthy and strong tribe. Don't tell anyone something is wrong with you. You'll never find a husband then! You are just so pretty and so smart, of course, of course—it's the evil eye!'*
>
> *I cannot be disabled. It's all in my head—my MS head, the part of my brain that has forgotten all about my identity as a Bedouin woman. How can I be disabled if no one else is? I feel a surge of shame begin to take over my already-numbed limbs. Tied to the diagnosis, choked by the stigma of being labelled damaged goods, I cannot turn to family any more. I am now othered, and my aunties have made the verdict clear.*

Bedouin women can also serve to keep traditions intact: 'Some people, including some Bedouin women (especially those who belong to an older generation), strongly support the traditions and values that control women's lives' (Julia & AlMaseb 2007: 82). In other words, they are patriarchal women who have internalized the voice of the patriarchal collectivist society. Aunties here embody forces of oppression and discrimination. As I entered my twenties as a disabled undergraduate student, these were the conversations that shattered me:

> *'She should stay at home! She should stay inside. She is already a burden; if she goes to university, she will become sicker. Who will marry her then? Hide her at home, it will make things better.'*
>
> *My father is silent, shaking his head, conflicted. What is he to say when there is no prior reference for this anomaly? Bedouin women don't always go to school. Disabled Bedouin women are just unheard of. He locks eyes with me, and I lower my gaze, knowing I have created more reason for controversy. I just want to be invisible. Oh, to be invisible would be a dream come true.*

I was the first member of my family to be diagnosed with an incurable disease—one that would place me on the margins of society. However, when my body began 'passing' as normal, others began to forget about my disability. They seemed to think I was cured. I acted as if I were able-bodied, but it felt disingenuous to deny my disability in front of my family, who are meant to support me in my illness. As Brune and Wilson note, most disabled people have had to consider 'the choice of hiding their disability or drawing attention to it and the question of what to do when others overlook it [...] their decisions weigh issues of stigma, pride, prejudice, discrimination, and privilege but rarely put the matter to rest' (2014: 1). I must contend with making these choices about how to present myself to others as I confront life with MS. The concept of 'passing' is multifaceted, particularly in the context of an invisible disability. MS is uncommon in the Arab world; it typically affects Caucasians and those living in cloudy regions, so my diagnosis made little sense. It is an underemphasized neurological disability that eludes early diagnosis, leading to complications that range from mild to severe. Even in the mildest of cases, MS symptoms wax and wane unpredictably. As someone who suffers from MS, I sometimes need a cane or a wheelchair to get around. On other occasions, I can move about freely and can even play games such as squash. The fluctuation of my symptoms means that many people do not believe I am disabled.

One is never truly 'out of the woods' with MS. To my aunties, I am a strong spinster fighting a disability. The PhD I earned was not seen as an accomplishment. Instead, getting an education further marginalized me. I was considered a solitary academic who made strange decisions, all to avoid society's judgement. Disabled women are often demeaned because they have 'failed' to perform ideal femininity, being unable to procreate and contribute to their tribe's population. The stigma and shame of disability are constant and ever-intensifying stressors, even when one tries to stay hidden. I feel like a captive in my own house; any move I make triggers an alarm that only I can hear.

I think of 'invisible disability' as not being seen at all, and 'visible disability' as being seen too much. But 'randomness' is a third space of disability I have learned to occupy, a space that oscillates between visible and invisible periods of disability; as such, I have frequently referred to MS as a 'random disability' (Alshammari 2017b). In forging a new definition of self in relation to others, I have begun replacing my aunties with a new circle of women: my feminist friends. These friendships relieve me of the discrimination and prejudice I confront daily, either from family or from society at large. In the Gulf, friendship is understudied as an essential community-building force among marginalized groups. However, one study examining Indian communities in Dubai demonstrates that friendship and shared values help community members establish intimate and supportive social bonds within a new environment (Sancho 2020). Friendship networks among Dubai migrants were instrumental in their well-being, and these networks replaced the role of the family (Sancho 2020). In the same way, my friendships offer me support, healing and a place in a community that fosters well-being. It is a feminist tribe that supports the stories of women: one where *suwalif* are everyday pleasantries and intimacies.

My friends are all mothers. I am the aunty who holds their children's hands, buys them gifts and entertains them whilst their mothers are away. These are new alliances that I have created, feminist friendships that will give me a sense of belonging (Gardiner 1996). I was present at my best friend's first ultrasound appointment, and later I became her daughter Lulu's favourite aunty. I am Juliet's godmother and Mimi's academic adviser. I am an aunty whose two-bedroom apartment is the home of sleepovers for many. The following are among the statements made by these friends:

> *'It's important to me that you are part of her life. I want you to be there and advise her when she needs you,' Nourah says.*
>
> *'I want you to get to know my daughter. She doesn't have any academic influences around her. I know how much you love children and couldn't have them—but it doesn't have to be this way. She will love you,' Nosh says.*
>
> *'Do you need help carrying her? If she's too heavy, don't worry about it,' Fatma offers.*

My role has shifted into different ways of being with others, in which my disabled identity is accepted. Disabled women often struggle with psychosocial conflicts produced by stigmatization and vulnerability to prejudice and discrimination, which affect their sense of self and well-being (Nosek & Hughes 2003). However, to better accept and cope with my disability, I have taken on unconventional social roles. Now, I have new-found hope that I will be able to manage my day-to-day life through finding meaning, namely from passion

GULF WOMEN'S LIVES

projects and interactions with my college students. Ellingson and Sotirin (2006) remind us of the value of 'aunting':

> Aunting moves us beyond the impasses and antagonisms of the mother/daughter trope as well. For third-wave feminists, the aunt figure offers the opportunity for female-centred intimacy without the intense identification of the mother/daughter relation. (37)

In academia, my relationship with my students (especially disabled students) continues years after they have graduated, as mentorship, friendship and allyship, in the same vein as Bernadette Calafell's significant work on feminist allyship and mentoring (2012; Ghabra & Calafell 2018). Because disabled women are marginalized, silenced and hardly noticed, most of my students are shocked to see me with a cane. It is a disturbing image for them to see me using a cane, while at other times I am fully functional. My academic performance as disabled faculty is part of the embodied scholarship I carry out. Even in using the cane I take this as a teaching moment, an opportunity to discuss what it means to be living with disability that is sometimes invisible. The invisibility of disabled faculty is a necessary conversation to have with students. I find myself under the burden of exemplariness as a disabled Bedouin woman who happens to be a successful professor, aiming to mentor, support and love through feminist allyship. When I share my disability with my students, they are shocked by my vulnerability and openness. I become their friend after they graduate, like an aunty figure guiding them through complex issues such as love and loss, as well as disability. In doing so, I aim to be more than just an academician. I aspire to redefine the notion of 'aunting'. Care is defined as 'living well and also an emphasis on the in-between spaces of individuals who are [...] not totally distinct under conditions of trauma and disability' (Harris & Fortney 2017: 21). 'Aunting' is an important practice for those who are othered, enabling them to challenge heteronormativity, traditionally maternal spaces and ableism. Aunting is a performative space in which lived experiences of discrimination and otherness can be reclaimed. However, I do not wish to be confined to being an aunty or an academic mentor. By applying embodied feminism to my everyday life, I merge the personal and political and favour speech over silence. I speak about disability from everyday personal experiences. I traced the importance of women's voices and *suwalif* to my own ancestral bloodlines, and so it became inevitable that I would take the path of writing.

On Writing Illness Narratives and Voice

Growing up, listening to *suwalif* was an integral part of my female interactions within my family. My paternal grandmother recited oral poetry and told stories of women who had experienced grief and loss. My understanding of grief and loss began by listening to women's poetry and narratives designed to make sense of it. I recall Shammar's tribal poetry being recited in everyday conversations to emphasize the feeling of loss. My grandmother had lost multiple sons and invoked other women's poetry and narratives to extract meaning from her own experiences. Although she was illiterate, she understood language's power to summon the universal human experience of loss. She also narrated the experiences of female friends, family friends, tribe members and ancestors, referring to the tales as *suwalif*. Each *salfah* was constructed to carry the voice of the original female storyteller. In a sense, each *salfah* performed informal autoethnography that positioned other women within the larger (tribal) sphere, allowing them to reflect on cultural practices, rituals and human emotions. The position of the narrator was significant because it raised communal and, at times, universal issues. Storytelling was not foreign to me, but oral or written narratives by disabled women were unheard of. As I approached writing my own disability narrative, I situated myself within the feminist politics of survival. Reclaiming my voice through writing came with an awareness that academia was a place from which I could 'talk back'. As hooks (2021) puts it,

> Moving from silence into speech is for the oppressed, the colonized, the exploited, and those who stand and struggle side by side a gesture of defiance that heals, that makes new life and new growth possible. It is that act of speech, of 'talking back,' that is no mere gesture of empty words, that is the expression of our movement from object to subject —the liberated voice. (166)

As I increasingly talked back to my aunties, to my tribe, and to the stigma that I lived with, I realized that my path was untrodden. Supported by my Palestinian, non-tribal mother, who believed in narrating trauma, constantly referencing Palestinian resilience in the face of occupation, I knew that writing was my calling. Resilience, in her world, was a place of growth and healing; a place where death did not exist. To give up, to have parts of myself die unnarrated, would go against her definition of resilience in the face of warfare. I had chosen to write about illness and disability, but there was nothing I could reference about these from Arab literary history, let alone from Bedouin oral or written narratives. Arab illness narratives are scarce, but Gulf illness narratives are virtually unheard of. As Hamdar notes (2016), 'Arab studies on chronic illness, disability, and other physical ailments have mainly provided statistical data and medical findings rather than targeted the social and cultural scope of these and other illnesses' (17). It comes as no surprise, then, that disability was non-existent in all of the *suwalif* I had heard. There were no stories to rely on; there was no compass I could use to help me navigate an understanding of my new-found disabled identity within my Bedouin culture. As an academic researching disability studies and illness narratives, I found a staggering gap in Arabic literature: women, disabled or not, have hardly written about illness or disability. I searched for disabled female heroines in Gulf literature, but I found only tragic depictions of disabled women. In Kuwaiti television serials, female disabled heroines were evil, pitiful or tragic (Alenaizi 2018). Iconic disabled characters like Khalti Gmasha ('my mother-in-law Gmasha') used a cane to harass her family, whilst others were shunned and marginalized, hidden from society's gaze. I knew I had to write my own body into the canon. I had a *salfah* to tell; talking back marked the beginning of my career in writing about the intricacies of the disabled body.

> '*Are you sure you want to write in English? You're Kuwaiti. Arab-blooded! You can't betray the language. Make sure that you write in Arabic.*'
>
> '*Are you sure you want to write about your illness? It's too personal! Only Westerners write about disability!*'
>
> '*Are you sure you want to write about yourself? That's just... self-indulgent. That's not real research.*'

As a disabled Arab female researcher and author, I have had to contend with all these unsolicited suggestions, questions and confusions. To occupy multiple positions at once means I must constantly explain my choices. I explain to fellow academics, friends, students and readers alike. More often than not,

FROM STIGMA TO SPEECH

I attend conferences where I must defend my writing. Writing becomes a place for both forgiveness and healing, and the language chosen is a simple tool of expression. Forgiveness of one's self and the other manifests in writing about the trauma, the grief and the stigmatization. Writing about my experience with liminality and illness situates my body at the forefront of the discussion. The language chosen does not preoccupy my thoughts, as I find that my 'affair' with the English language releases me from my commitment to Arabic (Kellman 2013). Having an affair with English is the way I write my *suwalif*, blending my Bedouin ancestral roots with a language that expands to fit my uncontainable disabled body.

As I write, I am increasingly aware that narrating the disabled body is a challenge. Disabled bodies are silenced not just in my Bedouin tribe, but also in the West. Western culture has continually regarded women's disabled bodies as inferior. This notion goes back to Aristotle, who, as Rosemarie Garland-Thomson (2002) reminds us, considered women 'mutilated males', whilst Western thought has 'long conflated femaleness and disability, understanding both as defective departures from a valued standard of able-bodied maleness' (78). Western thought, then, was not the sole reason behind my desire to write about illness and disability. I recall the oral poetry of women from the Shammar tribe, written around themes of love and the body. Numerous other examples remind me that women's voices are not always silenced; that this is a myth. Bedouin women have found a space to express their losses, loves and pain through poetry and *suwalif*. It should be expected, even predictable, that I would do the same, choosing to tell grander *suwalif* (textual narratives) and documenting personal histories. As a disabled academic, I have to defend my writing choices: autoethnography as a method and the subject being the disabled body—my own. As Spry (2001) puts it:

> We have been expected to accept the myth of the researcher as a detached head—the object of Thought, Rationality, and Reason—floating from research site to research site thinking and speaking, whilst its profane counterpart, the Body, lurks unseen, unruly, and uncontrollable in the shadows of the Great Halls of the Academy (Spry 2001: 720).

'The Academy' wants me to write objective research, Arabs want me to write in Arabic, and the tribe does not want me to write about disability.

GULF WOMEN'S LIVES

These conflicting demands place me at odds with many social settings. However, because I have reflected critically on these academic, cultural and social expectations, I have been able to continue writing about the body. My body carried *suwalif* and stories with me wherever I went. Sara Ahmed (2020) coined the term 'companion texts', suggesting that

> a companion text is a text whose company enabled you to segue on a path less trodden. Such texts might spark a moment of revelation [...], they might share a feeling or give you resources to make sense of something beyond your grasp. (16)

In my understanding, companion texts encompass both the *suwalif* and the written texts that I carry with me to situate my voice as a disabled Bedouin writer. The necessity of companion texts lies in what they offer us: a compass to navigate 'less trodden' places.

My companion texts included Nancy Mairs's *Carnal Acts* (1991) and Arthur Frank's *The Wounded Storyteller* (2013). Each of these Western texts has given me an understanding of illness and the language to use when writing about it. The work of Mairs (1991), a white academic living with MS, provided me with a new sense of hope. Although she was writing from a Western perspective of disability, I was able to make connections and find universal aspects in her work to which I could relate. Making connections between cultures, languages and illnesses did not mean I was unaware of differences. I was choosing to bridge the gap between two opposing cultures and languages, putting in the critical and reflective work required to tease out similarities and differences between the experiences of disabled women. Discrepant experiences, according to Said (1994), can be placed alongside each other to be interpreted together 'contrapuntally' (32). My contrapuntal readings of experiences (and texts) allowed the forging of new space, a path that blended cultures and languages, feminist scholars and Bedouin women's *suwalif*, and led me to write the first memoir of illness from the Gulf. It is this merging of cultures (and languages) that has allowed me to navigate my life with disability and writing.

As I began to form local feminist circles of friends, mentors and students, I wanted to write about my experiences, having read so many Western illness narratives. I moved from the local to the global through the written word, through writing two illness narratives. My first was *Notes on the Flesh* (2017a), an illness narrative that included many stories of ill and/or disabled women, including mine. Most of these stories were fictional, although my narrative was autobiographical. The illness narrative has been on the rise since the 1990s in Western literature and scholarship. Illness narratives fall under three different categories: restitution narratives, quest narratives and chaos narratives (Frank 2013). Restitution narratives aim for triumph over disease and the return of the individual to the normalcy of everyday life. Quest narratives offer insight into disease and human suffering, as the illness transforms the ill subject and they are then able to share their new-found wisdom with others (Frank 2013: 115). These illness narratives are mainly Western, and as a scholar trained in English literature and literary theory, I was very aware of the tradition of life writing in Western texts. As a wounded storyteller, I was able to come to terms with navigating the limits of my disabled body and with society's stigmatization of women's disabled bodies. My debut work was a 'chaos' narrative, one that did not fall into a strict genre category. It did not have a linear plot line, and it largely shunned the standard forms of narrative closure, eschewing literary traditions.

> *'But you are a literature professor! Literature professors study literary criticism! Give us an ending, a resolution. Let it make sense. Readers need closure. Otherwise, you have betrayed the reader,' says my literature colleague.*
>
> *'I don't have an ending. There's no ending to illness,' I respond, unsure how to defend my narrative and aesthetic choices.*
>
> *'Well, there has to be a narrative arc. We all know this.'*

The common belief that a life's narrative has to have a beginning, middle and end is an ableist one, because it assumes a resolution to the narrative arc and conflict. Illness interrupts life; disabled lives are structured and lived differently. This 'we all know' is the able-bodied academic in the ivory tower. Moreover, most narratives, whether they be oral or written, have a sense of temporality.

> The conventional expectation of any narrative, held alike by listeners and storytellers, is for a past that leads into a present that sets in place a foreseeable future. The illness *story* is wrecked because its presence is not what the past was supposed to lead up to, and the future is scarcely thinkable (Frank 2013: 55).

GULF WOMEN'S LIVES

All the stories I have read, as well as the *suwalif* that I have listened to, have had a common narrative arc and a resolution. As a literary critic, I am trained to identify and assess narrative arcs, and the ones with which I engaged did not accord with my own lived experiences with illness. Talking about my own experiences demanded a sense of distance that I only achieved by creating an alter ego, Sarah, who also navigates life with MS in my first book, *Notes on the Flesh* (2017a). Readers do not ultimately know what happens to Sarah, because I myself do not know what will happen in my life. I employed the same way of thinking in my full memoir, *Head Above Water: Reflections on Illness* (2022), which is a very long *salfah*. I was more committed to truth-telling, narrating the experiences of disability, and outlining my academic career. Drawing on theories of disability studies, autoethnography, trauma studies and illness narratives, I found myself writing out my conversations with influential people in my life. My memoir oscillates between past and present but mainly focuses on conversations. I consider the experience of being disabled and the trauma of being stigmatized for it, whilst attempting to make sense of my bodily experiences without victimizing myself. As a Bedouin woman who grew up very aware of women's agency in storytelling and poetry, I wanted to keep my writer's voice intact and narrate the narrative as my 'normal'. There was no ending, no clear compass, and, as I am still very much alive, the memoir ends abruptly. My 'new normal' took shape in my ability to accept the loss of 'normalcy' in favour of new definitions of family, friendship and life. While my life story is critically engaged with academic scholarship around autoethnography and life writing, it also insists on merging scholarship with everyday life.

Conclusion

My commitment to embodied activism manifests itself through my connec-tions to friends, students, and readers whom I have not met. It is a commitment to Bedouin women who tell their *suwalif* and to disabled women who have never told their *suwalif*. Autoethnography relies on making sure the researcher is placed within the subject of the research and, I would suggest, from a bodily perspective: 'The autoethnographic text emerges from the researcher's bodily standpoint as she is continually recognizing and interpreting the residue traces of culture inscribed upon her hide from interacting with others in contexts' (Spry 2001: 711). Spry (2001) contends that autoethnography (and I would add life writing in general) has a personal, professional and political emancipatory potential. Disabled Bedouin women's voices are unheard of for fear of stigmatization and shame. Gulf narratives of illness and disability (whether in Arabic or English) are scarce. There is a staggering lack of narratives about the body and its intricacies, failings and position within larger social settings. More autoethnographic research needs to be explored, and more disabled women's voices need to be at the forefront of any discussion on their bodies and lives. I have set out on an untrodden path, but it is my hope that it will be a path that many scholars (and writers) follow. As Frost puts it: 'I took the one less travelled by, and that has made all the difference' (2002: 105).

References

Abu-Rabia-Queder, S. (2006). Between Tradition and Modernization: Understanding the Problem of Female Bedouin Dropouts. *British Journal of Sociology of Education*, 27(1), 3–17. https://doi.org/10.1080/01425690500376309

Ahmed, S. (2020). *Living a Feminist Life*. Duke University Press. https://doi.org/10.1515/9780822373377

Al-Nakib, F. (2014). Revisiting Hadar and Badū in Kuwait: Citizenship, Housing, and the Construction of a Dichotomy. *International Journal of Middle East Studies*, 46(1), 5–30. https://doi.org/10.1017/S0020743813001268

Alenaizi, H.M. (2018). Portrayal of Disabled People in the Kuwaiti Media. *Disability and the Global South*, 5(1), 1315–36.

Alshammari, S. (2017a). *Notes on the Flesh*. Faraxa.

Alshammari, S. (2017b). Troubling Academe: Disability, Borders, and Boundaries. *Journal of Middle East Women's Studies*, 13(3), 458–60. https://doi.org/10.1215/15525864-4179111

Alshammari, S. (2019). Writing an Illness Narrative and Negotiating Identity: A Kuwaiti Academic/Author's Journey. *Life Writing*, 16(3), 431–38. https://doi.org/10.1080/14484528.2018.1514240

Alshammari, S. (2022). *Head Above Water: Reflections on Illness*. Neem Tree Press.

Brune, J.A. & Wilson, D.J. (2014). Disability and Passing: Blurring the Lines of Identity. *Journal of American History*, 101(1), 301–02. https://doi.org/10.1093/jahist/jau305

Calafell, B.M. (2012). Monstrous Femininity: Constructions of Women of Color in the Academy. *Journal of Communication Inquiry*, 36(2), 111–130. https://doi.org/10.1177/0196859912443382

GULF WOMEN'S LIVES

Chatty, D. (2020). Mikkel Bille, Being Bedouin around Petra: Life at a World Heritage Site in the Twenty-First Century. *Nomadic Peoples*, 24(2), 348–51. https://doi.org/10.3197/np.2020. 240213

Cole, D.P. (2003). Where Have the Bedouin Gone? *Anthropological Quarterly*, 76(2), 235–67. https://doi.org/10.1353/anq.2003.0021

Ellingson, L.L. & Sotirin, P. (2006). Academic Aunting: Reimaging Feminist (Wo)mentoring, Teaching, and Relationships. *Women and Language*, 31(1), 35–41.

Ellis, C. & Bochner, A. (2000). Autoethnography, Personal Narrative, Reflexivity: Researcher as Subject. In L.K. Denzin & Y.S. Lincoln (eds), *Handbook of Qualitative Research* (Issue 28, pp. 733–68). SAGE.

Frank, A.W. (2013). *The Wounded Storyteller: Body, Illness, and Ethics*. University of Chicago Press. https://press.uchicago.edu/ucp/books/book/chicago/W/bo14674212.html

Franz, K., Büssow, J. & Leder, S. (2015). The Arab East and the Bedouin Component in Pre-modern History: Approaching Textual Representations and Their Changing Settings in Life. *Islam—Zeitschrift fur Geschichte und Kultur des Islamischen Orients*, 92(1), 1–12. https://doi. org/10.1515/islam-2015-0001

Frost, R. (2002). The Poetry of Robert Frost: The Collected Poems. In R. Frost & E.C. Lathem (eds), *Owl Books* (2nd edn). Holt, Henry & Company, Inc.

Gardiner, M.E. (1996). *Parent–School Collaboration: Feminist Organizational Structures and School Leadership*. SUNY series, The Social Context of Education.

Garland-Thomson, R. (2002). Integrating Disability, Transforming Feminist Theory. *NWSA Journal*, 14(3), 1–32. https://doi.org/10.2979/nws.2002.14.3.1

Ghabra, H. & Calafell, B.M. (2018). From Failure and Allyship to Feminist Solidarities: Negotiating Our Privileges and Oppressions across Borders*. *Text and Performance Quarterly*, 38(1–2). https://doi.org/10.1080/10462937.2018.1457173

Hamdar, A. (2016). The Female Suffering Body: Illness and Disability in Modern Arabic Literature. *British Journal of Middle Eastern Studies*, 43(4), 684–86. https://doi.org/10.1080/13530 194.2016.1182263

Harris, K.L. & Fortney, J.M. (2017). Performing Reflexive Caring: Rethinking Reflexivity Through Trauma and Disability. *Text and Performance Quarterly*, 37(1), 20–34. https://doi.org/10.1080/ 10462937.2016.1273543

hooks, b. (2021). Writing Autobiography. In *Talking Back: Thinking Feminist, Thinking Black* (pp. 167–71). Routledge. https://doi.org/10.4324/9781315743134

Ingham, B. (1993). The 'Sālfah' as a Narrative Genre. *Asian Folklore Studies*, 52(1), 5. https://doi. org/10.2307/1178449

Julia, M. & AlMaseb, H. (2007). Kuwaiti Bedouin Muslim Women Achieving Control over Their Lives: Factors Supporting Empowerment. *Social Development Issues*, 29(1), 81–99.

Kellman, S.G. (2013). Promiscuous Tongues: Erotics of Translingualism and Translation. *Neohelicon*, 40(1), 35–45. https://doi.org/10.1007/s11059-013-0170-4

Mairs, N. (1991). *Carnal Acts: Essays*. Perennial.

Maisel, S. (2018). Tribalism and Family Affairs in the Arabian Peninsula. *Hawwa*, 16(1–3), 26–59. https://doi.org/10.1163/15692086-12341344

Nosek, M.A. & Hughes, R.B. (2003). Psychosocial Issues of Women with Physical Disabilities: The Continuing Gender Debate. In *Rehabilitation Counseling Bulletin*, 46(4), 224–33. https://doi.org/10.1177/003435520304600403

Said, E.W. (1994). Identity, Authority, and Freedom: The Potentate and the Traveler. *Boundary*, 21(3), 1. https://doi.org/10.2307/303599

Sancho, D. (2020). Facing Life Together. In E. Buscemi & I. Kaposi (eds), *Everyday Youth Cultures in the Gulf Peninsula: Changes and Challenges* (pp. 123–38). Routledge. https://doi.org/10.4324/9781003048626-11

Spry, T. (2001). Performing Autoethnography: An Embodied Methodological Praxis. *Qualitative Inquiry*, 7(6), 706–32. https://doi.org/10.1177/107780040100700605

Wall, S. (2006). An Autoethnography on Learning about Autoethnography. *International Journal of Qualitative Methods*, 5(2), 146–60. https://doi.org/10.1177/160940690600500205

Women Talking Back: In Conversation with *Sekka* Magazine's 'Managing Storyteller' Sharifah Alhinai

2

Ildiko Kaposi (0000-0003-1365-8939)

Sekka is Arabic for the narrow streets connecting neighbourhoods in traditional Arab settlements. *Sekka* is also a cultural magazine and media company founded by Emirati sisters Manar and Sharifah Alhinai in 2017 as a response to their growing frustration about the ongoing misrepresentation of the Gulf and the Arab world in Western media. Breaking centuries of misperceptions is no small task, but the Alhinai sisters represent a young generation of Emiratis exuding an assertive can-do attitude and confidence about the possibility of reclaiming the narrative of the Gulf. Their motto comes from Edward Said's call to replace outraged righteousness in the face of Western hostility with a 'conscious and forceful self-image' (Said 1997: 66).

Sekka is a sophisticated way of talking back to a Western world that has shaped the history of the Gulf in so many ways. It is also a product of the contemporary Khaleeji cultural scene whose origins, at least in the current leading centres of the UAE and Qatar, can be traced back to state-devised strategies of diversifying the economy from a near-total reliance on hydrocarbons towards serious investment in other sectors, including sports, media, arts and culture. The small size of these nations does not stop them from aspiring to a global presence and impact, and their governments are markedly fluent in the language of globalization in its market-centric vernacular. As are *Sekka*'s founders, who have benefitted from an enabling entrepreneurial environment in the UAE.

Ildiko Kaposi, 'Women Talking Back: In Conversation with *Sekka* Magazine's "Managing Storyteller" Sharifah Alhinai' in: *Gulf Women's Lives: Voice, Space, Place*. University of Exeter Press (2024). © Ildiko Kaposi. DOI: 10.47788/XSXW3918

Since its launch, *Sekka* has diversified its activities: it branched out into a creative and communications consultancy, established an annual literary prize awarded for emerging Arab writers, and launched a sister venture, a digital museum/art gallery showcasing art from the Arab Gulf region.[1] The magazine also transitioned from its original digital online publication to print in 2022, and relocated its headquarters to Covent Garden for proximity to London's global media hub. *Sekka* is printed in London and distributed through European and American retailers, while a collaboration with PressReader also makes its digital editions available on airlines globally.

Sekka showcases the region in its transcultural heterogeneity, inviting citizens and residents, men and women alike, to add their voices to the magazine. Issued three times a year, its editions are thematically organized around topics such as 'Aib [shame]', 'The Creative Giants', 'The Power of Words' and 'The Neo-Arabs'. *Sekka* does not self-identify as a women's magazine, but it championed womanhood in the Spring 2022 edition of the same title, and it has consistently tackled social taboos related to women, such as Arab feminism, the male gaze, disabled women and menstruation. Despite the avoidance of the women's market niche, the magazine's contributors and audiences are predominantly younger females from the Gulf, the USA and the UK.[2]

Talking to Sharifah Alhinai is an experience in demolishing conceptual pigeonholes that pit culture against commerce, idealism against pragmatism, journalism against public relations. Our conversation focused on the sisters' choice of a magazine as the medium for 'talking back', and the editorial and managerial nuts and bolts of running a sustainable media platform for regional voices.

Q: You have done journalism and media writing, but you have never started a magazine before the launching of *Sekka*. What skills and experiences did you bring to this new venture?

A: Prior to establishing *Sekka*, [my sister] Manar had written for a number of regional and local publications. Journalism was something she's been passionate about ever since we were children. We both have a passion for

---

1. The Khaleeji Art Museum can be visited 24/7 at https://khaleejiartmuseum.com/.
2. According to *Sekka*'s media kit, 64% of readers are female, 45.1% are in the 25–34 age group, and 28.9% are aged 18–24.

GULF WOMEN'S LIVES

writing, we believe in the power of the written word. It felt natural for us to tackle the misconceptions and stereotypes about the region and its people in this way.

Manar studied mass communication in university, and I have an undergraduate degree in law and an MSc in international politics from the School of Oriental and African Studies. When the idea of *Sekka* was born, I had just finished my master's, and I thought I would pursue a more traditional diplomacy or political career. I saw our work through that lens, that it is a form of cultural diplomacy, and that really excited me. I was very attracted to the idea of starting our own media company. It was not just that passion for writing, it was also this equal passion for bringing people together, starting cross-cultural conversations that are meaningful and impactful, and changing the narrative about the region.

Q: It seems like your skills and backgrounds complement each other beautifully. But what is it like to work with your sister on this enterprise that you are both passionate about?

A: You know, we get asked this question often. We enjoy working together, and we do complement each other as people, which I think is the reason why our partnership has been so successful. Manar is the one who is more outgoing, she is a force of nature. I am the one that is maybe a little bit more introverted or reserved in comparison. We balance each other out in that respect. In terms of other characteristics, I am very detail-oriented, I am a perfectionist. Manar is the kind of person who does things very quickly. So, while I take my time with things, she speeds things up, and in that way too we complement each other. Honestly, she is a person that I have looked up to ever since we were kids, because there is about a six-year age difference between us.

Q: Big sister? Six years your senior.

A: Yes, yes. She has always been my idol, and she has been a great mentor for me through this whole process. She is the one who had the media education, the experience of working for years as a contributing writer to many different publications and media companies. I learned a lot from her, and I owe so much of what I do and what I am able to do to her. When we were little, Manar started a magazine in elementary school, and she actually convinced a local bookseller to sell her magazine in his shop!

I was mesmerized by that, by my sister creating this magazine. Mind you, at the time I was maybe five years old. I was very inspired, and I thought that was the most amazing thing in the world. And when I got a little bit older, I also did the same thing. I started a magazine in school, I called it *Girl Zone* [laughs]. Then in the eleventh grade I co-founded my school's first newspaper, and it became a class where students would produce the newspaper and get graded for it. So you can see the beginnings of our interest in journalism, media and writing started very early on.

Q: And this is all in the UAE where you were growing up? The school and the magazines?

A: Yes. In the UAE.

Q: *Sekka* defines itself as an 'independent publication and integrated creative platform'. What does independent mean for you, and why do you feel it is important to emphasize?

A: When we say that *Sekka* is independent, we essentially mean that it was founded by Manar and I, and it has been self-funded as a business in the sense that we have not brought any investors on board. That is pretty much what we mean by independent: it has been independently owned and funded for the last five years.

Q: Setting *Sekka* up, how easy or challenging was it to launch? Launching a cultural magazine, acting as creative entrepreneurs in the UAE.

A: It did take a relatively short time to establish the magazine. But there were a lot of conversations that we had during that short time between the idea and the first issue about what this media company would look like, how we would differentiate it, how it will succeed in a world and at a time where so many media companies and magazines were struggling worldwide to survive. They were very important conversations to be had— and also included, of course, the name, what would the name of the magazine be, and how would we communicate our message through it. All of these conversations happened in approximately nine months.

It was a challenging time to start a magazine because of the global context that we were going to operate in. We even thought a number of times, should we even do this? Is it too risky? Should we be tackling these misconceptions and stereotypes in a different format? But the conclusion was always no, we have to do this format. This is the most suitable for us,

GULF WOMEN'S LIVES

and this is what we know best. And if we do not do it, who will? In 2016–17, there were not many publications from the region dedicated to the Arab world with such a mission and a global outlook. Because right from the beginning, our mission was to change the narrative about the region, to reclaim it and to tell our stories in our own voices, and for our message to be international as opposed to just speaking within the region itself.

In terms of setting it up as a media company, it was very easy to do. We did it in the matter of a few days. What has been challenging is producing content that stands out in a world that is already oversaturated with content, where there is a competition for eyeballs wherever you go.

This is something that we constantly have to think about: how do we produce content that is very appealing? And in addition to that, how do we promote it on social media? Because that is an important way of getting readers. It is not easy to create and promote content to people that come from a wide range of cultural backgrounds and different societies. We have to think about keeping up with our *Sekka* community, keeping them engaged and also growing it.

Q: Coming back to these early discussions, how did you decide to make *Sekka* a media company, as you say, implying also that it is a commercial business? You are publishing a magazine with higher cultural aspirations. So why did you decide on this commercial business framework for *Sekka*?

A: Given the goals we had in mind, we wanted to be producing not only digital issues, which we started with; we also wanted to create content and publish it on an online platform. We wanted to keep it quite flexible for future expansion of the services that we provide. So it made the most sense for it to be a media company, as opposed to just a magazine, and over the years we have expanded our products and services. In addition to the digital issues and the platform through which we publish more regularly articles outside the issues, we also ventured into print from 2022. Now our issues are available in print, and they are sold through retailers in Europe and the USA. And we are constantly looking to expand to new markets. In addition to all that, we also began a creative consultancy through which we advise government bodies, businesses, individuals on everything related to the creative economy, with regards to communication.

WOMEN TALKING BACK

That has led us to become more of an international media brand. The services we provide also really go back to our mission, which is to emphasize the arts and culture, literature and opinions of the region. Through the programmes and activities we now help curate and organize for different entities, and through the consultancy that we provide, we try to elevate the creativity and cultural sectors of the region, which has been our emphasis right from the get-go.

Q: The magazine started out digital, and then you made the decision to also have a print edition. With this one, you seem to be going against the tide or the trends of the existing print version also needing an online presence. So why did you want a print edition?

A: It is a very good question because it does seem like we are going against the tide at first glance. Essentially, we wanted to appeal to as many readers as possible. Despite the move to reading books or magazines digitally, there are a lot of people that still prefer to read in print. I am one of them, I still like to read books in print. Printing our issues was also something that a lot of our readers had asked for over the years. Almost every time we published a new issue, or we had somebody contribute to *Sekka*, we always had the question of 'Is this also available in print? I'd love to keep it.' There is always this idea that once you have it in print, you are able to keep it, it is going to live forever.

The issues are more of a crossover between a book and a magazine. The quality of the paper, the way it is printed, designed, it reminds you so much of a book, more than it does of a magazine. We have created them in a way that this is something that you buy and keep forever. In a nutshell, that is the thought we had behind the print: to cater to as many people as possible, to respond to our readers' demands, and to create something that people can keep for years to come.

Q: 198 pages with lots of gorgeous illustrations, *Sekka* looks like a coffee table book with some serious content. It is almost begging to leap off the digital and go to print. But on this note, how did you manage to arrange partnerships with international, overseas stockists to carry *Sekka*?

A: It was quite easy to get our magazine to be sold through international retailers because, and this is something that we heard from a number of them, they have been hungry for something like this. It has been a gap for them, this part of the world. I remember a conversation that we had with Casa Magazines in New York, which was the first store that stocked *Sekka* in the USA. The owner was very excited to have something from the Arab world in his store. On the cover was a woman who wore a hijab (that was the Creative Giants issue). The owner himself and the team decided to put *Sekka* in the window display because they were really excited to have something Arab that also represented Muslim identity, because the owner is actually a Muslim, he has South Asian origins. *Sekka* was placed right next to magazines such as *Vogue, L'Officiel, GQ* in the window [Figure 2.1]. That was symbolic and momentous because it meant that our voices were becoming an equal part of the global conversation. It was very symbolic not only for us, but also for our *Sekka* community.

> **Sekka**
> @sekkamag
>
> We promised we'd take the voices of the people from the Gulf and wider Arab world globally, and we have.
>
> Sekka is now available in New York's most iconic & famous magazine store Casa Magazines on its store window, on the first row, alongside the world's most known publications.

9:18 AM · Jan 6, 2022

Figure 2.1: *Sekka* announcing Casa Magazines partnership on social media.

WOMEN TALKING BACK

When we published that picture of *Sekka* in Casa Magazines' display on *Sekka*'s Instagram account, it was one of the photos that people have most interacted with because it also meant that they, our contributors, our community, had also made it. It was a moment where we also got a lot of emails and messages from people wanting to contribute to *Sekka* more because they also wanted to reach that global level. It was very exciting for everybody.

Q: Does the owner still sell *Sekka*?

A: Yes, our partnership has continued since then. It has sold well in the store and in other stores in New York, including different branches of Iconic Magazines. It has also performed very well in the Netherlands and in the UK because on their platforms or in their stores *Sekka* really does stand out as something from the Arab world. It is also visually appealing to a lot of people who are generally interested in arts and in culture. That was something that we worked very hard on, how to make it visually attractive and vibrant, while also having content that is meaningful and thought-provoking that gets people interested and curious about the region.

Q: The magazine is published in English. Did you get any criticism for not publishing in Arabic, or not incorporating Arabic more?

A: I would not consider it criticism. I would say that there was an interest to have the content also available in Arabic. We started off in English in 2017, and then we ventured into Arabic about a year later. We started publishing articles on an equivalent *Sekka* platform that was entirely in Arabic. We did that for a few years, and we did get engagement with the Arabic content, but unfortunately it was not to the level to keep it going. So we decided to switch back to our English-only focus. It really makes sense because our mission and outlook from the beginning was international. *Sekka* was always a message to people outside of the region, because that is really where we have the stereotypes and misconceptions that need to be corrected, that narrative that needs to be changed. We thought that publishing in Arabic, as much as we wanted to do that, did not really serve our mission in the end.

Q: Your plans for *Sekka* are clearly long-term, and it is not just about sustaining it because it has been expanding with all the other additional activities and projects that you are building around *Sekka*. But strictly for the

45

GULF WOMEN'S LIVES

magazine, concerning its sustainability, since you are running this as an enterprise, what sort of financial model did you decide to pursue? What revenue sources are you trying to base yourselves on?

A: Right from the beginning we knew that we did not want to bring in investors. And we have been successful in that pursuit. We rely on a number of different revenue streams for *Sekka*, which is something that a lot of media companies are doing now. They are diversifying their revenue streams. One of our revenue streams is advertising in the print issue, on the website and on our social media pages. In addition to that, we also have revenue from magazine sales, whether it is digital issues or print issues or yearly subscriptions. And a more recent one has been the creative and communication consultancy arm. The consultations that we provide and the programmes that we curate and the events we help hold have also been a revenue stream for us.

Q: You are not selling *Sekka* as a luxury good. It is £9 for a single digital issue, £25 or €35 for a print copy, and then at €90, the subscription is not outrageously expensive either. How did you settle on these price points?

A: We wanted to have a very balanced price because when we started off as a magazine, our content was available entirely for free. Our issues and access to our articles on the platform were for free. This was the case until we started making our issues available in print. We wanted as much as possible to not have any barriers to knowledge and acquiring knowledge. If we can provide knowledge for free, we are happy to do it. But at the same time, to ensure the sustainability of the magazine we had to put a price on it, and when it came to setting the price, we wanted *Sekka* to still be affordable as much as possible. The price of the digital and print issues stems from that, from wanting *Sekka* to be affordable to as many people as possible, while at the same time being able to cover our costs and to ensure our ability to continue and survive as a media company in such a challenging context for media outlets globally.

Q: I believe there is now a paywall up on the *Sekka* website, you are no longer sharing the magazine, the contents, for free. There is a teaser, enough to make people want to go and buy it.

A: Yes. Anything that we have published from 2022 onwards and made available on the website has had that paywall. But anything published

46

WOMEN TALKING BACK

between 2017 and late 2021 is still available to read for free. We are happy that we have been able to at least continue providing these articles free of charge.

Q: It is every media firm's problem, how to generate revenue from online when the digital culture is, 'here it is, read it, share it, it is free, love us, and advertise'. But the advertising market in the Gulf does have its problems. It is not as well developed as in some other parts of the world.

A: When it comes to advertising, I think a global challenge right now is that as a media company or a magazine you are no longer just competing with another media company or a magazine for advertisers, which was the case maybe twenty years ago. You are now also competing with social media influencers, because a lot of advertisers have turned to people who are well known on social media to do their advertising and to get to their target audiences. That is one of the reasons why relying on just advertising as a source of revenue is no longer a smart thing to do, because the competition just got tougher. Thinking about generating revenue is a continuous creative exercise that you have to revisit every once in a while, to make sure that you are able to continue as a magazine or media company.

Q: What was your readers' reaction to erecting the paywall?

A: We do still get emails from people who would like us to provide them with free copies or want free access to the magazine. This is something that happens pretty much with the release of any issue. As much as we would like to provide our content for free, unfortunately we cannot continue to do that if we want to ensure the survivability and continuity of the media company. It is something unfortunate, but it is something that we must do.

Q: What do you know about who reads *Sekka*?

A: The people who read *Sekka* are a mix from within and outside of the region. Some of our top readers are from the United Arab Emirates, Oman, Saudi Arabia. But at the same time in our top five are people from the USA and the UK. They are people who have a genuine curiosity about the Arab world and the Arab Gulf states in particular, and who want to know more, beyond the over-politicized and religion-centric image they often get through international media.

GULF WOMEN'S LIVES

We noticed these consistencies over the years, which is something that we are very happy about, because it is not easy to make content that is appealing to people who come from such diverse cultures and societies and backgrounds. Also, they are people who, in general, appreciate the arts. There is a lot of focus on arts and visuals in our magazine and on our website and social media pages. So it is usually people who have an interest in art, and people who also appreciate literature, culture and opinions, because that is also what we produce.

Q: How do you stay in touch with your readers, and what sort of reactions do you get from them?

A: In terms of how we stay in touch with our readers, we are, as much as possible, very responsive to them on social media, especially on Instagram, where we interact with them the most perhaps. They send us a lot of DMs, they tag us, they mention us. We are also open to receiving emails. We provide our email on the website, in our print issues and on our social media pages, you can contact us directly through email. That is the direct way that they have been communicating with us as a team. In addition to that, Manar and I constantly receive DMs from people who have contributed to *Sekka* or have become part of the *Sekka* community or the club. A lot of them have become our friends. Some of them have even become colleagues, and some business partners. They also stay in touch with us directly on Instagram, almost on a weekly basis. I always get somebody sending me something like suggesting a story to cover or somebody to feature, which is something that I am constantly grateful for because they help keep me abreast of everything that is going on. They help us curate our issues. In terms of what reactions we have gotten from people, a lot of the comments or correspondence that we get revolves around the same sort of subject, which is that a lot of people are very happy and grateful for the presence of *Sekka* because it has helped introduce them to so many really interesting personalities and talented people.

Sekka has played a great role in spotlighting emerging artists, photographers and writers. Many photographers and artists had their debut in *Sekka* and then went on to be featured in more international magazines and to become well known in their field. Similarly with contributing writers and interns. We launched a formal internship programme during

Covid as a way of supporting students and graduates of journalism, graphic design and arts. Many of the interns have gone off to do really exciting and inspiring things themselves. For example, one of our first interns is now a big editor in *Forbes*. She is doing amazing things that I am very proud of.

Sekka has been a way for people to really get to know the scene, to get to know some of its emerging and key players. *Sekka* has also inspired the emergence of two publications. We were directly told this by the founders themselves. They are publications from the region that likewise focus on art, focus on culture, on the emerging voices of the region. We are very happy about that.

Q: But that means you are sort of generating your own competition perhaps?

A: Honestly, I think there is space for everybody to shine, to provide something. We do still have a gap internationally when it comes to the region. We have been trying to fill it, but there is so much room for other players to come in and provide a more authentic narrative about the region, to share the region's rich stories and to highlight its people. Whenever we see the emergence of new media companies or new initiatives or collectives, it actually makes us very happy because that means more voices, more stories. That means the gap is slowly closing.

Q: As editors, you are spotlighting talent. Cultural curating becomes part of what you do, and that is a heavy responsibility. Your choices have consequences. Certainly, very positive ones for those you pick, but then there is a limit of roughly 200 pages, and inevitably, there are contributions that you need to leave out. I am wondering if you feel the weight of this responsibility when you are making editorial decisions.

A: Definitely. I felt that weight from day one, and I continue to feel it every day. Every time we produce an issue, no matter how good it is and how great a job the team has done, I always flip through it and say we could have done more, we could have put in more people, we could have highlighted this subregion or that subregion within the Arab world more. I would love to include everybody, because the world has been missing out on so many great stories from the region. I do feel limited by the number of pages, although to many people it feels like 200 pages is a lot. But it really is not. There is still so much to be covered, there are so many voices to be heard, so much work by artists and photographers to be seen. There is that feeling of responsibility, definitely, about what we publish and what we do not include.

Q: How do you choose the topics covered in each issue? Do you have a process, a routine, or is it more random? I am trying to imagine the storyteller-in-chief and the managing storyteller, the titles you and Manar gave to yourselves, at work.

A: There is definitely a process that goes into it. It is a very fun process actually. Apart from the responsibility, of course, it is a lot of fun to come up with the theme for each of our issues. We always make sure that the themes that we tackle are timely, but at the same time they have a universal appeal. The question is, how do you come up with something that is universal, but also timely and appealing to many people?

So we have a discussion every year, beginning in the summer and ending in the fall, about what themes we should highlight in the coming year. It is pretty much a collective exercise. Everybody in the team takes the time and thinks about and researches what they think we should be tackling next, what would be appealing to our readers and our community. Then we all meet, and everybody proposes their themes and explains their choices a bit more, gives an example of some of the stories that could be covered. Then we vote on what we want to cover.

Sometimes there are changes to those themes that emerge during our discussions, if we feel that there is a topic that suddenly a lot of people are talking about, and we need to address it as well. We work on our issues for months before they are released.

Q: How did the Womanhood issue come together? Can you share some of the details of that process?

A: The Womanhood issue [Figure 2.2] is one of my favourites, I really enjoyed working on it. We published it in March 2022, coinciding with International Women's Day. It sheds light on the incredible women of the Arab world who speak about the challenges they face, the successes they have enjoyed, and the issues that are of importance to them. It was important for us to have an issue dedicated to women of the Arab world and allow them to speak for themselves and represent themselves, because they are too often spoken for and misrepresented in international media. We

Figure 2.2: The Womanhood issue promoted on Sekkamag.com.

highlighted women from different backgrounds, from film to fashion to social media and art, because we wanted to hear from women in various fields.

They spoke about the female body, smashing stereotypes about Arab women through social media, and so much more. They were happy to be part of an issue that presented women of the region on their own terms on an international stage. Another reason why it was so important for us to have an issue that was dedicated to women is because the women of the region have been such an important and essential part of *Sekka*'s journey. Right from the beginning when we established *Sekka*, we put that call out for people to join us, whether they be contributing writers or illustrators or photographers, or just people who could be featured in the issue through an interview. Most of the people who have responded to us over the years have been women, especially young women of the region. This is not a feat that many media companies have achieved. As you know, women around the world are under-represented in the field of media. So being able to run a company with over fifty per cent of its contributors women from the Arab world is incredible. To have an issue dedicated to them, and to highlight them, is also to show our appreciation for them and the important role they have played in *Sekka*.

Q: You ended up with a who's who list of young regional talent. How did you choose the contributions? Did you have the ideas about whom you wanted, or were the contributors approaching you?

A: It was really a combination of what you mentioned. Sometimes we were driven by the person we wanted, for example with Layla AlAmmar, we really wanted her voice to be a part of the issue. We gave her the space to suggest a topic within the theme.[3] Or sometimes it was subject-driven. We wanted a story about the world of fashion or modelling, then we started searching for who would be appropriate to speak about this topic. Other times we approached people who had emailed us expressing their interest in contributing to *Sekka* before. Sometimes there is not enough space in a specific issue, or we had just closed work on our issues for the year, but we keep these people in mind after getting to know their areas of interest. So when a theme such as womanhood comes up, and they are relevant to it, we contact them and ask if they would like to take part. That is how we usually work on the issues.

Q: In the Womanhood issue, as in many of the others, you are pushing boundaries with some of the contributions. Quite a few of the topics are not the sort that you would regularly see in the regional press. You are challenging Western stereotypes, but you are also taking a good hard look at the region we are living in, with all its opportunities and its existing restrictions. You are highlighting artists and writers who are pushing the boundaries of Gulf sensitivity. So how did that play out?

A: Right from the beginning of our *Sekka* journey, we have always pushed to have important discussions, meaningful and honest discussions. This was something that we have become known for. We want to have bold, honest, meaningful conversations that are of importance to the people of the region and that also appeal to readers outside.

---

3. AlAmmar, a Kuwaiti novelist who writes in English, chose to cover language and identity.

We are a very visually driven magazine, which appeals to a lot of people, especially the youth. Another important area has been the kinds of topics we tackle through our issues and on our platform. It has been really interesting to work on this because when we have these conversations, we always try to strike the right balance in the sense that we want to have meaningful conversations, honest conversations on important topics, but we also want to be very respectful of our society and our culture and our people. So we always make sure that whenever we tackle a topic that is quite timely or that is viewed in many different ways, we do it in a way that is very respectful. We are very happy that we have been able to do that generally successfully and in a way that our readers have also appreciated. They have appreciated that we have been able to tackle important topics, but in a way that is respectful and objective and informative at the same time.

Q: Sounds like the recipe for how to push and challenge, but avoid having the 'unfiltered', as you call the voices you publish, banned in the Gulf.

References

Said, E. (1997). *Covering Islam: How the Media and the Experts Determine How We See the Rest of the World*. Vintage.

Bodies on the Margins: Nonconforming Subjectivities in Gulf Women's Literature

Emanuela Buscemi (0000-0003-2126-7858)

Introduction

Employing a postcolonial and decolonial framework, the present chapter intends to investigate nonconforming subjectivities and marginalized bodies in Jokha Alharthi's *Celestial Bodies* (2019), Shahd Alshammari's *Head Above Water* (2022a), and Laila Aljohani's *Days of Ignorance* (2014). The above-mentioned works powerfully delineate nonconforming subjects, especially women, who sit on or have been pushed at the margins of society by traditional arrangements and customary practices.

Celestial Bodies (Alharthi 2019) is the first book translated from Arabic to win the International Booker Prize. A multigenerational narrative of women and family relations in an Omani village, it underlines the tensions between tradition and modernity in a rapidly changing social and cultural landscape through the story of three sisters and their deceptive experience with marriage. Shahd Alshammari's *Head Above Water* (2022) is an autobiographical illness narrative on the author's experience with multiple sclerosis as a Palestinian-Kuwaiti young scholar and writer descending from a tribal family, and her positionality in academia, the family, the tribe and the wider communities that she carves for herself. Laila Aljohani's *Days of Ignorance* (2014) revolves around a hate crime perpetrated against Malek, a black resident, by the brother of his former girlfriend Leen. The novel, set in Medina, Saudi Arabia, between

---

Emanuela Buscemi, 'Bodies on the Margins: Nonconforming Subjectivities in Gulf Women's Literature' in: *Gulf Women's Lives: Voice, Space, Place.* University of Exeter Press (2024). © Emanuela Buscemi. DOI: 10.47788/LYZH2631

the hospital where Malek lies in a coma and the urban streets where Leen and her brother Hashem reminisce about their life, focuses on the strains between a conservative society (and its global terrorist-like derivations) and the attempts at navigating openness and a new role for women.

By centring their narratives on characters such as slaves, black non-citizens, migrants and people with disabilities, among others, these authors interrogate the current social and cultural practices, (re)claiming a de-invisibilization of the conditions of those who are neither showcased in the news nor take central stage in Gulf public discourse. These powerful explorations of race, gender and status, broadly intended, allow readers to glimpse into the gender, ethnic and tribal foundations of Gulf countries to interrogate the roots and polarities of contemporary Khaleeji societies by pushing to the forefront of the literary scene unconventional and uncomfortable characters and plot lines. By doing so, the texts contribute to opening up the discussion on contemporary Khaleeji identity, as well as social, political and cultural tenets.

The present chapter sets out to investigate nonconforming subjectivities and bodies in the light of power relations exacerbated by naming and recognition, genealogies of pain and mutating landscapes with reference to both the passing on of legacy and customs. It also contributes to the exploration of the accelerated changes that have occurred in the region, generated by the fast pace of oil-fuelled wealth, and the deployment of agency from and in the margins.

Women and the national project

Traditionally, women and their bodies have been central to national(istic) narratives, embodying the nation and its aspirations. In this respect, Floya Anthias and Nira Yuval-Davis individuate a number of instances through which the state regulates women's bodies and behaviour towards the national order: as biological reproducers; as reproducers of the boundaries of ethnic and national groups; as agents in the ideological reproduction and conveyors of culture; as signifiers of ethnic and national differences; as participants in national and military struggles (1989: 7). These multilayered implications of women in the perpetuation of the patriarchal order and its social, political and economic structures share a common element in the control over the performativity of the woman's body.

However, the relationship between gender and nation needs to be problematized with reference to the Global South and colonial experiences. It is important to note that the decolonial framework of analysis goes beyond the historic experience of colonization. It constitutes an epistemological standpoint that decentralizes the gaze while focusing on the *subalterns* (Spivak 1988), and it allows an adjustment of attention from the centre to the margins (Martínez Cairo & Buscemi 2022).

Kumari Jayawardena (1986) examines women's contributions and emancipation during anti-imperialist movements, emphasizing a stronger role for women in crafting new nations. By doing so, she simultaneously suggests women's active involvement while countering stereotyped depictions of women's passive subjection to political projects. In this sense, Chandra Talpade Mohanty signals the production of the 'Third World Woman' in the form of an ahistorical and monolithic subject (1988: 62). María Lugones builds on Mohanty's work, reconceptualizing intersectional theories of overlapping and concomitant axes of oppression through the *coloniality of gender* as a system created by the colonial experience and perpetuated through relations of domination and exploitation, affecting the structures of power and gender (Lugones 2008) beyond the colonial era. In the same vein, Gloria Anzaldúa's *mestiza consciousness* sheds light on the impact of colonial gender relations and the patriarchal organization of society by reclaiming ancestral cultural roots and feminine archetypes, as well as exposing the lived experiences in the peripheries (1987). *Border thinking* thus reappropriates the 'epistemological margins of modernity' (Motta 2013: 37). Moreover, *border thinking* and *mestiza consciousness* envision a multiplicity of forms of being, feeling, belonging, configuring a state of in-betweenness (Buscemi 2020) that characterizes minorities, ethnic groups, disabled people, and an array of bodies and beings that do not conform or are not constructed as viable or functional to the political project. The geographic but also symbolic borders can be thus regarded as sites of resistance, transformation and reform.

Women writing the body

Since the nation has been historically conceptualized as a masculine heterosexual construct, the production of social norms and hierarchies traditionally has been structured along patriarchal lines, whereby women and marginalized subjects have been discursively produced as Others (Mayer 2000). As gender roles have been critical in consolidating the national project, the woman's body can be regarded as a border in itself, 'a socially shaped and historically "colonised" territory' (Bordo 1999: 251) signalling the liminality of the Other (McClintock 1995).

However, women have crafted spaces of agency and resistance by devising arrangements with the patriarchy and creating communities of solidarity. They have also reclaimed their voices in politics, culture and society. Writing has been one such act of reclamation. Cherríe Moraga and Gloria Anzaldúa describe an engaged women's (and queer) literature as *theory in the flesh*, whereby 'the physical realities of our lives—our skin color, the land or asphalt we grew up on, our sexual longings—all fuse to create a politic born out of necessity' (2015a: 19). One way the authors suggest to 'bridge the contradictions in our experience' is 'by naming our selves and by telling our stories in our own words' (19). It is in the converging axes of oppression and liberation that writing empowers women and other marginalized subjects to tell their stories, bodies, affects and solidarities. By *opening the gates* (Badran & cooke 2004), literature becomes an act of affirmation written on and through the body: 'The very act of writing [...] is to bring into consciousness what only the body knows to be true' (Moraga 2015: xxiv).

Marginalized subjects, by virtue of being de-invisibilized, bridge discursive boundaries, politically acknowledge Other bodies, and expose their cultural hybridity through the sign of the difference located within the body. The peripheral status of subjects and characters invests physical, ethnic, cultural, social and linguistic boundaries as liminal areas. Trinh Minh-ha, in her critique of the Western male gaze over Other literatures, exhorts women to 'write— think and feel—(with) our entire bodies' (1989: 36). The body itself is a border, a political and spatial construction that is also the site and point of convergence of cultures, traditions, rituals and meanings, 'a politically inscribed entity [...] shaped and marked by histories and practices of containment and control' (Bordo 1999: 251). Liminality runs through the body-border, and discursively constructs acceptable and functional bodies that serve the national paradigm, while others are marginalized in the process (Buscemi 2016). It is in these identifications that the boundaries of women's embodiment overlap with irrationality, madness, emotional unrestraint and moral inferiority, whereby containment and control are deemed necessary to regulate and silence them.

However, when the body-border is claimed and reclaimed through women's writing, it can materialize as a place and space of acknowledgement, recognition, rehabilitation and redemption. As Toni Morrison observed in her Nobel Prize acceptance lecture: 'I stood at the border, stood at the edge, and claimed it as central. And let the rest of the world move over to where I was' (Morrison 1993, quoted in Emezi 2019). Gulf women writers, and in particular Alharthi, Aljohani and Alshammari, unveil the body-border and bring to light the painful intersectionalities and negotiations that marginalized subjects undergo, but also the communities that they form and the catharsis to be found in appropriating the border as a space and the border status as a condition and, eventually, a redemption.

Gulf literature and women's voices

In the Arabian Gulf, social and cultural norms rooted in the family as primary gatekeeper exert control over women's behaviour, sexuality, conduct and reproductive rights. More generally, power relations are organized along the lines of gender and age (de Bel-Air et al. 2018). Control and stigmatization are closely linked to nation-building processes and power preservation.

The rich Gulf literary scene, however, has been infiltrated by a growing number of Khaleeji women writers reclaiming agency and voice through their texts and choice of characters, plots and settings. In particular, a growing interest in the historical novel and the uncomfortable stories of a problematic past have been addressed by Gulf women writers, notably Raja Alem and Badriya al-Bishr (Saudi Arabia), Bothayna Al-Essa and Laila al-Othman (Kuwait), Salha Obaid and Maha Gargash (United Arab Emirates), Fatma al-Shidi (Oman) and Bushra al-Maqtari (Yemen), to name only a few. Gulf women writers not only engage with women's stories and lives, but they also explore the body as a space of struggle and negotiation. Moreover, across the region, writing the body and through the body amounts to 'an exposure [...] which goes against the traditional norms of hiding the female body [and] the need for concealment and keeping women's bodies outside the public sphere' (Alshammari 2022b: 57). The authors of the literary works here examined appropriate the narrative from a gender standpoint to highlight intersecting and overlapping single stories within the broader history of the region. This also allows to de-exceptionalize the Arabian Gulf often depicted through a mix of excesses and opulence, tradition and oppression, complicating our understanding and deconstructing preconceived notions on the region.

However, storytelling can also be powerfully employed as a tool for agency, or possibly a literary end result, focusing on telling her-story, their-stories, as Mona Kareem notes: 'I felt that there [is] a relationship between literature and freedom' (Elgayer 2020). Building on the idea that the personal is political, and even more so for women writers who are invested with a sense of moral and social duty to rectify the past and highlight the margins, bodies are employed as tropes and synecdoches of non-inclusive and highly segregated societies (Buscemi 2022).

Going against ahistorical essentialism, the three texts problematize intersecting and multiple layers of oppression (Moraga 2015) by insisting on the docility and obedience imposed on and performed by the body, but also the rebellion and resistance that are manifested through it. Writing and storytelling become self-saving tools that contribute to expose Others, confront trauma and mitigate the pain in the urban space as a geographic and symbolic construct of modernization, hybridization, loss of authenticity and ultimately border crossing. As Gloria Anzaldúa eloquently puts it: 'To survive the Borderlands / you must live *sin fronteras* / be a crossroads' (1987: 195).

Nonconforming subjectivities: naming, power and recognition

In recent years nonconforming subjects and subjectivities have become a growing focus in Gulf literature. The exploration of relations of power and identity-building as part of the national(istic) project are investigated by the three literary works examined here. Jokha Alharthi's *Celestial Bodies* (2019) digs into Oman's and more widely the Arabian Gulf's relationship with slavery. As in other parts of the world, historically slaves were the property of their owners, crossing the productive and reproductive realms by functioning simultaneously as labour and capital (Shildricks & Price 1996: 5). While they were essential to the local economy, they were also employed in the domestic sphere in wealthy extended-family homes. The advent of a fast-paced oil-driven modernization, however, was confronted with new international laws. On the verge of the abolition of slavery, the wealthy Merchant Sulayman objects to the institutional interference into his private affairs: 'Sanjar is mine, he doesn't belong to the government. The government can't free my slaves. I bought his mama Zarifa [...], I fed her [...]. My slave, mine' (Alharthi 2019: 24). What Alharthi highlights here is not only the control over slaves' bodies and choices, but also over their identity and mobility, both physical and social.

A significant element in the asymmetrical relations of power between slaves and their owners was the former's naming. Names connect human beings with their identity, delimit their individuality and trace a (hi)story. Claiming the right to name or rename exemplifies structural social inequalities as political acts of conquest that recall the naming of areas by will of the colonizers: renaming is wiping out a past, stories and genealogies; it is linked to kinship and lineage while it also symbolizes filiation and infantilization. Liminality passes through the body, and is epitomized by race and gender, as the slave Ankabuta's story reveals. As a child Ankabuta was renamed in Arabic to erase her past and her roots, as well as her language and identity, to shape her into a slave-woman. Forced marriage, rape and motherhood also established the physical border between the slave and the master's family, signalling a gendered biological function as well as the reproduction of boundaries between ethnic groups (Anthias & Yuval-Davis 1989). Ankabuta embodies the essentialized woman subject produced by the colonial discourse (Mohanty 1988), as well as the coloniality of gender reproduced through relations of domination (Lugones 2008).

Mayya, one of the protagonists of *Celestial Bodies* (2019), shares a similar fate: denied the possibility to explore a love interest she only cultivated from afar, throughout the years she resorts to a progressive self-annihilation, withdrawing herself from family and society. However, she attempts to forge a different life for her daughter. London's name causes the family innumerable troubles and inspires gossip, as it does not align with tradition or with the family's genealogy. The burden placed upon London's shoulders will not lead her to meet the expectations that her bold name evokes: despite becoming a doctor, she struggles to get out of an abusive relationship and her white coat, symbol of social mobility and an increased ability to make decisions for herself, only serves to highlight her anorexic body. London's body is a place of

BODIES ON THE MARGINS

enunciation from which the woman invokes the contradictions of her society, a body historically shaped by social conventions and discourse (Bordo 1999).

Similarly, in *Days of Ignorance* a minor character is renamed after her husband's profession, contributing to erasing her identity and independence: 'Her own name was long forgotten since people had started calling her simply Muezzin-Wife' (Aljohani 2014: 31). This practice recalls the renaming of parents after their first son (or, in the absence of sons, the name of the eldest daughter): 'She'd once been Selma, and was now "Umm Hashem"—Mother of Hashem […]. Her existence had at last been validated' (Aljohani 2014: 86). The perceived aberration of generating daughters (Aljohani 2014: 76) is relieved by the blessing of a son for Leen's mother, although he is a fundamentalist who ultimately decides to purify the family blood by plotting the murder of his sister's former boyfriend. Again, we are reminded of women's embodiment of the rigid delimitations among different ethnic and national groups (Anthias & Yuval-Davis 1989), as well as the sign of difference that Moraga (2015) identifies within the woman's body.

In her autobiographical illness narrative, Alshammari (2022a) convincingly defictionalizes and decolonizes stereotypes around Arab women's passivity and submissiveness, as well as the taboos surrounding disability and illness that are intimately correlated to pain and the need for it to be named, whereby the body is converted into a place of acknowledgement: 'You wanted to be listened and heard. Sometimes we aren't really looking for immediate solutions, only that your pain is valid. That it isn't all in your head' (Alshammari 2022a: 24).

The validation of pain and illness de-invisibilizes disability while placing stigma on the ill subject, marking the boundaries of embodiment. The young multiple sclerosis patient's relation with the wider world is mediated by her father, a respected Kuwaiti professional and the voice of the family in the face of institutions: 'Doctors and nurses took me more seriously when my father introduced himself as a lawyer. My father spoke for me' (Alshammari 2022a: 28). Illness and shame obliterate the woman's voice, accentuating the liminality of the disabled subject as Other (McClintock 1995). The discursive construction of the ill body interacts with the gendered stigma related to women's perceived natural biological processes: the father is mobilized as social protector and mediator. Alshammari poses here important questions regarding the space for illness and the validation of socially and culturally appropriate bodies, whereby normative and regulatory practices establish binary power dynamics with regard to the healthy/ill dichotomy. In this context, the ill body is not only viewed as defective and marginal, but it can also be considered as a bearer of stigma: the woman's body carries the pride and shame of the tribe and its significance lies at the intersection of nation and gender (Mayer 2000).

Similarly, another challenge presented in the illness narrative is the power to name a love that grows on the margins of heteronormativity, patriarchy and gender binaries. Alshammari produces stories of friends and acquaintances who come to her when she enters a coma after a complicated health procedure. These visitations are employed as literary devices to zoom out of Alshammari's own memories in order to investigate the people inhabiting her surroundings. Danah accepted a marriage arranged by her mother, even though she was in love with another woman: '[She] killed herself and left behind two little girls. [Danah] couldn't tell her [mother] who she really wanted to be with and how she had no way out […]. Freedom was not an option for her' (Alshammari 2022a: 83).

Alshammari's text, as well as Alharthi's and Aljohani's, signals the liminality of women's nonconforming bodies and subjectivities, and the multiple layers of oppression woven into their identities and struggles. The borders dividing racial identities and communities are always ethnosexual, whereby mixed relationships are highly controlled, sanctioned and discouraged (Ghigi & Sassatelli 2018: 182). It is by acknowledging their own condition and performing agency and resistance that marginal subjectivities can truly inhabit and reclaim the margins as spaces of political elaboration. Interestingly, the three women authors appropriate their own names in telling stories set in their countries. Contrary to a tradition of forced literary modesty and disguise performed by pioneering Arab women writers for safety and protection, but also for creative freedom (Ashour 2008), Alshammari, Aljohani and Alharthi assert their subjectivities and belonging, as opposed to the many women characters who appear nameless or are renamed in their narratives.

Genealogies of pain against mutating landscapes

The representations of marginalized bodies and subjectivities in the three literary works here examined are intertwined with the geographic and historical backdrop against which they are set. The fast-paced modernization that occurred in the wake of the discovery of oil generated rapid changes in Gulf societies, and accelerated the urbanization of the territory while it enhanced the education of its population and started attracting a growing migrant population too. An element of continuity was elaborated through genealogies, both intended as family lineage and the continuum of pain endured across time by marginalized subjects, leading to other legacies of suffering. The three literary works acknowledge and investigate the control over women's bodies and mobility, the enduring trauma of displacement and diaspora, as well as the stigma placed on disability, especially when affecting women.

Celestial Bodies (2019) is particularly invested in depicting the contradictions and failings of the sudden wealth and modernization of Oman, and the celebration of the past and of heritage, while also looking into slavery, gender roles and trauma. One of the leading themes of the book, and an element in common with the other literary works here examined, is the liminal space between memory and forgetting. *Head Above Water* is a collection of 'retellings and re-imagined truths' (2022a: 3) that interrogate disability and trauma through a variety of diary entries, memories, dreams, and dialogues with friends, family and students. *Days of Ignorance* (2014) similarly interweaves the official history with personal fictional memories, adopting the insertion of journalistic vignettes to tell another official story, that of the United States' dominant one-sided narrative on war, human rights and terrorism: 'Iraq has given UN inspectors a huge file of documents and information on its weapons programs and previous activities which [...] confirms that Iraq has no banned weapons in its possession' (Aljohani 2014: 113). The three writers seem to collectively invoke the prejudices of the West towards the Middle East, an area where the heavy interference of Western countries has constructed invented traditions of violence and backwardness to justify their own geopolitical goals (Abu-Lughod 2015).

Reference to this can be found in Alharthi's depiction of the role of education and how it was seen as a potentially dangerous endeavour. The author mentions a 1940s exchange between a senior Omani civil servant and a British representative, whereby on realizing that 'the mere idea of educating Omanis terrified the rulers', the civil servant accused the British representative: 'Are we going to educate Omanis like you educated the Indians, and so they revolted against you, and soon they'll oust you entirely?' (Alharthi 2019: 149). The denial of accessible and free education becomes an element of dispute in a wider colonial discourse while also insisting on nation-building prerogatives.

The urban space is synonymous with openness, possibilities and border crossing to overcome the dualistic construction of margins and centre. However, the city is also the place of violence, conflict and segregation, whereas the countryside is often depicted as a space of fixed identities and elaborations, tighter norms and timeless hierarchies. London's grandmother exemplifies the rejection of modernization and the resistance to a more modern lifestyle by refusing to be seen by a doctor: 'no creature ever saw my body [...]! These days you all go to the hospitals in Maskad, where those Indian women and those daughters of the Christians see every inch of you' (Alharthi 2019: 18).[1] The perceived chasm between nature and culture troubles Salima, who considers nature immutable and consistent with tradition and values, whereas imported modernization and medicine, practised increasingly by non-Muslims, revolve for her around the state capital with a changed name that she refuses to acknowledge. In the small oasis village, 'people were firm believers in the past; they did not look to the future' (Alharthi 2019: 136).

In the same village, the 1970 abolition of slavery was considered a break away from tradition and an endangerment of community stability, as noted in a previous passage on Merchant Sulayman's objection to institutional inter-ference. In much the same way, Aljohani's *Days of Ignorance* (2014) refers to a pre-Islamic past of divisions and the lack of religious guidance. Here the author appears to interrogate contemporary Saudi Arabia as a place of obscu-rantism and further sectarianism where a 'transparent partition [...] was raised like a protective barrier between different colors, races and ethnicities' (70). In this passage the author reflects on the confrontation between Leen's love and devotion for a black resident and structural racism in Saudi society. Leen and Malek connect through a notebook where she illegally registers the stories of pain, abuse and deceit of the girls and women attending the care centre where she works. The love that develops between them is thus based on a shared

---

1. For a thorough analysis of women's socialization in the Omani oases before 1970, refer to Khan's contribution in this volume (Chapter 7).

experience of affliction, be it the pain that Leen feels as a daughter neglected by a mother who sees her son as her sole validation, or the pain in the form of the in-betweenness that Malek faces as a long-term resident whose mother and brother depend on his visa to stay in the country, and as a black man referred to by Leen's father as 'slave' (Aljohani 2014: 117). Both characters' writing is thus an embodied act (Moraga 2015) of acknowledgement and recognition.

The stories that Leen collects uncover genealogies of unperceived pain borne by women victims of domestic violence. Fifteen-year-old Muznah was married off by her father to a man older than him. In an exchange that reminds of Sheikh Sulaiman's acquisition of Ankabuta for a lower price than a sack of rice, Muznah's future husband offers her father a minivan, ironically a symbol of consumerism and modernization, urban mobility and wealth. When Muznah runs away three days after her wedding and meets Leen at the care centre, she shares a story that is similar to many others that Leen has collected: 'she hadn't been able to bear the pain [...]. [T]hey'll summon her father or her husband, and whoever comes will sign a pledge not to do her harm. Then he'll [...] take her away' (Aljohani 2014: 74–76).

Muznah's story, like others found in *Celestial Bodies*, *Days of Ignorance* and *Head Above Water*, establishes the peripheral status of the victims of domestic violence, where the body is a border that primarily contributes to nationalistic and nation-building purposes that discipline and sanction its performativity (Anthias & Yuval-Davis 1989). Aljohani locates the structural element of violence in the country's prerogatives, 'where people said what they didn't do and did what they didn't say [...]. Like a vast unpolished silver surface [...], her country needed a little hellfire to melt it down, purify it and reshape it' (Aljohani 2014: 100), just like the flames had consumed another woman who passed by the care centre: Sharaf had set herself on fire to escape the circle of violence. Genealogies of pain can thus be traced in a country where '[n]obody smiled at anybody. Everybody looked glum' (Aljohani 2014: 18).

The body-border accumulates oppressions in an intersectional configuration that links genealogies and lineage with gender and health: 'My grandfather used to refer to a beautiful woman as a *mahra*, innocent, chaste, gentle [...], with excellent reproductive abilities [...]. An ill *mahra* is a cause of contamina- tion [...] and likely to poison the healthy bloodline' (Alshammari 2022a: 37).

GULF WOMEN'S LIVES

Belonging and collective identity also transcend geopolitical structures and the wider histories that take place beyond people's homes. As Alshammari's mother is Palestinian, she was raised in the knowledge of the complications of the concept of home, not only as a physical place, but also as her own ill body. The ill woman cast aside from a tribal society is left to find alternative arrangements, to fashion a renewed sense of belonging beyond the materiality of her surroundings or the body, signalling the enunciation of border thinking (Anzaldúa 1987) as a non-binary, non-dichotomous concept that highlights the multiplicity of being.[2] The concept of home and belonging is further complicated by the author's hybrid identity: 'even if I had a home, and I was only "half" Palestinian, I would always carry pulsating diaspora in my veins [...]. Except I felt that the state of diaspora and exile was from the land of the healthy' (Alshammari 2022a: 110). Alshammari powerfully appropriates the diasporic identity that Anzaldúa refers to as the *mestiza consciousness* (1987) to signify not only her roots and conflictual relationship with tribal expectations, but also her exile and marginalization from the canon of healthy and (re)productive subjects—a condition that she then amplifies to evoke the liminality shared by women in a genealogy of pain:

> So many beautiful women around me got sick [...] of holding on to hope [...], of the law [...], of suffocating in their huge houses, windows closed, doors locked. [A] slow self-annihilation [...]. Their bodies weren't their own and at the end of the night he would come in and take what was legally and rightfully his [...]. As they began to feel less at home in their bodies, they started spiralling downwards into depressive fits [and] medicating. [They] felt that that was the only way out. (Alshammari 2022a: 61)

Alshammari here hints at the generalized illness not just displayed by women trapped between self-awareness and duty, but more broadly of an entire society that places upon them expectations that are out of sync with modern countries inserted in the global economy—countries that yet turn to the past for their approach to relationships between genders. In these countries being a woman feels like 'a burden' (Alshammari 2022a: 106), with the aggravation of disability

---

2. For a more thorough analysis of the Bedouin and tribal affiliation for women, refer to Alshammari's chapter in this volume (Chapter 1).

BODIES ON THE MARGINS

as 'a scarlet letter' (107) in its 'grotesqueness, its crossing of boundaries' (121). With no clear way out, Alharthi, Aljohani and Alshammari suggest finding consolation and agency in the margins, where nonconforming subjectivities have been relegated.

Agency in the margins

The body as a border can be interpreted not only as a place of containment and control (Bordo 1999), but also as a place of acknowledgement, recognition and, eventually, redemption. Nonconforming subjects and subjectivities resist and fight back from the margins, and while pursuing their agency they become crossroads and bridges (Moraga & Anzaldúa 2015a).

In *Celestial Bodies* (2019) we notice an increasing visibility of the women slaves who voice their liminality or take action to refuse their own marginalization. Zarifa had always been the only slave to eat together with the other women of the house (Alharthi 2019: 33). Throughout the novel, she demands to be acknowledged as 'the person in charge of [the] household, not to mention [the patriarch's] long-time mistress [...] and a concubine. She would be his beloved, and the only woman who was ever close to him' (Alharthi 2019: 126–35). Zarifa asserts her right to a relationship of physical proximity, while reclaiming her place at the table through her own patriarchal arrangements. In the same vein, she also performs *zar exorcisms* that were passed on to her by her mother in the form of days-long ceremonies where food, drinks, music and dance would lead to trance, intoxication and ecstasy. Recuperating ancestral memories and performances, Ankabuta and Zarifa recover part of their identity and assert themselves in positions of power as organizers of the exorcism and mediators with the people attending them, embodying a crossroads of cultures and traditions, and a cultural hybridity through their bodies and their gestures (Anzaldúa 1987).

Other marginal subjects reclaim their place in the world and a new active position in society. Unmarried Najiya lives in the desert where she tends to the family farm, which she eventually inherits after her father's death. She marks her first step into a better socio-economic life by accessing modern household upgrades, symbolically rejecting the tent and the camels as tenets of the past and of nomadic life. When she chooses her lover, she comes across

GULF WOMEN'S LIVES

him in the desert. She is insouciant towards his social standing as an established married man in the community. In the love relationship, she renames herself to mark her new life: 'I am Najiya. I am Qamar, the Moon' (Alharthi 2019: 48). She thus rejects the gendered relations of domination (Lugones 2008) to embrace her *mestiza consciousness*, suspended between the past and the present, submission and autonomy, nomad and dweller, nature and culture (Anzaldúa 1987). Her freedom and independence charm Azzan, Mayya's father, who desperately falls in love with a woman who 'had taught him his own body [and] enticements that shattered his old existence to pieces [like] he hadn't known anything at all about anything before he knew her' (Alharthi 2019: 90). In an interesting reversal of roles, Najiya/Qamar is the initiator to the pleasures of intimacy, the one who leads the relationship, effectively crossing borders to surpass her peripheral status.

Mayya, on the other hand, struggles in a loveless marriage with Abdallah, and once her children grow up, she finds solace in a progressive self-effacement through silence and sleep. She reclaims her body to enter a trance state not dissimilar to the one produced during the exorcisms presided over by Zarifa, a liminal place of quasi-death that recalls the comatose state of a nation trapped between the past and the future. Similarly, Aljohani (2014) reflects on the in-betweenness of Malek as the victim of a hate crime that comes to symbolize a whole country stuck in an antiquated vision of social, ethnic and gender relations. Leen retrospectively sees her relationship with Malek as an escape from bigotry and double standards, just as the predominantly young women she meets at the care centre try to escape the decisions made for them by their fathers, or the patriarchal arrangements devised by their protectors. These figures all try to assert their agency, or lack thereof, by confronting the social norms and defying the gender control operated by elder male members of their family by way of policing and censoring conduct and performance (Anthias & Yuval-Davis 1989; Bordo 1999; Ghigi & Sassatelli 2018).

Similarly, Alshammari decides to fashion for herself alternative communities in which to feel seen and acknowledged, and ultimately to belong (2022a: 35). Academia allows her to tell and collect stories, but also contributes to a filiation of sorts with some of her students in the form of a 'politics of love' (Alshammari 2022a: 138). As she points out in another powerful passage: '[i]n shared vulnerabilities, I have found a third space, a space of belonging'

BODIES ON THE MARGINS

(Alshammari 2022a: 182). Going against the grain of the values of a family-based society, the author underlines the determination to act and perform her own familial ties in a community of volition and choice, and a true sense of acceptance and membership in the margins (Moraga & Anzaldúa 2015a). She finds a community of gathered pain and vulnerabilities in a circle of friends: 'Always, together, knowing that family was […] a women's circle that wanted to ensure you stayed alive' (Alshammari 2022a: 168–69). Women's bodies and proximities create new ties and refashioned families based on 'the element of healing, giving, and receiving' (Alshammari 2022a: 175–81).

Bridging the pain, sharing marginalities and marginalizations, the circle of love and friendship rests on 'the privilege of vulnerability' (Alshammari 2022a: 187). This *theory in the flesh* (Moraga & Anzaldúa 2015a) defies the established social order and subverts canons through the sign of difference (Moraga & Anzaldúa 2015a) located in the bodies of these women on the margins. The *mestiza consciousness* (Anzaldúa 1987) operates by way of the body as a border through storytelling and narration. Border thinking shapes agency and resistance while it reconfigures geographic and symbolic frontiers and liminal spaces of in-betweenness (Anzaldúa 1987), where women's bodies bridge societal restrictions to confront taboos, stigmatization, othering, and eventually find mutual recognition and redemption.

Conclusions

In the course of this chapter the liminal and peripheral subjectivities of women characters in two Gulf novels and an autobiographical illness narrative were analysed, in order to interrogate the construction of women's bodies as body-borders exemplifying the social, ethnic and class differences of national states through their productive and reproductive functions. The chapter also set out to individuate and problematize the resistance and agency built from the margins through alternative communities of choice where consciousness and relations of mutual support are cultivated and cherished.

As Cherríe Moraga eloquently maintains, the issue 'is not always a matter of the actual bodies in the room, but of […] what is *missing* in that room; and responding to that absence' (2015b: xix). In this sense, it is possible to argue that these three Gulf women writers accept Moraga's challenge and put at the forefront of their texts nonconforming, uncomfortable, powerful characters who crack wide open the silenced histories of marginalized subjects. Following other Gulf writers in the de-invisibilization of marginalized and liminal characters, Alharthi, Aljohani and Alshammari uncover and legitimate the inclusion of forgotten and uncomfortable stories as a political stance against official narratives of public memory and remembrance.

In the aftermath of turmoil and social unrest, it is possible to infer that Gulf women writers' literature has progressively become more political by addressing social and cultural issues, employing a growing selection of unconventional characters, de-stigmatizing social taboos, and righteously giving relevance to women's contributions to society in the context of patriarchal and othering structures. These three literary works open up the floor to an investigation of the structural othering and marginalization of women's stories and bodies through embodied knowledge. Pulling the margins towards the centre stage of the public discourse exemplifies a *theory in the flesh* (Moraga & Anzaldúa 2015a) that is political precisely for its reappropriation of bodies, embodiment and knowledge though storytelling and writing. When women *write their bodies* (Minh-ha 1989), they repudiate taboos to envision prefigurative possibilities: 'How can we [...] not use our bodies to be thrown over a river of tormented history to bridge the gap?' (Moraga & Anzaldúa 2015: xxxvii).

Acknowledgement

I am indebted to Audrey Fabbri for support and assistance on this chapter.

References

Abu-Lughod (2015). *Do Muslim Women Need Saving?* Harvard University Press.
Alharthi, J. (2019). *Celestial Bodies* (trans. M. Booth). Sandstone Press.
Aljohani, L. (2014). *Days of Ignorance* (trans. N. Roberts). Bloomsbury Qatar Foundation.
Alshammari, S. (2022a). *Head Above Water*. Neem Tree Press.
Alshammari, S. (2022b). Life Writing by Kuwaiti Women: Voice and Agency. *IAFOR Journal of Cultural Studies*, 7(1), 53–63. https://doi.org/10.22492/ijcs.7.1.04
Anthias, F. & Yuval-Davis, N. (1989). Introduction. In N. Yuval-Davis, F. Anthias & J. Campling (eds), *Woman-Nation-State* (pp. 1–15). Macmillan.
Anzaldúa, G. (1987). *Borderlands/La Frontera*. Aunt Luke Books.

BODIES ON THE MARGINS

Ashour, R. (ed.) (2008). *Arab Women Writers: A Critical Reference Guide, 1873–1999.* American University in Cairo Press.

Badran, M. & cooke, m. (eds) (2004). *Opening the Gates: An Anthology of Arab Feminist Writing* (2nd edn). Indiana University Press.

Bordo, S. (1999). Feminism, Foucault, and the Politics of the Body. In J. Price and M. Shildrick (eds), *Feminist Theory and the Body. A Reader* (pp. 246–57). Routledge.

Buscemi, E. (2016). Abaya and Yoga Pants: Women's activism in Kuwait. *AG About Gender— International Journal of Gender Studies*, 5(10), 186–203. https://doi.org/10.15167/2279-5057/ ag.2016.5.10.350

Buscemi, E. (2020). Bamboo and Bougainvillea: Literary Perspectives on Identity and Belonging in Contemporary Kuwait. In H.S. Ghabra, F.Z.C. Alaoui, S. Abdi & B.M. Calafell (eds), *Negotiating Identity and Transnationalism: Middle Eastern and North African Communication and Critical Cultural Studies* (pp. 236–59). Peter Lang.

Buscemi, E. (2022). The Pact(s): Gender Identity and Social Order in Kuwaiti Literature. In S. Hopkyns & W. Zoghbor (eds), *Linguistic Identities in the Arab Gulf States: Waves of Change.* Routledge.

de Bel-Air, F., Safar, J. & Destremau, B. (2018). Marriage and Family in the Gulf Today: Storms over a Patriarchal Institution? *Arabian Humanities*, 10. https://journals.openedition.org/cy/4399

Elgayer, A. (2020, 9 September). A Stateless Poet Finds Her Home and Identity in Literature. *Al Fanar Media.* https://al-fanarmedia.org/2020/09/a-stateless-poet-finds-her-home-and-identity-in-literature/

Emezi, A. (2019, 7 August). This Letter Isn't for You: On the Toni Morrison Quote that Changed My Life. *Them.* https://www.them.us/story/toni-morrison

Ghigi, R. & Sassatelli, R. (2018). *Genere, corpo e societá.* Il Mulino.

Jayawardena, K. (1986). *Feminism and Nationalism in the Third World.* Zed Books.

Lugones, M. (2008). Colonialidad y género. *Tabula Rasa*, 9(1), 73–101. https://doi.org /10.25058/20112742.340

McClintock, A. (1995). *Imperial Leather: Race, Gender, and Sexuality in the Colonial Contest.* Routledge.

Martínez Cairo, B. & Buscemi, E. (2022). Latin American Decolonial Feminisms: Theoretical Perspectives and Challenges. *Les Cahiers ALHIM: Amérique Latine Histoire et* Mémoire, special issue on Feminist Territories in Latin America: Peripheral Voices, 42, 9–21. https://doi. org/10.4000/alhim.10153

Mayer, T. (2000). Gender Ironies of Nationalism: Setting the Stage. In T. Mayer (ed.), *Gender Ironies of Nationalism: Sexing the Nation* (pp. 1–22). Routledge.

Minh-ha, T. (1989). *Woman, Native, Other. Writing Postcoloniality and Feminism.* Indiana University Press.

Mohanty, C.T. (1988). Under Western Eyes: Feminist Scholarship and Colonial Discourses. *Feminist Review*, 30(1), 61-88. https://doi.org/10.1057/fr.1988.42

GULF WOMEN'S LIVES

Moraga, C. (2015). Catching Fire: Preface to the Fourth Edition. In C. Moraga and G. Anzaldúa (eds), *This Bridge Called My Back: Writings by Radical Women of Color* (4th edn, pp. xv–xxvi). SUNY Press.

Moraga, C. & Anzaldúa, G. (2015a). Entering the Lives of Others: Theory in the Flesh. In C. Moraga & G. Anzaldúa (eds), *This Bridge Called My Back: Writings by Radical Women of Color* (4th edn, p. 19). SUNY Press.

Moraga, C. & Anzaldúa, G. (2015b). La Jornada: Preface, 1981. In C. Moraga & G. Anzaldúa (eds), *This Bridge Called My Back: Writings by Radical Women of Color* (4th edn, pp. xxxv–xli). SUNY Press.

Motta, Sara C. (2013). 'We Are the Ones We Have Been Waiting For': The Feminization of Resistance in Venezuela. *Latin American Perspectives*, 40(4), 35–54. https://doi.org/10.1177/0094582X13485706

Shildricks, M. & Price, J. (1996). Breaking the Boundaries of the Broken Body. *Body & Society*, 2(4), 93-113. https://doi.org/10.1177/1357034X96002004006

Spivak, G. (1988). Can the Subaltern Speak? In C. Nelson & L. Grossberg (eds), *Marxism and the Interpretation of Culture*. Macmillan.

PART II

Spaces

Unmasking Patriarchy: Emirati Women Journalists Challenging Newsroom Norms in Pursuit of Equality

Noura Al Obeidli

Introduction

There is a reason why the issue of feminism and gender in the media industry of the United Arab Emirates (UAE) has been underexplored: gender equality, as a modern Western ideal, has no foundation in the indigenous culture of the UAE. While Islamic law or sharia mentions men and women's rights when it comes to education, inheritance and the ownership of businesses and investments, for example, Emirati women continue to live in a closely guarded tribal patriarchal society, and practise only limited duties outside the realm of the home. Women have little or no authority in political, economic and social affairs, despite the state's continuous nation-building schemes to champion their access to education and emancipation in the workforce. There is a gap in feminist media studies focused on the UAE, and the issue of gender in the media industry, in particular, is highly under-examined.

Yet gender came to the forefront in the UAE in 2007 after the publication of the United Nations' Gender Inequality Index (GII),[1] which revealed the

---

1. The UAE ranked 105 out of 128 countries for gender equality, according to the 2007 Global Gender Gap Index (GGGI). In 2017, under the patronage of the vice president, the Gender Balance Council was launched to enhance the nation's efforts to drive

low proportion of Emirati women involved in political decision-making. However, since the UAE is a tribal and patriarchal nation, the term 'gender' did not emerge as a social, economic and political force; rather it began to permeate the UAE's traditions, Arabic language and religious frameworks without a solid mechanism to deal with it having been developed. As Emirati scholar Suaad Al Oraimi put it, 'the concept of gender requires feminist intellectual unity, based on belief in the unity of women's identity, and this does not exist in the UAE' (2011: 80).

Against this backdrop, I have become determined to research 'gender' and 'feminism', two particular concepts that are alien to Emirati society and only became part of the state's modernization and nation-branding schemes in 2005, when participation in the elections to the Federal National Council (FNC) was granted to women, as the state aimed to position itself favourably on the international scene (Allagui & Al Najjar 2018). In particular, I have become determined to understand the sociocultural factors that affect Emirati women's presence in the vital industry of the media.

For the past four decades, the media environment in the UAE has become engulfed by state-controlled propaganda, censorship and institutionalized gender politics, clustering in the newsroom where Emirati female journalists have discarded their journalistic roles in fear of breaking the patriarchal gender contract or losing their jobs. Living in a closely guarded system rooted in tribalism has an impact on Emirati women's consciousness and self-worth, manifest in feeling shame as well as fear of damaging their families' tribal reputation and honour. Tribal patriarchalism has also impacted Emirati women's contribution to public life, due to the lack of equal opportunities in various sectors and professional fields, including journalism.

As experienced by female journalists worldwide, entering the newsroom and working in the media industry have proven difficult for Emirati women

---

women's participation in the development of the UAE, with the ultimate aim of making the UAE one of the world's top twenty-five countries for gender equality by 2021 (UAE Cabinet 2019). The leadership's endeavour to close the gender gap in political empowerment was achieved, as documented in the Global Gender Gap Report released in March 2021. The report stated that 'only one country [in the Middle East], the United Arab Emirates, ranks among the top 25 countries globally' (World Economic Forum 2021: 26).

because of the patriarchal stereotypes and sexist attitudes (Al Malki et al. 2012) that Emirati and Arab expat men often demonstrate. Gender-related biases compound the systemic problems of the oppressive media environment that works to erase memories of the remarkable role Emirati journalists and intellectuals played in the past. Ignorance of this history was addressed by Emirati journalist and novelist Dhabiya Khamis on Twitter (2020), when she mourned the loss of two pioneer Emirati journalists in 2020: Hussein Ghubash (1951–2020) and Thani Al Suwaidi (1966–2020). Khamis's commemoration blamed the patriarchal state, the government-funded cultural authorities and the adaptable multifaceted Emirati intellectuals for ignoring their historical contribution to journalism and the literary and cultural movements in the UAE (Khamis 2020).

In a series of tweets, Khamis chronicled her personal journey and the early stages of the cultural movement in the UAE following its political independence.[2] She has acknowledged the early generation of pioneer Emirati journalists and intellectuals for being rebellious, a characteristic that shaped their news production and writings (Khamis 2020). From the early 1970s until the 1990s, the early generation of pioneer Emirati journalists and intellectuals were bold and critical, but suffered the consequences of free speech as media surveillance increased following specific internal and external political changes. As Khamis tweeted:

> Unlike the current generation of tamed intellectuals, Emirati literary writers of the eighties and nineties were never treated with fairness. We were marginalized, while some suffered from bitter and incomprehensible hostilities that led to their isolation, displacement, writing anxiety, and imprisonment. Our books were confiscated, banning the Emirati society from accessing our literary production. I was the first Emirati female writer to be detained for publishing a news feature under the title *The Palm Graveyard* in 1987. Unfortunately, our writers and ingenious intellectuals die without being recognized and their literary work unread by their people in the Emirates. (2020)

---

2. The tweets were posted on 6 and 21 July 2020. Translated from the original by the author.

Methodology

In the current chapter, I investigate three under-examined areas of media development and culture in the UAE: gender dynamics and the attitudes around gender roles experienced by Emirati female journalists; censorship and self-censorship practices in the newsroom; and the link between tribal patri-archalism and the empowerment of female journalists in the UAE. To this purpose, I rely on semi-structured interviews and participant observation. The interviews were conducted in 2017 with thirty female and ten male journalists who represented two generational cohorts: the early generation, who had been active between the 1970s and the 1990s and were between the ages of 47 and 65; and journalists from the new generation, who have been active since 2000 and were aged 27 to 41. The interviewees represented nine local print and broadcast media corporations: Abu Dhabi Television Channel One, Emirates News Agency (WAM), *Al Ittihad* newspaper (an Abu Dhabi daily), *Al Bayan* newspaper (a Dubai daily), *Al Khaleej* newspaper (a Sharjah daily), *Al Roeya* newspaper (an Abu Dhabi daily), *Zahrat Al Khaleej* women's weekly magazine (Abu Dhabi), *Al Azminah Al Arabiya* weekly magazine (Sharjah), and *Awraq* weekly magazine (Sharjah).

The interviewees came from different schools of thought, influenced by their culture, education and previous experiences in journalism in other Arab countries. Of the ten male journalists, six were Arab expats from Egypt (four) and Palestine (two), each with more than twenty years of experience, and who expressed concerns about the oppressive media environment in the UAE. The remaining four male journalists were Emiratis who were born between the 1950s and 1970s, and have had a relatively positive experience in journalism. As for the thirty female journalists, they too were influenced by their culture, education and previous experiences in journalism, in careers that spanned from two to thirty years. Twenty-one were Emiratis, while the remaining nine came from Jordan, Morocco, Syria, Egypt and Iraq.

The participant observations were conducted in 2017 at two popular news centres in the UAE: Dubai News Centre, operated by Dubai Media Incorporated (DMI), and Abu Dhabi News Centre, operated by Abu Dhabi Media Company (ADMC). Upon receiving approval for access, I was advised by the director generals for both centres to spend three hours inside the newsroom starting at 6 pm,[3] when most of the editorial staff would be actively present, and witness for myself the work routine and the production of news before the daily broadcast of the one-hour local evening news,[4] which was aired at 8 pm from The Gallery.[5] The diary entries detailing my observations aim to provide the reader with a vivid picture of the everyday journalistic practices that I observed in the newsrooms.

The mixed research methods allowed me to gather evidence of the complexity surrounding gender dynamics and their association with the social constructs of Emirati tribal society. I also analysed the influence of these social constructs on the media landscape, which is seen as patriotic and loyal to the state (Ayish 2021). The observations and interviews undertaken have elicited how gender and authoritarianism dictate journalistic practices and routines in the newsroom, where prior censorship is commonplace (Duffy 2014: 31) and barriers are created to limit Emirati female journalists' progress in the field.

The suffocation of beautiful minds

Historically, beautiful minds have existed in the UAE. However, over time, gendered and censored media cultures have had a detrimental effect on Emirati women's contribution to literature and journalism. The practices of investigative journalism and literary production remain as restricted for Emirati women today as they were before the country's 1971 independence, due to complex sociocultural factors along with the state's powerful grip on journalistic expression.

In the pre-oil era, women's creative contributions were hampered by limited literacy rates and the various social customs governing conduct among literate elites. Before the establishment of government-funded schools, access to

---

3. A desk was allocated for me inside both newsrooms, where I spent three hours observing the newsroom norms (from 6 pm to 9 pm) for fourteen days.
4. Both news centres broadcast the news at the same hour on national television, from 8 pm to 9 pm.
5. A large glass-panelled office full of screens and technical equipment inside both newsrooms, designed for the editing and directing of the live news broadcast, staffed by a team of editors, technicians, producers and directors.

GULF WOMEN'S LIVES

homeschooling was only possible for Emirati women who belonged to families privileged by either their alliance with the royal family through politically arranged marriages, or by their prosperous businesses and inherited wealth. Yet their privileged position made creative Emirati women writers reluctant to publish their work—mainly poetry—under their real names (Soffan 1980), and most of these authors preferred to use pseudonyms to avoid the prejudice of male-dominant circles. Women of the Trucial States were confined to preserving and maintaining one particular moral custom within the tribe, honour (*sharaf*), which had to be reflected in their manners as family members, as married women, as mothers, and as supporters to their husbands in all the complementary work they took on outside the home to survive, such as selling clothes, food and fish.[6]

This form of support led the Trucial women to temporarily establish a strong matriarchal system within society, in which they were in absolute control of family affairs, finances, investments and business transactions at the market-place, acting as breadwinners and childbearers, especially during the pearl-diving season that extended from June to October (Sonbol 2012: 153). However, the influence of tribal honour and other patriarchally oriented customs predating the dawn of Islam in the Arabian Peninsula, and the reforms thereby introduced, made women submissive, a social behaviour referred to as 'passive acceptance' (Al Malki et al. 2012: 112), in which women have come to believe that they are inferior, secondary to men, and accustom themselves to traditional duties.

Nevertheless, the new-found oil wealth brought gradual advancements to Trucial society, and its women in particular, who became exposed to rising Arab liberation and feminist movements, as well as to Arab literature, through the modest availability of print publications (Obaid 2000) and the establishment of schools across the region.[7] Consequently, the local cultural scene witnessed the emergence of two generations of creative Emirati female writers

---

6. The Trucial States were a group of tribal sheikdoms that resided in the south-eastern Persian Gulf, such as the Al Qawasim tribe, which established treaties for an informal protectorate by Britain from 1820 until 1971.

7. Local grocery shop owners published newsletters such as Ibrahim Mohammed Al Medfaa's *Oman* and Mosabah Obaid Al Dhaheri's *Al Nikhi* ('Chickpeas') (Obaid 2000).

from the 1960s to the late 1980s, which is viewed as the golden age of literature and the journalism movement in the UAE.[8]

Viewed today with nostalgia for being permeated by critical writing, emotional speeches and pan-Arabism, and for women pushing social boundaries by travelling for education and removing the veil (Al Nowais 2017), this golden age also witnessed a few Emirati women coming to shape the early phase of the journalism movement in the UAE. These women challenged tribal customs by choosing to study journalism instead of academic degrees and employment in 'respectable' fields such as nursing or teaching, where gender segregation is imposed. They travelled to study in neighbouring countries like Lebanon and Egypt, as the United Arab Emirates University (UAEU) did not establish an academic journalism programme until 1977 (Simonson & Park 2016: 485). On their return home, they found employment in local print and broadcast media corporations. They partnered with local media outlets, which were funded by the state and developed in collaboration with regional media corporations such as Kuwait TV and the Egyptian Radio Networks (Al Darmaki 2014).[9] As a consequence, they forced public acceptance for women's presence in the media as journalists and broadcasters who appeared without a veil and wearing Western clothes. Moreover, they appeared as guests on television debating various societal and cultural issues, including Emirati women's empowerment and contributions to local arts and literature.

Their actions defined a more liberal era for women in the social history of the nation and media. Among those pioneers is Hessa Abdullah Lootah, who wrote features on social issues in *Al Azminah Al Arabiya* weekly magazine. Another example is the Sharjah-born Mouzah Khamis, who contributed

---

8. Popular names from the period include Ousha bint Khalifa Al Suwaidi, who published a series of Nabatean poetry, or verses written in Emirati dialect, in the early 1970s under the nickname of Bint Al Arab; and novelists Amal Khalid Al Qassimi and Nama Al Qassimi (Salih 1983).

9. In 1973, a five-year agreement was signed between Egypt and the UAE to develop the media infrastructure and exchange expertise. During this period, thirty-two Emirati technicians and broadcasters were trained by eighty-six Egyptian media professionals to administer and broadcast news at Sharjah Radio Station, Dubai TV and *Al Ittihad* newspaper in Abu Dhabi. Among the trainees was Emirati journalist for *Zahrat Al Khaleej* magazine Abla Al Nowais, who received an internship in Egypt (Al Darmaki 2014, pp. 121–23).

GULF WOMEN'S LIVES

weekly columns in *Al Khaleej* newspaper and published special features on various topics, including pearl diving, herbal medicine, agriculture and heritage, in the early 1980s. Khamis was also passionate about broadcast media and became the first Emirati female TV host, working for Dubai Channel 2 in 1973 (Salih 1983: 357). Hessa Al Ossaily, like Khamis, was passionate about broadcast media and had the opportunity to study Arabic literature abroad, in one of Egypt's most reputable universities, Ain Shams. In 1965, she became the first Emirati female radio host to work for Dubai's Sout Al Sahel radio station.[10] By the mid-1970s, she worked as a host for Kuwait Television which had an office in Dubai. Later, she moved to Abu Dhabi Television, where she became the first Emirati woman to hold the position of broadcasting director (Hassan 2011: 21).

Furthermore, the launch of the Emirates Writers Union (EWU) in 1984 by thirty members (Gulf News 2012) presented potential opportunities for freedom of the press and freedom of expression for the second generation of writers. However, literary production and investigative journalism remained challenging because of state-imposed censorship and the fear of punishment under the media law. First introduced in 1980 and imposed on media corporations and journalists without updates since, the media law limits free speech by allowing for the imprisonment and fining of journalists, or for the suspension of the activities of a newspaper if prohibited content is published (UAE Federal Government 1980).

The media law of 1980 came as a reaction to the relative freedoms of speech and critical writings by Emirati authors during the golden age, and as a reaction to external political changes at the time. It imposed heavy restrictions on print and broadcast media as well as local publishing houses, affecting literary production and investigative journalism and increasing the practise of self-censorship. The story of *Al Azminah Al Arabiya* illustrates these shifts. The political weekly magazine was founded in 1979 by the late Emirati journalist Mohamed Obaid Ghubash. It was known for endorsing Emirati female journalists, including Khairiyah Rabei who wrote special features about Palestinian women's rights, as well as Rafia Obaid Ghubash and Hessa Abdullah Lootah

---

10. Arabic for 'voice of the sea coast'.

who covered art and literature in cultural features. The magazine, however, was banned in October 1981 for a cover story celebrating the assassination of Egypt's president Muhammad Anwar El Sadat. The Arab press generally portrayed Sadat as a betrayer of Arab unity for signing a peace treaty with Israel at Camp David in 1979, and *Al Azminah Al Arabiya*'s cover story was released with a bold front-page headline that read: 'The Arabs' Betrayer Has Fallen' (Salih 1983: 357). The public sarcasm and celebration of Sadat's assassination sparked demonstrations across the Arab region—an external threat the leadership of the young UAE wanted to avoid. The government preferred to see its neutral foreign policy and moderate political views mirrored in the press, and it wanted to preserve internal political stability and coexistence between Emiratis and Arab expats. The magazine's approach violated a number of clauses in the media law, such as the prohibitions against the 'blemishing' of heads of Arab states and 'agitation' that would cause a strain on the relations between the UAE and other Arab countries (UAE Federal Government 1980). In 1983, two years after its ban, Ghubash obtained a licence to print the magazine in London, but it closed down for good in 1994 due to lack of funding (Salih 1983).

If the two early generations of Emirati female journalists in the 1960s to 1980s faced unceasing criticism for defying patriarchal social norms and the media law, the third generation (1990s to the millennium) were exposed to a different range of challenges imposed on them by the local media corporations. These corporations discriminate between journalists on the basis of gender, challenging women's presence in the field with prejudices against their feminine attributes and emotional intelligence, which stands against their professional growth and intellectual contribution. Women's empowerment is often rejected due to the practice of institutionalized gender clustering in the workplace via male executives, evidencing the deficiency of Human Resources policies on tackling female journalists' rights. The latter go unnoticed and unrecognized by the UAE government, affecting female journalists' presence and performance in this field as they remain exposed without protection to the male bullying culture inside the newsroom—a dilemma that was not prevalent during the golden age of journalism in the Emirates.

GULF WOMEN'S LIVES

Another challenge that the third wave of Emirati female journalists endure is imposed by media regulators such as the National Media Council (NMC)[11] and the Security Media Department.[12] Heavily imposed regulations have limited the practise of investigative journalism, increased self-censorship, and turned the younger generation of Emiratis and media graduates away from this vital field out of fear of the authorities.

Chronicling newsroom norms and gender politics in the UAE

The observations and in-depth interviews conducted for this research have covered and analysed three main themes: (1) the journalistic experience of Emirati women in comparison with those of their female counterparts elsewhere, in terms of dealing with dynamic gender politics inside the newsroom, (2) how gender as an identity marker intersects with other markers such as tribe, family and class in the UAE, and (3) the state's role in Emirati women's empowerment, and the anomalies that arose with the Emirati government's approach to empower women while at the same time holding them accountable as the carriers of 'traditions' that those in power select and reinvent according to their own purposes. This chapter highlights two specific issues from the original research agenda: the gendered and stereotypical portrayal of Emirati women in the newsroom, and the practise of censorship and self-censorship. I unveil a selection of evidence and statements from the twenty-one Emirati women journalists who shared their stories of intentional institutionalized engagements inside the newsroom that resulted in the emergence of gender inequality, discrimination and the excessive practise of censorship and self-censorship in Emirati media. The stories of these Emirati female journalists, a number of whom preferred to use pseudonyms, reveal beliefs that 'men take charge' while women 'take care', confirming their inferiority in the

---

11. The NMC was founded in 2006 following the termination of the Ministry of Information and Culture. In June 2021, the council was merged with the Ministry of Culture and Youth. Following the merge, the ministry launched the Media Regulatory Office to draft regulations, conduct media-related research and offer licensing services (Ministry of Culture and Youth 2022).
12. The Security Media Department was established in 2008 to act as the governmental communication arm of the Ministry of Interior and Abu Dhabi Police.

workplace and the resultant discrimination in career development. Their statements prove that Emirati women remain under-represented in the media. They are either eclipsed in hard news, or fantasized about as 'eye candy for the viewers' (Darwish 2009: 285), exemplifying how the top management at media corporations 'give women jobs that require wearing a smile all the time, or on the basis of external beauty' (Al Malki et al. 2012: 21). In the media, Emirati women's presence is limited to gender-segmented news coverage of topics like childcare, family welfare, fashion and cookery. Alternatively, they are portrayed as beauty objects, especially those who work as news anchors and broadcasters for talk shows dedicated mainly to women, which will be discussed in the following section.

Too beautiful for brains

The sexist culture inside the newsroom has impacted the mental health and the intellectual power of Emirati female journalists. They feel pressured to submit to the masculine newsroom practices that focus on their biological nature and feminine attributes. Some of them failed in their attempts to cover politics or the economy because they were not able to 'respond to news in a male pattern' and couldn't 'avoid being labelled "too soft"' by their male editors (Chambers et al. 2004). During the interviews, a number of Emirati female journalists affirmed that they had encountered direct verbal harassment belittling their creative work, and that they had been barred from promotional opportunities because male colleagues appeared to be of the view that women are unreliable and incompetent in reporting politics and economy news.

'Rawdha', age thirty-five, reflected on her early career experience when she worked as a journalist for a daily Arabic-language newspaper, covering both entertainment and the economy. She said:

> When I succeeded in doing an exclusive interview with [a prominent Arab political figure], the entire editorial content with statements was never published in the newspaper! I knew later that an Emirati male senior editor did not want my name and profile as a journalist to be raised. The former editor-in-chief of the newspaper was a misogynist. He disliked the idea of empowering women, and never allowed female journalists to reach leading

GULF WOMEN'S LIVES

positions in the newspaper, especially as section heads, and instead of promoting me, he hired a male journalist from Saudi Arabia for the position.

Meanwhile, P.Q., twenty-nine, an editor of international politics in a daily Arabic-language newspaper, had to put up with her male colleagues' sarcasm. She explained: 'They would say: "You are a girl! What do you want to do with politics!" or "You are very pretty, why don't you write in entertainment instead of politics?" I've also been offered a promotion, but only if I give up my current job position!' 'Leila', thirty-six, an executive news editor at a news agency based in the UAE, had to put up with sarcasm and stereotypes presupposing that Emirati women are incapable of covering hard-hitting news from every angle. In 2017, 'Leila' decided to step down from her position because she was not being recognized or encouraged or given credit for her work:

> As a woman, I find it very difficult and a challenge to be taken seriously. I had to speak so much louder to get my point across. If I want to say something, I have to keep repeating it and proving and chasing, trying to explain 'please let's think about this.' I think my boss was harsher on me. There was a lot of resistance from the misogynistic older men that I managed, basically. They didn't like it. I asked to have my pay increased to reflect my position because I had much more responsibility. That didn't happen.

Arab media play an influential role in maintaining gendered conceptions and stereotypes not only about gender roles, but also about appearance, promoting for women in an unrealistic, flawless and ultimately sexist image on television through newsreaders (Mitra 2014). This is evident in Arab news broadcasting channels, and the culture of female satellite television presenters (Darwish 2009) has been investigated frequently. In 2006, the leading Kuwaiti daily newspaper *Al Qabas* published a feature stating that 'female presenters have become the dream girls or model women for Arab teenagers and men in general. Every young man sees Arab female presenters as the model of beauty he seeks in his dream girl' (Darwish 2009: 285). In the Emirati context, the portrayal of female news anchors and broadcasters as eye candy or 'dream girls' was apparent when I observed Emirati female news anchors' exotic looks, heavy eye make-up and embellished veiling.

Unlike Emirati female field reporters, who get approximately twenty seconds of face time in front of the camera and require less make-up, the Emirati female news anchors I observed seem to accept their treatment as beauty objects and do not find it discriminatory. They pay attention to their glamour, as opposed to their intellectual power, to enjoy their fifteen minutes of fame in the media. However, some Emirati female field reporters have openly expressed their disagreement with the beauty versus brains treatment. M.A., twenty-eight, who reports for an Abu Dhabi-based channel, said:

> Senior editors and managers here always have an excuse: either that the female voice is desirable for human interest stories only, or that women do not have the capabilities to create influential news like men! They told me that they don't like female voices, except for reading the LVO [Live Voice Over] from the teleprompter, which apparently a female news host is allowed to do.

Furthermore, the Emirati female news anchors I observed at the Dubai and Abu Dhabi News centres are evidently concerned with their makeup, hair and clothing. They tend not to follow the professional dress codes given to them by the appearance department at both news centres,[13] preferring to outsource to local designers for their attire, often to a popular designer boutique which will receive credit at the end of the broadcast. In addition, Emirati female news anchors do not depend on the professional make-up experts employed by the studios, preferring popular Lebanese or Emirati make-up artists who specialize in weddings and special occasions. This particular attitude has itself become a source of laughter and teasing by male colleagues. In an Abu Dhabi newsroom, a senior male editor joked as an Emirati female news anchor was busy fixing her make-up: 'There's no need to add more make-up or to fix it!' Then, in front of the entire team in the newsroom, he peeked into her small Harrods utility bag, took her perfume and tried it on himself. However, I also observed Emirati male news anchors paying attention to their

---

13. The appearance department is typically responsible for coordinating the wardrobe and make-up of on-air talent, including TV hosts. This may involve selecting clothing and accessories that are appropriate for the host's role and the show's overall style, as well as providing make-up and grooming services to ensure that the host looks polished and professional on camera.

own appearance. On one occasion, during a commercial break, I observed a young Emirati male news anchor for Dubai Television's *Akhbar Al Emarat* news broadcast looking in a mirror hidden under the table to adjust his *ghutra*,[14] and taking a selfie for his followers on Instagram.

The management at both television news centres is responsible for portraying Emirati news anchors, regardless of their gender, as beauty objects. They choose young, attractive Emirati men and women who conform to the ideal body shape, which perpetuates the stereotype of beauty over brains. This phenomenon seems universal since satellite networks, especially in the Arab region, 'use women as attractive commodities to increase audience ratings' (Arab Media Forum 2014). This was demonstrated in 2016, when the Egyptian Radio and Television Union (ERTU) decided to suspend eight female presenters who had been attacked by the Egyptian public on social media and labelled as *bakabozza*, meaning fat. To protect the reputation of Egyptian state television, the presenters were ordered to follow a weight-loss plan for a month and resume work only once they had achieved the standards of beauty and appearance set by the state channel (Cairo Scene 2016).

Observing the sexist portrayal of Emirati female journalists made me reflect on my short-lived journalistic experience. In 2008, after completing a four-week extensive one-to-one training programme on television and radio broadcasting for a news anchor job position at an Abu Dhabi-based media outlet, I was rejected immediately during the job interview, in which the managing director of the newsroom offended me by commenting negatively on my body in front of other HR representatives: 'Simply put, you're not photogenic enough to appear in front of the camera!' In another incident one year later, my self-esteem hit rock bottom when an HR representative at a Dubai-based media outlet cancelled a job interview by email without any justification after I submitted a couple of professional portrait photographs of myself, confirming disapproval of my 'not so ideal' physical appearance.

---

14. Better known in the Middle East as *keffiyeh*, *ghutra* is an Arabic word for a long garment used by men in the Arabian Gulf to cover their head and shoulders, as part of their traditional day-to-day clothing. It is tied on the head with a black piece of cord, known commonly as *aghal*.

Silencing Emirati journalists

Apart from gendered stereotyping and discrimination, Emirati female journalists have to grapple with the excessive practise of self-censorship impacting their journalistic writings and skills, putting limitations on their freedom of expression and, as a consequence, inhibiting a free press in the country. The earlier generations of Emirati journalists formed the golden age of the Emirati press through publishing bold news stories pushing against the red lines, or so-called triangle, that determine the three main taboo subjects: religion, politics and sex. That pioneer spirit seems lacking in their contemporary counterparts. Just like the Emirati female news anchors who seem to accept the gender stereotyping in the newsroom, the new generation of Emirati female journalists seem confident in the practise of self-censorship to save them from trouble and help them produce news that is loyal and conforms to the national agenda.

The Emirati female journalists I interviewed acknowledge the reality of media and journalism practice in the UAE, confirming that it is dominated by self-censorship. Some of them even reflect on it as an exercise of patriotic journalism, in which they produce responsible news material to make the public aware of and secure from external threats. For instance, F.A.S., thirty-four, an executive at an Abu Dhabi-based media outlet, said:

> Freedom of practice should be in parallel with the government's mission. We should refrain from broadcasting things that may cause negative reactions or retaliation. The media should follow the government's mission and support it. In the end, you don't work to harm your nation.

Others admit that this specific reality has divorced them from exercising true journalism and from playing the role of watchdog, a dynamic not recognized in the UAE. They also understand that Emirati women's representation and empowerment in the media sector is used merely as an element in the country's Islamized state-feminism scheme, in which their public roles should focus on preserving Emirati sociocultural components including heritage, religion, traditions and national cohesion, to achieve unity and identity-building.

A few of them are frustrated about the current media landscape, but they have done nothing to change it, and even if they tried challenging the status

GULF WOMEN'S LIVES

quo, any bold features that they proposed were eventually sidelined, as the following testimonial reveals. 'Mahra', sixty-five, a former journalist for *Al Azminah Al Arabiya* and *Awraq* magazines,[15] believes that the rules of censorship in the UAE during the early 1980s were not clearly identified by the censors and local authorities. Even though Emirati journalists, women and men alike, were bold and forward in their writings at that time, they still worked with an awareness of the sensitive religious and cultural norms in the UAE. When their writing was censored despite this awareness, they found the censors' standards needlessly oppressive and meaningless. 'Mahra' recalled:

> A few of my features were censored either by deleting paragraphs or photographs. For instance, a censor decided to delete a photograph of an art painting that was supposed to be published in one of my cultural features because—from his perspective only—it featured nudity. Most of the time, we weren't aware of the nature of the editorial or pictorial content that censors might delete, they just didn't tell us, it wasn't clear, so we ended up having paragraphs deleted or an entire edition of the magazine censored. One time, a censor deleted a picture, it was a painting by Picasso, because 'it reveals a woman's bosoms', he said! When I practised journalism, the level of press freedom was quite high, and we were able to write bold and critical subjects on politics and culture, but afterwards, the level of press freedom declined dramatically due to the political environment in the Arab world at that time.

The observations and interviews chosen for this chapter reveal mixed views that reflect either submission or resistance towards the reality of media practices in the UAE. Journalists get silenced one way or another, as the neo-patriarchal governing leadership is very successful at co-opting potential dissent inspired by the issue of gender inequality. This issue is still viewed as a political aspiration only by critics of the government's policies, especially external media observers and international organizations such as the Committee to Protect Journalists (CPJ), Human Rights Watch, and the United Nations Entity for Gender Equality and the Empowerment of Women. Moreover, inequality is

---

15. *Awraq* was a weekly cultural magazine founded by the late Emirati journalist Habib Al Sayegh (1955–2019). Privately owned and run, the magazine was published from 1982 to 1995.

overshadowed by tribal patriarchalism, enshrined gender-defined roles, expectations and sociocultural norms, which are often given religious legitimacy.

Conclusion

Contradictory state education and emancipation campaigns have had significant impacts on three generations of Emirati women's consciousness regarding gender and their rights, and on their desire to achieve autonomy and to implement a social discourse for change. Yet there are elements that stand in the way of Emirati women generally. These include a lack of the confidence needed to achieve their potential due to being confined consciously and unconsciously by gendered sociocultural bias, limited access to full participation in the nation-building scheme, the deficiency of state-backed campaigns in granting Emirati women equal rights in family law, and the state's attempts at Islamizing feminism that have been politically instrumented in fear of losing the nation's hegemony and cultural identity (Pomeroy 2017: 19).

Despite the state's efforts towards empowering Emirati women through Islamizing feminism, this particular factor did not change the distinctive structure of tribal patriarchalism in the UAE. On the one hand, Emirati women have become visibly integrated in the public sphere through access to education, employment and government-regulated political practice, while on the other, they have become increasingly trapped in the confines of tribal arranged marriages, which are part and parcel of tribal belonging to maintain blood ties. Women are bound within roles chosen for them by male relatives because of misinterpreted religious and traditional values, with no right to choose (Al Suwailan 2006).

In the absence of a collective consciousness of gender disparity, activism and progressive social movements in the UAE, Emirati women's fight against tribal patriarchalism, with its suffocating notions and mindset, will not achieve social change, nor will it eliminate discrimination (N'Guessan 2011). Steering the course of social change is achievable if Emirati women of all social classes, but particularly those who belong to the largest demographic of middle-class tribes in the UAE, create a collective response. Currently, these Emirati women are functioning dynamically in the cultural and literary scenes, but their collective work is absent from the picture, alongside the absence of women's political parties and affiliations. It is important to mention that bargaining with the patriarchy, which sits at the core of a conservative tribal society that has only embraced modernity and adapted to the rapidly changing conditions of contemporary life in the past half-century, will continue to be a challenge for Emirati women who still bargain implicitly and explicitly with family members endorsing patriarchal and matriarchal kinship relations, as well as with the bureaucrats and representatives of the state apparatus.

With this in mind, the media needs to play a vital role in promoting a decent and balanced portrayal of Emirati women to educate and influence public opinion, while Emirati women of all social classes need to collectively launch domestic feminist movements and NGOs aimed at gaining an influence in the national political landscape, and to increase their participation and presence in the regional and international arenas, building solidarity with their peers. Their efforts in contributing to Emirati women's press and literature, including filmmaking and the publication of books, will further shed light on their rights, and will eventually put pressure on the government to adopt new policies, which in due course will result in progressive social change. As Palestinian author Hisham Sharabi states: 'Women's movement is the detonator which will explode neo-patriarchal society from within. If allowed to grow and come into its own, it will become the permanent shield against patriarchal regression, the cornerstone of future modernity' (Sharabi 1988: 154).

Acknowledgements

I am indebted to my colleague, Marwa Koheji, whose introduction to the project was instrumental in shaping its direction and focus. Her insights, alongside the support of the NYUAD Humanities Research Fellowship Program on the study of the Arab World, have been invaluable throughout this journey.

References

Al Darmaki, Q. (2014). العلاقات الإماراتية المصرية. Hamdan bin Mohammed Heritage Centre.

Al Malki, A., Kaufer, D., Ishizaki, S. & Dreher, K. (2012). *Arab Women in Arab News*. Bloomsbury.

UNMASKING PATRIARCHY

Al Nowais, S. (2017, 28 August). No Tree Without Roots. *The National*. https://www. thenationalnews.com/uae/special-report-the-first-emirati-women-to-travel-abroad-for-education-1.623688

Al Oraimi, S. (2011). The Concept of Gender in Emirati Culture: An Analytical Study of the Role of the State in Redefining Gender and Social Roles. *Museum International*, 63(3–4), 78–92. https://doi.org/10.1111/muse.12009

Al Suwailan, Z. (2006). The Impact of Societal Values on Kuwaiti Women and the Role of Education. Tennessee Research and Creative Exchange. http://trace.tennessee.edu/cgi/viewcontent.cgi?article=3141&context=utk_graddiss

Allagui, I. & Al Najjar, A. (2018). From Women Empowerment to Nation Branding: A Case Study from the United Arab Emirates. *International Journal of Communication of the University of Southern California*, 12, 68–85. https://ijoc.org/index.php/ijoc/article/viewFile/7319/2217

Arab Media Forum (2014, 24 May). Are Television Channels Attracting Viewers with Beauty over Brains? http://www.arabmediaforum.ae/en/media-center/press-releases/are-television-channels-attracting-viewers-with-beauty-over-brains.aspx

Ayish, M. (2021). United Arab Emirates: Media for Sustainable Development. In C. Richter, N. Abdulhaq & K. Hafez (eds), *Arab Media Systems*. Open Book Publishers.

Cairo Scene (2016, 11 August). Egyptian TV Banning Female Presenters for Being Fat? http://www.cairoscene.com/Buzz/Fat-Women-Are-Not-Allowed-On-Egyptian-State-Television

Chambers, D., Steiner, L. & Fleming, C. (2004). *Women and Journalism*. Routledge. https://doi.org/10.4324/9780203500668

Darwish, A. (2009). *Social Semiotics of Arabic Satellite Television*. Writescope Pty.

Duffy, M. (2014). *Media Law in the United Arab Emirates*. Kluwer Law International.

Gulf News (2012, 27 December). The UAE Writers Union. https://gulfnews.com/uae/the-uae-writers-union-1.1124627

Hassan, A. (2011). *Our Media Identity*. Fujairah Media and Culture Authority.

Khamis, D. (2020). Tweets [@dhabiya1]. Twitter. Retrieved 6 July 2020, from http://www.twitter.com/dhabiya1

Ministry of Culture and Youth (2021, June). About the Media Regulatory Office. https://mcy.gov.ae/en/mro/

Mitra, B. (2014). Audience Responses to the Physical Appearance of Television Newsreaders. *Journal of Audience & Reception Studies*, 11(2), 45–57.

N'Guessan, K.G. (2011). Gender Hierarchy and the Social Construction of Femininity: The Imposed Mask. *Acta Yassyensia Comparacionis*, 9, 185–199. http://www.literaturacomparata.ro/Site_Acta/Old/acta9/n.guessan_9.2011.pdf

Obaid, A. (2000, 18 April). الصحافة في الامارات من البدايات الى آفاق العالمية. *Al Bayan*, http://www.albayan.ae/one-world/2000-04-18-1.1083118

GULF WOMEN'S LIVES

Pomeroy, B. (2017). *Mediated Nationalism: Press Freedom, Mass Media, and Nationalism* [unpublished master's thesis]. Calhoun Institutional Archive of Naval Postgraduate School. https://calhoun.nps.edu/bitstream/handle/10945/56785/17Dec_Pomeroy_Brenton.pdf?sequence=1&isAllowed=y

Salih, L. (1983). أدب المرأة في الخليج العربي. Dar Al Yaqatha Publications.

Sharabi, H. (1988). *Neopatriarchy: A Theory of Distorted Change in Arab Society*. Oxford University Press.

Simonson, P. & Park, D. (2016). *The International History of Communication Study*. Routledge.

Soffan, L. (1980). *Women of the United Arab Emirates*. Routledge.

Sonbol, A. (2012). *Gulf Women*. Bloomsbury Qatar Foundation Publications.

UAE Cabinet (2019, 2 May). Mohammed bin Rashid Assigns the UAE Gender Balance Council to Oversee the Implementation of the 'Gender Inequality Index'. The Media Centre, UAE Cabinet. https://www.uaecabinet.ae/en/details/news/mohammed-bin-rashid-assigns-the-uae-gender-balance-council-to-oversee-the-implementation-of-the-gender-inequality-index

UAE Federal Government (1980). Federal Law No. 15 for 1980 Concerning Publications and Publishing. Ministry of Information and Culture.

World Economic Forum (2021). *Global Gender Gap Report*. https://www3.weforum.org/docs/WEF_GGGR_2021.pdf

5 A Critical Analysis of Women's Petitions and Gender Reform in Saudi Arabia

Nora Jaber (0009-0008-7173-8033)

Introduction

Women in Saudi Arabia are often the subject of reductive and homogenizing narratives. In 'Western' media and scholarship, they are regularly constructed and represented as '*objects* of passivity, silence, submission, veil and seclusion' (Abdo 1995: 141).[1] They are often depicted as never rising above their object status and have been subjected to a larger process of 'discursive homogenization and systematization of the oppression of women in the Third World' (Mohanty 1988: 338). Reductive depictions of women in Saudi Arabia are not only produced externally but are also articulated within and as a result of the state's official historiographies and legitimacy narratives, in which the country is presented as a place without social divisions and in which the people are portrayed as 'not having political will or sensibilities' (Bsheer 2020: 222). Even in the work of scholars from and of the Arab region, the Saudi state's mythical narrative has been reflected, elevated and popularized, resulting in what Bsheer (2020: 8) calls a 'secondary Orientalism that dominates knowledge

---

1. 'Western' in this context is not limited to feminist discourse and scholarship produced by those who, as Mohanty explains, identify themselves as being geographically or culturally from the West; rather it applies to anyone who uses analytic strategies, principles and methods that furthers rather than challenges the reductive objectification of Third World women (2003).

Nora Jaber, CC BY-NC-ND, 'A Critical Analysis of Women's Petitions and Gender Reform in Saudi Arabia' in: *Gulf Women's Lives: Voice, Space, Place*. University of Exeter Press (2024). © Nora Jaber. DOI: 10.47788/JREF4746

GULF WOMEN'S LIVES

production on Saudi Arabia' and that feeds into consolidating the state narrative, rather than deconstructing it.

Simplistic depictions of Saudi women have been hugely beneficial to the state. In fact, gender constructions have always played into myths of national and collective identities, which has made capturing the authentic voices of women a challenge and a necessity. In Saudi Arabia, women have been consistently instrumentalized by the state to embody and symbolize the various images it has sought to project, ranging from that of an icon of Islamic piety, to—particularly since the announcement of Vision 2030 in 2016—a Kingdom of progressive modernity and reform within a 'moderate' Islamic framework.[2] As the country undergoes important changes, so too does the official gender discourse, altering the scope of women's rights in the country. Two of the most widely noted gender reforms, which encapsulate the state's recent emphasis on 'women's empowerment' as part of its self-promotion as a hub of cosmopolitan modernity, have been lifting the ban on women driving and the reduction in the scope of the male guardianship system (MGS) in 2017. Importantly, the result of the ongoing homogenization of Saudi women, at both international and local levels, is that their agency and their modes and discourses of resistance are often unaccounted for. In such accounts, it is the state that is charged with bringing about the necessary reforms, thereby establishing society as the cause of underdevelopment and the state as the primary agent for progress, where progress, as it is defined by international agencies, is increasingly linked to a neoliberal discourse of progressive secular modernity (Hasso 2009).

This chapter challenges such culturalist and uncritical accounts, which not only contribute to the reductive homogenization of Saudi society but also take part in the concealment of decades of women's advocacy demanding the recent reforms that have been portrayed as top-down (Friedman 2017). To do so, the chapter takes an innovative approach to capturing the voices of Saudi women by analysing petitions authored by them between 2011 and 2016, which challenge the (former) ban on driving and the MGS. By analysing the petitions as expressions of Saudi women's voices, the chapter offers a new and

---

2. Vision 2030 is an economic diversification strategy that encapsulates a series of economic, social, legal and political reforms accompanied by discursive shifts, ultimately designed to reduce the Kingdom's dependence on oil.

WOMEN'S PETITIONS AND GENDER REFORM IN SAUDI ARABIA

critical perspective on how Saudi women construct themselves as gendered selves, how they negotiate legal rights and gender hierarchies, and how they navigate the legal and social restrictions imposed on them. The analysis also sheds light on the way in which women petitioners, whilst challenging discriminatory laws and frameworks, often end up reproducing dominant state narratives and reinscribing other hierarchies and inequalities. In this sense, the chapter complicates the binary between resistance and compliance and makes an appeal for a more transnational and inclusive feminism that empowers all women, rather than only those who fit within the new state project.

Petitions as voice

Petitioning is a global practice that can be found throughout history. In the literature, different definitions of petitions have been offered, the essence of which is 'writing upwards' (Lyons 2015: 317). Petitions, as they will be analysed in this chapter, are best described as letters addressed to figures of governmental authority in which citizens express certain grievances and make appeals or demands for reform. As with any form of writing, they transcend physical and spatial boundaries; they establish the petitioner's presence even in contexts and in times in which they are physically absent. In light of this, they have been a popular mode of political expression in Saudi Arabia (Kechichian 2012). In the absence of other avenues of communicating grievances to the state, citizens resort to a medium that allows them to assert their presence in a context in which their absence has been manufactured and manipulated.

Although they remain understudied in scholarship on Saudi civil society (Al-Rasheed 2015b; Kechichian 2012; Lacroix 2011), petitions have been very important for Saudi women—who until recently were excluded not only from the political sphere but also from the public sphere, where their invisibility has been engineered by the state as a hallmark of its piety and religious legitimacy. Saudi women have, particularly since public education was made accessible to women in the 1960s, engaged in different forms of writing as a means of challenging their enforced invisibility. Al Fassi explains that 'writing has come to serve as a means for women to share their experiences and negotiate their rights, power, and space depending on where they stand ideologically, intellectually and socially' (2016: 189). Like other women who took to the pen, Saudi women

GULF WOMEN'S LIVES

petitioners 'are seeking recognition and a voice in writing' (Al-Rasheed 2013: 176). By petitioning, they assert their presence, obtain visibility and endurance, and reach otherwise inaccessible audiences. Therefore, petitions offer a unique opportunity to hear Saudi women's voices, which are so often concealed by homogenizing narratives. They are also a significant lens through which to understand gender politics and power dynamics in the Kingdom. They tell us about the place of women within the Saudi sociopolitical context, and equally about who is excluded not just by the state but also by Saudi women's rights activists, who, in these petitions, demand rights themselves, to the exclusion of others. Hence, they are one of the few documentary sources available that offer an understanding of how Saudi women have negotiated, challenged, reinscribed and played a part in constructing the existing gender order (Alozie 2019: 354).

Methodology and limitations

This chapter focuses on two petitions, one from 2011 which challenges the ban on driving, and one from 2016 that challenges the MGS. These two petitions were selected because they capture two significant historical moments in which the state's narrative visibly changed, particularly with regard to its construction of Saudi women and their place in state and society. Both petitions were authored by Saudi women activists in Arabic.[3] The author names will not be divulged, though the petitions were written by Saudi women who have been actively involved in mobilizing against gender-based discrimination in Saudi Arabia through other means, such as awareness-raising initiatives, online campaigns and street demonstrations. While petitions have traditionally been circulated and delivered by hand, they can now be published and shared on international petitioning platforms and via other forms of online communication (email, messaging platforms, and social media platforms such as Twitter and Facebook) to gather signatures (Briassoulis 2010). Because state officials do have a heavy presence on social media platforms, Twitter in particular, a petition reaches them without the need for in-person delivery, although Saudi women's activists still do try to deliver petitions by hand.

---

3. They have been translated to English by the author of this chapter and direct quotes from the author's translation will be included in the analysis below.

WOMEN'S PETITIONS AND GENDER REFORM IN SAUDI ARABIA

To analyse the text of the petitions, this chapter employs feminist critical discourse analysis (FCDA), which conceives of discourse as a form of social practice, implying a dialectical relationship between texts and the situations, institutions and social structures that shape and are shaped by them (Lazar 2007). FCDA allows for an examination of the role of petitions in the challenge and reproduction of dominance, intended as any exercise of social power by elites, institutions or groups that results in social inequality, including political, cultural, class, ethnic, racial and gender inequality (van Dijk 1993: 250). More specifically, it allows for an examination of 'how power and dominance are discursively produced and/or [counter-]resisted in a variety of ways through textual representations of gendered social practices' (Lazar 2007: 150). FCDA exposes the ways in which Saudi women petitioners challenge, transform or reinscribe power relations and hegemonic gender norms, which are embedded in patriarchal, nationalist and religious discourses/state narratives.

While petitions are unique sources in which Saudi women's voices are heard and in which their concerns, desires and subjectivities are revealed, they have limitations that must be noted. As written texts, they only allow the researcher to work with what the text does or does not say. Petitions are also constrained by their form and by discursive boundaries. All petitions have certain elements in common: van Voss (2002: 2) explains that 'whatever form or context, petitions [are] usually written in a deferential style, showing that the petitioner did not intend to question the established power structure'. In other words, they recognize and affirm the authority of the addressee. Additionally, in Saudi Arabia, petitioners are also seeking to minimize risks to their safety, which informs the language they choose, the demands they make as well as how they are framed, and the legal and normative frameworks to which petitioners appeal. Finally, in addition to tailoring the petition to the addressee, petitions mould their content to their targeted signatories. The more signatures a petition obtains, the more attention from the authorities it commands. This can affect the types of demands and the justifications they put forward for making the stated demands. The petitions do allow the signatories to include some information about themselves, namely their name, occupation, location (city) and gender. However, the current analysis is limited to the text of the petitions themselves, as the main focus of the chapter is on the relationship between the petition text and the state narrative to which it responds.

GULF WOMEN'S LIVES

Because FCDA requires a reading and analysis of the petition texts in light of the context(s) in which they are situated, it must be preceded with an exploration of the necessary contextual background against which petitions are produced. The following section provides an overview of the sociopolitical context within which Saudi gender hierarchies are constructed and negotiated, and emphasizes the role of the state in producing the existing gender order.

The construction of the Saudi gender order

Women are consistently incorporated in national projects and visions in a manner that affects their legal rights and their lived and embodied experiences (Al-Rasheed 2013: 3). Le Renard (2014) observes that the Saudi state has gone from promoting a model of 'Islamic femininity' towards promoting a 'liberal ideal of femininity' in which women are educated and empowered by the state, within a moderate Islamic framework that does not clash with its neoliberal modernizing vision. In doing so, the government has 'formulate[d] a normative project shaping the possibilities, opportunities, and spaces accessible to Saudi women' (Le Renard 2014: 3).

Women as icons of piety

Until the early 2000s, the Saudi state promoted itself as a bastion of Islamic authenticity. It secured and maintained its own legitimacy by basing it on its role as the true protector of Islam. In forming the Saudi state and in securing the population's loyalty to the ruler, the Al-Saud dynasty has relied heavily on the support of the religious establishment to bolster its legitimacy. This resulted in a 'form of power-sharing between the princes and the clerics', with the former having full control in matters of governance and the latter 'being put in charge of defining and enforcing social norms' (Lacroix 2019: 97). The political–religious alliance between the state and the religious clerics, therefore, has been mutually beneficial and has underpinned the functioning of the Saudi Arabian political and legal system, often to the detriment of Saudi women. The state's religious legitimacy narrative was consolidated through the state fostering a sense of religious nationalism (Al-Rasheed 2013: 17), as 'a form of nationalism in which religion was the bond that was to unite people living

WOMEN'S PETITIONS AND GENDER REFORM IN SAUDI ARABIA

in Saudi Arabia', which was especially useful in the absence of a colonial history like that of its neighbours (Bsheer 2020: 11).

Because of the politico-religious alliance, which led to the prevalence of religious discourse in both official discourse and in public life in Saudi Arabia, discriminatory laws and practices in the country have often been attributed to restrictive interpretations of Islam and to the society's cultural conservatism. The reality, however, is much more complex and the state's role in determining the status of Saudi women cannot be ignored. On this note, Al-Rasheed (2015a: 293) has argued that 'the subordination and exclusion of Saudi women is a political—rather than simply a religious or social—fact', as Saudi women have been used by successive Saudi rulers as tangible markers of the state's Islamic credentials, as 'godly women', signs of the authenticity of the nation and its compliance with God's law (Al-Rasheed 2013: 17). They have also been used as symbols and transmitters—as mothers and teachers—of the state's religious nationalism project. They have been obliged to become the personification and embodiment of piety and to project it in their daily lives to promote the image of an Islamic nation. Women both became the stage on which the Islamic credentials of the state would play out, and—to borrow from Shahrokni's analogy describing the politics of gender segregation in Iran—they were 'included as unwitting protagonists in a play whose script was being written during its staging' (2020: 111). In constructing its image as a religious and masculine state, Saudi Arabia has depicted women as being in perpetual need of protection and control, resulting in an entire legal and social framework that institutionalizes and entrenches their subordination and infantilization. Saudi women's legal and social marginalization was particularly exacerbated since the late 1970s in response to the rise of political Islam across the region, as well as to internal challenges to Al-Saud's religious legitimacy by Islamist groups (Cerioli 2019: 55). Control over women's lives and bodies was conceded to religious authorities who, in turn, restricted and policed their rights and behaviour with the backing of the state.

Importantly, the state's linking of its Islamic credentials to a set of practices and tangible markers, most visibly its gender order, ultimately also 'produced a set of ideological and practical contours that shaped the state itself' (Shahrokni 2020: 115). The state was therefore not only enabled by religious nationalism but also constrained by it. This became a major issue in the early 2000s, when

GULF WOMEN'S LIVES

the government sought to adopt a new legitimacy narrative to which religion would no longer be central.

Therefore, the government has, until recently, been cautious with the implementation of progressive gender reforms to avoid potential backlash, particularly from the religious establishment and patriarchal family units who had long been given control over women and their bodies. The official religious establishment has, at times, opposed government policy through fatwas, particularly around gender reform (Alhargan 2012: 131). The government could not introduce major reforms to women's status without reshaping its legitimacy narrative and promoting a new nationalist discourse that did not have Wahhabi doctrine at its core. This would allow it to gradually marginalize the religious establishment without losing popular support.

Women as symbols of progressive modernity

In the new millennium, a series of events pushed the state to rethink its legitimacy narrative and reconfigure its internal and external political alliances. Most notable were the 11 September 2001 attacks on the Twin Towers in New York City, due to Saudi nationals participating in plotting and carrying out the attacks and their reliance on religious justifications, which echoed the religious teachings propagated by the Saudi educational system at the time (Lacroix 2011: 48). Following this, Saudi Arabia became the target of severe international criticism. The government's partnership with the religious establishment and its instrumentalization of religious nationalism to secure domestic legitimization became unsustainable, particularly once it came at the cost of its international reputation which became 'synonymous with terrorism, radical religious teachings, persistent gender inequality and stumbling economic development' (Al-Rasheed 2019). In light of this, Al-Rasheed observes that, in the state's post-9/11 narrative, Islamism was portrayed as the cause of various issues, including radicalization and gender-based discrimination and violence (Al-Rasheed 2010: 31). Islamism became akin to a foreign disease that had made its way into the country and had managed to spread and radicalize the minds of the Saudi populace. This allowed the state to conceal its own role in fostering and benefitting from the ideology underlying the attacks.

WOMEN'S PETITIONS AND GENDER REFORM IN SAUDI ARABIA

To improve its international reputation and ensure its political legitimacy and survival, the regime propagated an *iṣlāḥ* or reform narrative that embraces 'moderate Islam' (Alhussein 2020: 6). This strategic shift allowed the ruling family to retain its Islamic legitimacy whilst curtailing religious influence, asserting a separation between religion and politics, and centring Al-Saud as the political authority at the heart of a new approach which would herald sociopolitical and economic liberalization. While the phrase 'moderate Islam' was initially used in the Kingdom immediately following the 11 September 2001 attacks, it became a staple of the state's narrative when the Crown Prince Mohammed bin Salman declared at an economic conference in Riyadh in 2017 that: 'We are returning to what we were before—a country of moderate Islam that is open to all religions, traditions, and people around the globe' (BBC News 2017). In other words, this signalled a shift to an era in which the state would selectively invoke religion, but no longer rely on religious legitimacy to rule. The shift is seen in the form of nationalism propagated by the state, a renewed national narrative emphasizing secular identifications within the collective Saudi identity. In effect, it is a 'Saudi first' nationalist narrative within which Islam is retained as part of the state's identity, but only insofar as it does not clash with its political and neoliberal economic project (Alhussein 2019).

To consolidate the shift towards an era of modernization and religious moderation as means of improving its international status, the government again relied on women to portray the new image of the state: women 'became the soft face with which the state launched its charm offensive against critical international condemnation of Saudi society and religion' (Al-Rasheed 2013: 40). Therefore, since the early 2000s, the Saudi state has promoted a liberal discourse of women's empowerment, which has been accompanied by a series of legal and social reforms with the aim of elevating the status of Saudi women. This began with King Fahd's (1985–2005) decision to issue women ID cards in 2001, followed by King Abdallah's (2005–2015) appointment of women to the Shura (Consultative) Council in 2013, and then King Salman's (2015–present) decision to allow women to vote and run as candidates in municipal elections in 2015 and to drive in 2017. Crucially, the state's promotion of a neoliberal discourse of women's empowerment, particularly since the launch of Vision 2030 in 2016, has allowed the state to assert itself as the primary

GULF WOMEN'S LIVES

agent for progress—the ultimate arbiter of rights and protections in the face of a society that is highly religious and resistant to change.

The petitions

Against this background, two petitions authored by Saudi women will be analysed with a focus on how Saudi women not only negotiate and challenge discriminatory laws and frameworks, but also reproduce and legitimize state narratives in their activism.[4] In doing so, they advance certain rights for Saudi women whilst reinforcing other inequities based on class, race and nationality. In other words, they fall into a pattern of 'resist[ing] hegemonic power at [...] the interpersonal level, while reinscribing it at the national or international levels', which may render the effects of women's activism 'circumscribed and incremental, rather than fundamental or consistent' (Pratt 2020: 222–23). Therefore, the analysis below will not only mediate the connection between language and the social context in which it is used, but will also be highly attentive to hidden, or less obvious, hegemonic influences of power and dominance.

2011 driving ban petition

The 2011 petition was authored and circulated as part of the Women2Drive campaign, which was launched by Saudi activist Manal Al-Sharif in 2011 calling on Saudi women to drive their cars on 17 June 2011 in defiance of the driving ban. This was not the first petition in which Saudi women called on the state to end the ban. However, it was significant because it marked the reignition of Saudi women's rights activism challenging the driving ban, after a two-decade-long hiatus.[5] The 2011 petition mirrors the state's discourse

---

4. The petitions discussed here, either the original Arabic versions or the author's English translations, can be obtained from the author upon request.
5. In November 1990, Saudi women organized a demonstration against the ban on driving, which was preceded by a petition addressed to Prince Salman, Governor of Riyadh at the time. The women were met with a harsh state response that deterred them from engaging in organized activism until the Women2Drive campaign in 2011, inspired by the wave of Arab uprisings.

WOMEN'S PETITIONS AND GENDER REFORM IN SAUDI ARABIA

of reform, women's empowerment and religious moderation in which the Saudi woman is constructed as a visible and active participant in social and economic life who is no longer limited to the private sphere of the home, but who nevertheless remains protected from society by the masculine and paternalistic state. It differs significantly from a petition authored in 1990 by a group of Saudi women, known as the 'Ladies of November', who participated in the first ever organized driving demonstration in the Kingdom on 6 November 1990.

In the 2011 petition, the authors emphasize the social and economic dimensions of the driving ban. They explain that the driving ban has effects on their domestic life and their work life, both areas of importance under the state's narrative. This is done explicitly, for example, when they write that the obstacles that arise from the lack of transportation negatively impact 'one of two things: either related to domestic issues with regards to children and parents, or going to work'.

Therefore, the first justification the petitioners put forward for demanding the right to drive is that it would allow them to handle domestic matters more easily, such as 'tak[ing] care of children, patients and elderly people'. In beginning the petition in this way, the petitioners mirror the dominant narrative that the Saudi woman belongs first and foremost in the domestic sphere. In doing so, they uphold traditional gender roles within a patriarchal family structure that are deeply entrenched in Saudi society and institutionalized through the MGS. However, in emphasizing their role as carers, the authors of the petition present the Saudi woman not as a mere dependant, but a more active player in family life. In fact, they expressly reject their role as dependants in the family and manifest discontent with the impracticality of 'women's reliance on some family members such as the brother, the father or even the husband to see to their affairs' and complain that this 'disrupts their interests and exposes them to the humiliation of asking' a male relative to drive them. However, this does not extend to explicitly challenging the MGS as a structure, which only comes later in the 2016 petition.

The authors' act of linking demands to end the driving ban with women's role in the family recalls Fernea's (1998) notion of 'family feminism', in which 'Islamic feminists strive to create equality, not for the woman as an individual but for the woman as part of the family, a social institution still seen as

105

GULF WOMEN'S LIVES

central to the organization and maintenance of any society', the dominant form of feminism among Gulf women (Fernea 1998: 416).[6] Therefore, rather than endorse a liberal notion of individual autonomy and freedom, the petitioners' '"contextual self" emerges as an identity that may be tied to family, tribe, and religion, rather than a Western notion of individual autonomy' (Strobl 2010: 63). In this, the petitioners also replicate the state's construction of Saudi women as mothers who transmit to their children the values of the nation. This makes gendered analysis even more important, considering how the petition 'appeal[s] to paternalistic codes' and upholds patriarchal values and established gender norms in Saudi Arabia (Irfan 2020: 81).

Moreover, as they emphasize their role as workers, the authors also link the driving ban to the financial disadvantages that lack of transportation presents to women and their families. In particular, they complain about the need to hire a foreign driver to whom they must pay part of their 'salary that does not even suffice to cover their own needs'. In highlighting the legitimate economic burden that ensues from hiring a driver, the authors appear dismissive of the reality that many Saudi women cannot afford to hire one, thereby ignoring and reinforcing class disparities between Saudis, as well as reinscribing the dominance and inequality produced through the *kafala* (visa sponsorship) system, an unequal and abusive legal framework based on labour exploitation and border control and violence. On this matter, the petition refers to 'the great harm that comes with drivers due to their lack of discipline and moral deviation which threatens family members, for there have been many recorded cases of abuse'. In doing so, the authors reproduce harmful and exclusionary racialized stereotypes that equate foreignness with immorality. The petition shows no regard for the manner in which restrictions on Saudi women's mobility result in their own complicity in the everyday control and exploitation of migrant workers, as well as the double burden to which migrant women are subjected, both as women whose internal mobility is restricted by the

---

6. Islamic feminism is a gendered epistemology that grounds women's rights in Islamic sources rather than in other domestic or international legal sources. To do this, proponents engage in a methodology of independent reasoning to reinterpret religious texts in a more egalitarian manner. Although many Saudi women reject the term feminism, it is a useful term for understanding the methodology, strategies and discourses employed by the authors of the petitions when making rights claims.

WOMEN'S PETITIONS AND GENDER REFORM IN SAUDI ARABIA

driving ban, and as women whose bodies and lives are more largely and pervasively constrained by the *kafala* system. In addition to the relations of dominance that this reinforces, it also presents a combination of paternalism and exclusionary nationalism, as the petitioners ('daughters of the nation') are seeking this protection from the King ('our dear father'). By referring to the King as a father figure and as protector of his citizen daughters, the petitioners construct themselves within the same political and cultural narrative the state has propagated about Saudi women's need for masculine protection.

Additionally, the petition mirrors and reinforces the state's religious legitimacy narrative. The authors emphasize their Islamic identity by speaking in the name of the 'Saudi Muslim woman' and by invoking Islamic principles and frames of reference throughout the petition. The authors express that they 'want to exercise [their] legitimate right to drive a car'. The use of the term 'legitimate right', which refers to a right grounded in sharia, indicates that they are not referring to secular human rights, but rather a right grounded in Islam. Therefore, in addition to endorsing a 'family feminism', the authors also ground their rights claims in local normative frameworks and frames of reference. According to Yamani (2006: 13), women's rights activists in Saudi Arabia employ religious discourse because it is 'the legitimate language of the nation', in the sense that it is more difficult for both the state and the religious authorities to refute. The use of religious frames of reference also signals an awareness of the importance of religion to the state's legitimacy narrative and as a national value. This is clear when the authors of the petition write that if allowed to drive, in exercising their right, they would do so 'with full respect for the values of their generous nation and its Islamic roots'.

In requesting the right to drive, the petitioners reflect and reinforce the state narrative. In addition to reinforcing a paternalistic dynamic between the government and Saudi women citizens, the petitioners also invoke and reinscribe nationalist, religious and increasingly neoliberal discourses, all of which are propagated by the state. Importantly, the reproduction of hegemonic terms in the petitions should not be taken at face value, as the employment of a certain term or code does not necessarily signify acceptance. Irfan argues that it is often a 'performative tactic deliberately designed to increase the likelihood of an appeal's success' (2020: 82). The invocation of paternalistic and patriarchal discourses may also be a way of achieving 'subversiveness through

GULF WOMEN'S LIVES

reappropriation' whereby a woman writer 'plays with her cultural subordination in the symbolic order by replicating herself in the syntax of its familiar grammar, but always as a commentary on it' (Zaeske 2002: 158).

2016 MGS petition

The year 2016 marked a clear shift in the Saudi state discourse. The new regime, led by King Salman and Crown Prince Mohammed bin Salman, accelerated the pace of gender reforms and made women's empowerment a key component of the state's new economic agenda, encapsulated in Vision 2030. The state's increasingly neoliberal narrative emphasized the role of women as citizens, active participants in the prosperity of the nation, and importantly, successful economic actors. Saudi women saw in this an opportunity to shift their efforts to target what many regarded as the core of their marginalization: the MGS.

The focus on activism challenging the MGS began in 2016 when Saudi women launched the I Am My Own Guardian campaign (Doaiji 2017). The launch was timed to coincide with the release of a report by Human Rights Watch titled 'Boxed In', which was released on 17 July 2016. The campaign largely focused on spreading local and global awareness about the daily forms of discrimination Saudi women faced, and in turn on applying pressure on the Saudi government to take action to abolish the guardianship system. The 2016 petition, authored around the same time, is the most important petition to have circulated in Saudi Arabia with a focus on the MGS.

A first draft of this petition was authored in August 2016 by a prominent women's rights activist and was edited by twenty-five fellow-women activists. In August 2016 it was published online as a Google Document and was promoted on Twitter as part of the I Am My Own Guardian campaign in order to gather signatures. When it was taken offline after a month, it had gathered 14,682 signatures, at which point the petition was delivered in person to the Royal Court by Saudi activist Aziza al-Yousef on 26 September 2016.

The most noticeable feature of the 2016 petition is that it is largely framed within a narrative that has already been adopted and heavily propagated by the government, particularly since the launch of Vision 2030. Because of this,

WOMEN'S PETITIONS AND GENDER REFORM IN SAUDI ARABIA

there is a clear difference in the references employed between the MGS petition and the driving ban petition discussed above, but not in the strategy, which once again is largely based on situating demands within and reflecting the official state narrative. So, many demands made by the petitioners have been put forward in a way that demonstrates to the government how adopting them would benefit the state itself and help achieve the goals it has set for the country, rather than asserting them as rights claims that the state is under an obligation to guarantee its citizens.

Although the petition does not mention Vision 2030 explicitly, it does refer to the government's National Transformation Plan (NTP), one of the 'Vision Realization Programmes'. The petition begins by referring to the state's announcement of the NTP and the rest of the petition follows within this established narrative, 'with its emphasis on economic participation and individual responsibility' (Doaiji 2017: 1). In fact, throughout the petition, the MGS is challenged with reference to how it 'impedes the realization of the NTP', which the state is committed to achieving.

By referring to what the state has already endorsed and even propagated, the petitioners position themselves as merely asking the state to make good on its own promises. This is exemplified when the petition refers to the government's announcement of the NTP in which it 'confirmed its commitment to continue developing the talents of [female] citizens and empowering them'. They situate their demands within the bounds of what the state has already committed to do, effectively minimizing the boldness of the petition, adopting 'a language that gave them permission to speak, drew in state intervention, and allowed them to (re)define in some measure the meaning of justice, even while ostensibly sticking to the terms of officially acceptable discourse' (Chalcraft 2005: 318).

Although the petitioners limit their challenge of the MGS to areas the state has already expressed a commitment to reforming, and continue to seek empowerment from the state, their use of the word 'citizens' (*muwatinat*), which is feminized in the Arabic text, is significant. It is an assertion that Saudi women demand to be recognized as full citizens in terms of how they are treated under the law, and not merely in official discourse. Moreover, in asserting their citizenship, the petition departs from the father–daughter dynamic prevalent in the driving ban petition. Instead, it employs a

GULF WOMEN'S LIVES

citizen–state dynamic, which is notable because the attainment of full citizenship is the core aim of those seeking to abolish the MGS.

Again, in this petition the authors ground their demands within an Islamic normative framework. For example, they assert that 'the existence of the [MGS] cannot be reconciled with legitimate Islamic opinions which confirm a mature woman's guardianship over herself and her residence and her money and the management of all her affairs'. Here the petitioners point to the plurality of religious interpretations while working within the confines of state discourse as they begin the sentence with 'Considering the position of the kingdom in the Islamic world'. This is a direct reference to Vision 2030, which according to its website 'draws on the nation's intrinsic strength', the first of which is that 'Saudi Arabia is the land of the Two Holy Mosques which positions the Kingdom at the heart of the Arab and Islamic worlds' (Vision 2030 2022). It is important to note that Islamic feminism had by then become part of the state narrative, exemplified by the announcement that women would be included in the Council of Senior Scholars, due to the efforts of Saudi women's rights activists to use it to challenge dominant interpretations of Islam which have been used to discriminate against women.[7] Therefore, while in the driving ban petition the use of Islamic feminism did reflect the state's religious legitimacy narrative, it also transformed it by creating a space for alternative interpretations that granted women more rights.

Conclusions

This chapter has argued that the 'Saudi woman' has been repeatedly homogenized and constructed to support and advance shifting state narratives and political agendas. It argued that women are consistently instrumentalized to serve national projects and visions in a manner that affects their legal rights and their lived experiences. While attentive to the ways in which the state

---

7. The Council of Senior Scholars is Saudi Arabia's highest religious body. Established in 1971, it advises the King and provides religious support for royal decrees. Including women in the Council recognizes the importance of women as producers of religious knowledge and creates an opportunity for their issues to be voiced and reflected within official spaces.

consistently reshapes its gender politics to suit its legitimacy narratives, the chapter emphasized that women are not merely passive objects whose subjectivities are entirely defined by the state. One way in which they have asserted their presence and negotiated their rights is through petitioning.

By conducting a feminist critical discourse analysis of two petitions from 2011 and 2016, this chapter identified shifts in the frames of reference and discursive strategies employed by Saudi women activists when challenging the ban on driving and the MGS. The analysis of the petitions not only revealed the ways in which petitioners challenged the ban on driving and the MGS, but also other inequities reinscribed in their discourse. The analysis showed that the demands and justifications put forward by the petitioners were often framed within discursive bounds set by the official state narrative. In doing so, they reinscribed paternalistic and patriarchal relations and advanced certain rights for Saudi women whilst reinforcing other hierarchies based on class, race and nationality in particular.

Regardless of whether these discourses are truly endorsed by the authors of the petitions or whether they are strategic performative tactics employed to increase the likelihood of the petitions' success, it is necessary to recognize the legitimizing effect that the reproduction of hegemonic discourses has, as well as the possibilities for more inclusive forms of living that they preclude.

References

Abdo, N. (1995). Feminism and Difference: The Struggle of Palestinian Women. *Canadian Woman Studies*, 15(2), 141–45. https://cws.journals.yorku.ca/index.php/cws/article/view/9490

Al Fassi, H.A. (2016). Saudi Women and Islamic Discourse, Selected Examples of Saudi Feminisms. *Hawwa*, 14(2), 187–206. https://doi.org/10.1163/15692086-12341306

Al-Rasheed, M. (2010). *A History of Saudi Arabia* (2nd edn). Cambridge University Press.

Al-Rasheed, M. (2013). *A Most Masculine State: Gender, Politics and Religion in Saudi Arabia*. Cambridge University Press.

Al-Rasheed, M. (2015a). Caught Between Religion and State: Women in Saudi Arabia. In B. Haykel, S. Lacroix & T. Hegghammer (eds), *Saudi Arabia in Transition: Insights on Social, Political, Economic and Religious Change* (pp. 292–313). Cambridge University Press. https://doi.org/10.1017/CBO9781139047586.018

Al-Rasheed, M. (2015b). *Muted Modernists: The Struggle over Divine Politics in Saudi Arabia*. Hurst.

GULF WOMEN'S LIVES

Al-Rasheed, M. (2019, 21 March). The Saudi Lie. *London Review of Books*, 41(6). https://www.lrb.co.uk/the-paper/v41/n06/madawi-al-rasheed/the-saudi-lie

Alhargan, R. (2012). Saudi Arabia: Civil Rights and Local Actors. *Middle East Policy*, 19(1), 126–39. https://doi.org/10.1111/j.1475-4967.2012.00529.x

Alhussein, E. (2019). *Saudi First: How Hyper-Nationalism Is Transforming Saudi Arabia*. European Council on Foreign Relations.

https://ecfr.eu/publication/saudi_first_how_hyper_nationalism_is_transforming_saudi_arabia/

Alhussein, E. (2020). *Saudi Arabia Champions 'Moderate Islam,' Underpinning Reform Efforts*. The Arab Gulf States Institute in Washington. https://agsiw.org/saudi-arabia-champions-moderate-islam-underpinning-reform-efforts/

Alozie, B.C. (2019). 'Female Voices on Ink': The Sexual Politics of Petitions in Colonial Igboland, 1892–1960. *Journal of the Middle East and Africa*, 10(4), 343–66. https://doi.org/10.1080/21520844.2019.1684719

BBC News (2017, 25 October). Crown Prince Says Saudis Want Return to Moderate Islam. https://www.bbc.com/news/world-middle-east-41747476

Briassoulis, H. (2010). Online Petitions: New Tools of Secondary Analysis? *Qualitative Research*, 10(6), 715–27. https://doi.org/10.1177/1468794110380530

Bsheer, R. (2020). *Archive Wars: The Politics of History in Saudi Arabia*. Stanford University Press.

Cerioli, L. (2019). Driving in the Middle of the Road: Paradoxes of Women's Role under the New Saudi Arabian Nationalism. *Ex Aequo*, 40, 49–64. https://doi.org/10.22355/exaequo.2019.40.04

Chalcraft, J. (2005). Engaging the State: Peasants and Petitions in Egypt on the Eve of Colonial Rule. *International Journal of Middle East Studies*, 37(3), 303–25. https://doi.org/10.1017/S0020743805052098

Doaiji, N. (2017). *Saudi Women's Online Activism: One Year of the 'I Am My Own Guardian' Campaign*. The Arab Gulf States Institute in Washington. https://agsiw.org/saudi-womens-online-activism-one-year-guardian-campaign/

Fernea, E.W. (1998). *In Search of Islamic Feminism: One Woman's Global Journey*. Anchor Books.

Friedman, T.L. (2017, 23 November). Saudi Arabia's Arab Spring, At Last. *New York Times*. https://www.nytimes.com/2017/11/23/opinion/saudi-prince-mbs-arab-spring.html

Hasso, F.S. (2009). Empowering Governmentalities Rather than Women: The Arab Human Development Report 2005 and Western Development Logics. *International Journal of Middle East Studies*, 41(1), 63–82. https://doi.org/10.1017/S0020743808090120

Irfan, A. (2020). Petitioning for Palestine: Refugee Appeals to International Authorities. *Contemporary Levant*, 5(2), 79–96. https://doi.org/10.1080/20581831.2020.1815408

Kechichian, J.A. (2012). *Legal and Political Reforms in Saudi Arabia*. Routledge.

Lacroix, S. (2011). *Awakening Islam: The Politics of Religious Dissent in Contemporary Saudi Arabia*. Harvard University Press.

WOMEN'S PETITIONS AND GENDER REFORM IN SAUDI ARABIA

Lacroix, S. (2019). Saudi Arabia and the Limits of Religious Reform. *The Review of Faith & International Affairs*, 17(2), 97–101. https://doi.org/10.1080/15570274.2019.1608650

Lazar, M.M. (2007). Feminist Critical Discourse Analysis: Articulating a Feminist Discourse Praxis. *Critical Discourse Studies*, 4(2), 141–64. https://doi.org/10.1080/17405900701464816

Le Renard, A. (2014). *A Society of Young Women: Opportunities of Place, Power, and Reform in Saudi Arabia*. Stanford University Press.

Lyons, M. (2015). Writing Upwards: How the Weak Wrote to the Powerful. *Journal of Social History*, 49(2), 317–30. https://doi.org/10.1093/jsh/shv038

Mohanty, C. (1988). Under Western Eyes: Feminist Scholarship and Colonial Discourses. *Feminist Review*, 30(1), 61–88. https://doi.org/10.1057/fr.1988.42

Mohanty, C.T. (2003). *Feminism Without Borders: Decolonizing Theory, Practicing Solidarity*. Duke University Press.

Pratt, N.C. (2020). *Embodying Geopolitics: Generations of Women's Activism in Egypt, Jordan, and Lebanon*. University of California Press.

Shahrokni, N. (2020). *Women in Place: The Politics of Gender Segregation in Iran*. University of California Press.

Strobl, S. (2010). Progressive or Neo-Traditional?: Policewomen in Gulf Cooperation Council (GCC) Countries. *Feminist Formations*, 22(3), 51-74. https://doi.org/10.1353/ff.2010.0028

van Dijk, T. (1993). Principles of Critical Discourse Analysis. *Discourse & Society*, 4(2), 249–93. https://doi.org/10.1177/0957926593004002006

van Voss, L.H. (2002). *Petitions in Social History*. Cambridge University Press. http://public.ebookcentral.proquest.com/choice/publicfullrecord.aspx?p=4641302

Vision 2030 (2022). *Vision 2030 Overview*. https://www.vision2030.gov.sa/v2030/overview/

Yamani, M. (ed.) (2006). *Feminism and Islam: Legal and Literary Perspectives*. Ithaca Press.

Zaeske, S. (2002). Signatures of Citizenship: The Rhetoric of Women's Antislavery Petitions. *Quarterly Journal of Speech*, 88(2), 147–68. https://doi.org/10.1080/00335630209384368

6 Divorce: The Narratives of Qatari Women

Maryam Al-Muhanadi

Introduction

An important principle of feminist research is that the personal is political. Matters pertaining to women's inequalities are manifested in social and political structures where they cannot be separated from one another, an important entanglement when analysing the experiences of women and the issues that concern them. Hiba Ra'uf 'claims that "politics is personal," or the "private is political"', challenging the 'division between public and private, politics and the family' (McLarney 2010: 2). As a result, issues deemed as 'private' family matters are no longer considered personal concerns in feminist research—especially since the state infiltrates the family unit through its laws and legislation. As Joseph (2010) states, the 'assumptions of separations of public and private, kinship and state, civil society and state, religion and state do not necessarily hold up in Arab states' (15).

Violence against women takes on several forms: physical, structural, cultural, emotional and economic. Divorce processes and proceedings are structurally violent, with violence taking on several forms at several levels before, during and after the divorce. In this chapter, I examine the ways in which the process of divorce is violent towards women structurally, culturally, emotionally and economically. The chapter aims to portray the lived experiences of select research participants to showcase their own journeys through divorce. The notion of women's lived experience has played a key role in framing women's

Maryam Al-Muhanadi, 'Divorce: The Narratives of Qatari Women' in: *Gulf Women's Lives: Voice, Space, Place.* University of Exeter Press (2024). © Maryam Al-Muhanadi. DOI: 10.47788/VNZT1371

political actions, forms of resistance and demands. According to Hesse-Biber, 'the concrete lived experience is a key place from which to build knowledge and foment social change' (2012: 2). Women's life stories and experiences are of importance because they provide us with insights and details that could enhance the inclusion of more pressing public policies on these matters. This research does not aim at generalizing from these experiences, and it does not claim to be representative and speak for all divorced Qatari women; rather, it proposes a qualitative nuanced narrative on divorce that situates individual life stories within their wider structural and cultural context.

This chapter focuses on three primary research questions: What are the lived experiences of Qatari women in marriage and divorce? What do their lived experiences reveal about the violence they have faced? Where and how is violence manifested? Ultimately, I wish to uncover the hidden patterns of violence which are manifested in the family, the state and its laws. I argue that Qatari women face constraints in terms of their divorce choices as a result of these laws, economic structures, and cultural and societal norms.

Theoretical framework

The continuum of violence is a concept designed to understand how gendered violence takes on a structural and pervasive form in society. It is a framework which understands 'violence in the public sphere [and] violence in the private sphere [...] as linked through the thread of gender' (Adra et al. 2020: 6). It does this by linking individual acts of violence to an overarching social structure which legitimizes and reproduces the attitudes that lead to violence. Thus, the responsibility lies not only with those who perpetrate gendered violence, but also the wider structures, institutions and systems that produce certain masculine attitudes. This is especially the case since 'patriarchy no longer functions "as usual" and currently requires a higher level of coercion together with the deployment of more varied ideological state apparatuses to ensure its reproduction' (Adra et al. 2020: 8).

Suad Joseph (2010) contends that the structure of Middle Eastern families is determined by a combination of patriarchal, often religious, norms which uphold a wider legal structure of gendered 'citizenship'. The interplay between dominant norms, legal structures and religious institutions which produce this

GULF WOMEN'S LIVES

gendered citizenship therefore requires a concept like a gendered continuum of multiple forms of violence, to understand how it is sustained and reproduced. By positing laws as a form of structural violence, we can see how 'Arab states [have] privileged a masculine citizen', as women are impacted by the gendered personal status laws (Joseph 2010: 8).

The legal framework in Qatar

It is imperative to look at the role of the state, given its 'interventions in family relations and structures' (Joseph 2018: 2). The Family Law and Personal Status Law regulate and impact gender equality and family dynamics. Moghadam (2005) claims that the countries in the Middle East are best described as 'neopatriarchal' states, as the 'neopatriarchal state and the patriarchal family reflect and reinforce each other. Most states have sought the apparently contradictory goals of economic development and strengthening of the male-dominated, patriarchal family' (31). This is apparent in Qatar, where women are encouraged to enter the workforce and education but reforms to citizenship and family laws are not addressed. Furthermore, the Qatari legal system has 'no provisions for dealing with violence against women', as there is no specific law that criminalizes domestic violence (Al-Ghanim 2009: 82). Domestic violence is not listed as one of the grounds on which a woman can initiate a judicial divorce; what is listed as one of the grounds is 'detriment' or 'harm', which is ambiguous and vague and does not reflect the wide range of abuse or violence that women face in their marriages. Al-Noaimi echoes Moghadam's point by claiming that 'what can be understood from the recent codifications family law has undergone in the Gulf region is that it is a product of "state patriarchy"' (2014: 8). The state has an instrumental impact on families, as it has 'worked to shape family structure, authority within the families, men's and women's roles, and control over children [...] through legislation' (Joseph 2018: 8).

The legal grounds for divorce, as written in the Family Law, are gender-biased. Although the five Islamic schools of law tend to explain that both men and women have equal access to divorce, in codified law women face many constraints (Rahman 2012: 349). According to Aldosari (2016: 12), Gulf Cooperation Council laws grant several grounds for divorce when initiated by the woman, including a husband's chronic illness, imprisonment, abandonment and financial irresponsibility. If a wife wants a divorce, the husband has to consent to it, and if the husband decides not to give his consent, then the divorce process gets prolonged as 'the case goes through a judicial process in which a judge decides the legitimacy of the woman's claim to divorce' (Rahman 2012: 349–50). Another way for a woman to be granted a divorce is through *khul*, or annulment upon compensating her husband, usually done when no valid evidence can be provided to claim divorce (Aldosari 2016: 3). *Khul* allows the wife to initiate a divorce without her husband's consent, but she has to waive all her financial legal rights and refund the dowry money (Law No. 22 2006: art. 122). *Khul* lets women initiate a divorce for personal reasons, and it is 'the preferred choice for many women when a faster legal solution is desired or when marital harm is difficult to prove' (Aldosari 2016: 12). The main problem is that a woman cannot repay her *mahr* (dowry money) if she is financially dependent on the husband, and thus would have to opt for a judicial divorce which can be a long and rigorous process.

Methodology

I conducted in-depth interviews with Sara and Aisha, who are sisters, to gain insight into their lived experiences and journeys with divorce and the court processes. Some of the interviews were scheduled to occur in the participants' homes and others were in my house, depending on the participants' preference. To protect anonymity, participants are referred to using pseudonyms. It is important to highlight that because I have known my participants for several years, I had earned their trust, and as a result they spoke openly to me about their experiences. I provided a space for them to share their insights, a 'space where the personal transforms into the political' (Hesse-Biber 2012: 2).

Sara, fifty-three years old at the time of the interview, was married at nineteen. Her marriage lasted for twenty-eight years before she got divorced in 2014. She has five children. After graduating from high school, Sara was employed in the public sector but retired after ten years to focus on family matters. During her employment, Sara's ex-husband had access to her bank account, thus having full control of her finances. At the beginning of her marriage, Sara chose to help her ex-husband pay off his debts, but then he continued to withdraw money from her bank account. Consequently, Sara was

GULF WOMEN'S LIVES

financially dependent on her ex-husband during her marriage, especially after her retirement, as she had no savings left.

Her sister Aisha, fifty-two, was married at the age of twenty-two and separated from her husband in 2017. Her marriage lasted for twenty-seven years. Separation in Aisha's case entails her living apart from her husband, as she moved out of her husband's house without his consent, and she is still 'legally married'. Aisha has five children. After graduating from university, Aisha worked in the public sector but retired after seventeen years. Aisha was financially independent, as she did not allow her husband access to her income.

I am grateful that I was able to interview women with whom I have a close relationship, and who have previously shared and discussed with me their struggles and hardships over the years. Therefore, I felt that our dynamic during the research process did not comprise a 'researcher' and a 'researched'. I was an 'insider', as I was already part of their lives, which meant that the women were comfortable in answering my questions. Not once did my participants and I feel that I was an unemotional and neutral 'researcher' delving into their personal narratives. Even though I am aware that the 'eventual power rests with the researcher as she eventually writes the account of this encounter', I made sure to capture the women's own accounts and perspectives of their personal narratives and to avoid misinterpreting the information they offered (Allen 2011: 38). My aim was to place their narratives within the wider social and political arena, to bring attention to the often unheard struggles. At the same time, I acknowledge that I was 'seeking information on a sensitive and private topic, which had the possibility of embarrassing or retraumatizing the participants' (Allen 2011: 38). The long history I have with the two women allowed me to ask them extremely sensitive and personal questions. It was admittedly difficult—on the one hand, for me, as I was hearing the details of their violence, and on the other hand, on my participants for having to recount the details of what they have gone through. Both I and my participants, however, were mindful of the importance of discussing such issues.

Before the divorce

Sara said that 'The beginning of our marriage was nice and quite normal, but after several years of problems, I thought about getting a divorce for my

DIVORCE: THE NARRATIVES OF QATARI WOMEN

children's comfort.' Sara's ex-husband started to change; he was getting suspicious and distrustful, constantly checking her mobile phone. He was also physically abusive towards her. After a physical abuse incident Sara would stay over at her stepmother's or aunt's house for a few days. She was unable to take her children with her, since the houses are fairly small and would not fit six extra people. The stepmother and aunt were unaware of the physical abuse; Sara would only inform them that she and her husband had an argument and she needed to distance herself from him for a while. When I asked her why she returned to the marital home, she said, 'I couldn't stay away from my kids longer; I missed them so much in those few days.' Clearly, the first level of violence started with the husband's controlling behaviour and emotional abuse, then progressed into physical violence.[1] Linking everyday forms of violence with physical abuse allows us to trace the 'wider range of forms of abuse and assault which women experience' (Kelly 1987: 51) as invisible forms progress to physical (direct) violence.

Sara also recounted forces pushing her to stay with her husband:

> There was pressure from my family to stay with my husband, and the idea of my children staying with my husband and not me was the reason why I was hesitant about getting a divorce, and also because of this idea of us being a complete family, but after several years of problems and issues I decided to get divorced.

Women are sometimes pushed into upholding an appearance of the ideal family, as a result of a combination of familial and societal pressures. This appearance is manifested and maintained in multiple areas, such as the wider family itself and the state: 'States in the Arab region typically identify "the family" as the unit of society within their constitutions, giving the idea of the Arab family, and a unity, legal standing' (Joseph 2018: 7). Similarly, Qatar's constitution stipulates that 'The family is the basis of society. The Law shall

---

1. The World Health Organization defines controlling behaviours as a combination of 'isolating a person from family and friends; monitoring their movements; and restricting access to financial resources, employment, education or medical care' and emotional (psychological) abuse as 'insults, belittling, constant humiliation, intimidation (e.g. destroying things), threats of harm, threats to take away children'. It also defines physical violence as slapping, hitting, kicking and beating' (World Health Organization 2012: 1).

GULF WOMEN'S LIVES

regulate as necessary to protect the family, its structure, strengthen its ties and protect mothers, children and the elderly' (Permanent Constitution of the State of Qatar 2004: art. 21). Thus, the importance of the family is upheld and enforced through society as well as the state. Joseph states that in 'Arab countries in which the family has been valued over and above the person […], identity has been defined in familial terms and kin idioms and relationships have woven through society, connective relationships are necessary for successful social existence' (Joseph 2010: 14). Therefore, the continuum of violence in this case operates from *'indirect violence = structural violence*. Indirect violence comes from the social structure itself' and is then legitimized by cultural violence (Galtung 1996: 2).

When Sara's ex-husband started getting physically abusive, she called the family consulting centre Wifaq to ask about the divorce process.[2] She felt 'defeated' after talking to them because she wanted to gain some information and they kept telling her to 'be patient', warning there was no guarantee that she would 'get the house' that she resided in with her husband and children. Sara did not mention the physical abuse to Wifaq, so this may have been one of the reasons why the centre offered her no proper guidance. Nevertheless, the centre failed Sara, who had no information regarding her rights on child custody and her living situation, which deterred her from initiating divorce proceedings.

Sara then decided to seek the advice of a private lawyer, who failed to listen to her while trying to steer her away from getting a divorce. At such a difficult time in her life, Sara was let down by the various institutions that were meant to support and help her. Galtung (1996) argues that structural and cultural violence is rarely contained only within family units. Rather, these forms of violence are social and collective processes which involve many different actors within a given society: 'There is also violence frozen into structures, and the culture that legitimizes violence' (Galtung 1996: viii). This structural violence is evident in Sara's experience where the family centre and the lawyer failed to exhibit due care and sensitivity to her concerns, depriving her of resources

---

2. Wifaq (the term meaning 'agreement' or 'understanding') is a private institution of public interest established in 2002 by the consort of the former ruler of Qatar. The centre provides services such as guidance, counselling, family reconciliation and family court case assistance.

DIVORCE: THE NARRATIVES OF QATARI WOMEN

in a way that trapped her in an abusive marriage. A systemic failure is indicated here by the difficulties she encountered when trying to seek divorce-related information.

Sara's story illustrates how violence can begin in the home and continue into institutional domains, negating the dichotomy between the private and the public. Sara faced violence both in the private realm of her home and in public institutions, and the domains reinforced each other. For this reason, it is imperative to 'seek the roots of violence in the intersection between social structures and interpersonal processes' (Sev'er 1998: 5). Violence does not occur randomly; it is sustained and perpetuated through different domains. When intimate partner violence is perceived as a 'private family matter', it is attributed to individualistic and episodic instances of violence, thus ignoring the wider system that is gender discriminatory and sustains this violence. As Cockburn (2004) states, 'long before a man uses physical violence against a woman, she may experience "structural violence" in a marriage in which her husband or a constraining patriarchal community holds power over her' (30).

A couple of months into Aisha's marriage she noticed that her husband had anger issues and was verbally abusive. The violence escalated and he started physically abusing her. One of these instances occurred in the early years of her marriage, when her husband punched her nose and she started bleeding heavily. He took her to the hospital, claiming that she had tripped: 'It was obvious to [the doctor] what had happened; I felt like he wanted to say something, but he didn't.' Rather than speaking to Aisha on her own, the doctor chose to treat her with her husband present. This shows how, even when behaviours cross from typical to aberrant, they may still be categorized as 'normal' by institutions since they are considered a 'private family matter'. Getting a divorce was not an option for Aisha: '[It was] instilled in me throughout the years that my husband would take my children away from me.' For this reason, Aisha's children were one of the main factors making her hesitant about the divorce.

Just as institutional domains play a role in sustaining gendered violence, so does the interplay between societal norms and the law. Furthermore, some family members play a role in maintaining the violence experienced by women because of their beliefs that are structured by the wider society. Aisha's mother played a partial role in this by not supporting her daughter's decision to get

GULF WOMEN'S LIVES

a divorce, possibly out of a desire to protect her daughter. Legally the age limit for custody of children granted to women is thirteen for boys and fifteen for girls (Law No. 22 2006: art. 173). This helps us understand why it took Aisha twenty-seven years to separate from her husband: although she had to live under the same roof with her abusive spouse, she was able to raise her children and stay with them until young adulthood.

The cultural violence that Aisha experienced took the form of implicit norms and ideas instilled in her, encouraging her to endure various forms of violence for her children's sake. The accompanying structural violence, meanwhile, derives from the law itself. Thus, family becomes a way to re-embed gendered domination, where access to children is construed (as a result of the law) as a resource of which women can be deprived. In this way it is used to coerce women into accepting a range of behaviours, from control to physical violence. My analysis of the women's narratives on their experiences in marriage shows structural and cultural violence primarily mediated by certain gender norms. These norms infiltrate many of the obstacles women face to being taken seriously regarding their marital problems and experiences of abuse. In this way, a range of actions—from institutions, informal forms of family pressure, and the violent, controlling and/or neglectful acts of the interviewees' husbands—exist on a continuum of violence. This demonstrates how 'patriarchy found in the domestic sphere is also found in governmental and non-governmental spheres [...] The incorporation of patriarchal family modes of operation by the state is not perceived as a disruption to state and family boundaries, but continuous with them' (Joseph 2010: 15).

During the process of divorce

After an incident of physical abuse at the hands of her ex-husband, Sara's oldest nephew (Aisha's son) drove her to the hospital in order to protect her children. Sara was informed by the staff that they would provide her with a medical report, and they asked whether she wanted to report the case to the police. She declined as she did not want the situation to get worse. In contrast, when Aisha went to the hospital, she was not informed about the possibility of obtaining a medical report of her injuries or about the option to report her husband. This may be due to the differing time frames: Aisha went to the

DIVORCE: THE NARRATIVES OF QATARI WOMEN

hospital in the early 1990s, whereas Sara went in around 2012. This suggests that the medical staff are now more aware of intimate partner violence cases, and the ways in which they are meant to address these. 'There is a system of response to cases of violence against women and children [...]. The medical staff at the hospital are obliged to report suspected cases of violence' (National Human Rights Committee 2018: 51). On the other hand, they might have offered Sara the option to report her case because she was not accompanied by her abuser, as was the case with Aisha.

Sara recounts having to essentially blackmail her husband into granting her a divorce. She threatened to report her husband to the authorities, showing as evidence the medical reports, which indicated that the injuries she had sustained were consistent with physical abuse. Her husband proceeded to pronounce the formula 'I divorce you', and a few days later he informed her that the divorce had been ratified by the court.[3] According to Qatari law, a husband can divorce his wife by going to court to file the paperwork, no questions asked (Aldosari 2016).

Immediately after the divorce, Sara was granted custody of her children. She was told that her children had the right to choose which parent they would stay with, advice that contradicted the Family Law's provisions, but fortunately for Sara, the ex-husband did not want custody.

Sara also recounted the difficulty of post-divorce life. The house, as is typically the case, was in her husband's name. He returned to court in order to be allowed to sell the house and move his ex-wife and children into a smaller one closer to his family's home. Sara was forced into a long court battle, during which he would often refuse to show up to hearings in order to prolong the process. No formal mechanisms were available to sanction him. Eventually, the judge ruled in Sara's favour. However, the house is still owned by the ex-husband (it is registered under his name), which is an ongoing worry for Sara.

Aisha witnessed first-hand her older sister's experience with divorce. Sara did not receive adequate help or advice from the family centre or the lawyer, and had to visit the court multiple times to be allowed to live in her home.

---

3. 'Men are granted a unilateral right to divorce by stating "I divorce you" three times on one or multiple occasions' (Aldosari 2016: 11).

GULF WOMEN'S LIVES

Knowing about her sister's ordeal, Aisha was determined not to go through the same experience: 'it comes as no surprise that oftentimes women perceive court proceedings with trepidation knowing that family laws are gender biased, coupled with the stigma society attaches to women going against their fathers or husbands by fighting for their rights' (Al-Noaimi 2014: 20). Therefore, Aisha decided to separate instead of asking for a divorce. She is still married legally, but she moved out of her husband's house without his consent.

Since her husband would not give her a divorce, *khul* was the only option for Aisha. In her case, judicial divorce would be permitted only if she was able to provide grounds such as detriment or harm. Article 129 of the Family Law (2006) states:

> The wife, before or after consummation of marriage, shall have the right to request separation on the ground of detriment which makes marital life impossible to continue for her like. The Judge shall attempt to reconcile between the spouses. If reconciliation cannot be achieved and detriment is proved, separation shall be decreed. Detriment may be proved by Evidence including hearsay testimony.

This particular article, which allows a woman to file for a judicial divorce, fails to explicitly identify what constitutes detriment or harm. In practice, harm in the Personal Status Law is considered to be 'irreconcilable conflicts', which leaves judges with discretionary power to decide between marital reconciliation or divorce (Aldosari 2016: 12). Therefore, Aisha decided to buy a house and move out.

It took Aisha around five years to find a house that was within her budget: 'Whenever I saved money, the prices of the houses would keep increasing.' She wanted to own something of her own to secure her living arrangement. She did not want to rent a house, especially considering how expensive it may be. Renting a two-storey house in the city of Doha often costs around US$2,700 to 4,100 per month, and Aisha saw it best to invest her savings in owning her own property instead. In 2017, she finally managed to buy a house, though she had to spend all her savings on the purchase. Eventually, Aisha and her children moved out of her husband's house without his consent. This reflects how women have to sometimes strategize around ways to exit a violent relationship, as a result of the challenges they face with the divorce proceedings.

DIVORCE: THE NARRATIVES OF QATARI WOMEN

The gendered doctrine embedded in Qatari law serves to reproduce gendered control, as Sara and Aisha had to find their own solutions and negotiate with their husbands in order to end their marriages.

After the divorce

One might assume that the women's ordeal ends once they are divorced or separated. However, while divorce releases women and their children from marital conflicts, it creates a new set of issues. Financial constraints and social pressures may worsen their livelihoods due to stigma and ostracization (Al Gharaibeh & Bromfield 2012: 447–48).

Sara's case illustrates how a lack of regular employment and steady income can result in financial problems in the post-divorce period. As a result of her retirement, Sara did not have a source of income when she separated from her husband, and thus had to look for employment again to support her children. Her situation relates to Moghadam's point that even though laws 'compel husbands and fathers to provide financial support to their wives and daughters, cases of divorce, separation or death of the breadwinner often impoverished women' (2005: 32). While 'impoverished' does not accurately describe Sara's situation after the divorce, she still faced financial constraints. According to Numbeo's Cost of Living Index, Qatar ranked first in the Gulf countries as the most expensive place to live in from 2019 to 2022, and was the second most expensive country from 2014 to 2018 (Numbeo 2022). Even though Sara's ex-husband paid child support for her youngest daughter,[4] US$1,100 per month was not sufficient to run a household of six when the estimated monthly costs for a family of four are US$5,200 (Expatistan 2022).

One of the major problems extending to the post-divorce period concerns the father's legal authority as opposed to the mother's custody. Article 176 of the Family Law states that 'the guardian of the Child may retain the passport of the Child save for when traveling when it shall be delivered to the female custodian of the Child' (Law No. 22 2006). Since the law recognizes only the

---

4. Sara's youngest daughter was around sixteen at the time of the divorce, and the only child that was not employed. Therefore, the ex-husband had to pay alimony for the youngest daughter only, as she did not have an income like her siblings.

GULF WOMEN'S LIVES

father as the guardian while the mother is a mere custodian, he is able to prevent his children from travelling with their mother. Although the mother can seek judicial intervention, the process is often lengthy and costly (Aldosari 2016). This illustrates the gender biases of the law, which assign fathers a higher position with more responsibilities in decision-making concerning their children's welfare and freedoms, while disempowering and discriminating against mothers by denying them legal authority over their children. As Joseph summarizes, 'the non-negotiable sacred arena of the family is the means by which Arab paternal patriarchy is constituted' (Joseph 2010: 13). The family is a key unit through which the state genders society.

Sara discovered at the airport that her ex-husband had put a restriction on his daughters' travel. He was able to do so without informing his ex-wife and daughters, as the law gives the father the right to control his offspring's movement, establishing a space for men to retaliate and limit the freedoms of ex-wives and children. This incident showcases the ways in which 'constitutional law not only protects the state-envisioned gender roles and moral behavior of the family, but also entrusts the state to act as the guardian for the family' (Aldosari 2016: 6).

Aisha emphasized multiple times how grateful she was for her financial stability, especially for being able to provide a house for herself and her children. She expressed how glad she was that she had not let her husband have access to her income. If Aisha had let her husband take care of her money, she might not have been able to separate, and she would have had to get a divorce like her sister Sara—an especially dispiriting prospect after witnessing the ordeal that Sara went through. Aisha's case illustrates Kandiyoti's concept of 'patriarchal bargain' that encompasses how women 'strategize within a set of concrete constraints' which also 'influence the potential for and the actual forms of women's active or passive resistance' (1991: 27). Kandiyoti observes the material basis of patriarchy, where women's control over their finances creates a space that allows them to manoeuvre through patriarchal structures. Aisha was able to strategize to get out of the marriage through her material resources. By looking at the ways in which women deal with male power, authority and patriarchy in general, we can understand how and why women work within the 'set of concrete constraints' (Kandiyoti 1991: 27). Aisha used her financial independence as a strategy to separate from her husband, whereas

DIVORCE: THE NARRATIVES OF QATARI WOMEN

Sara used the medical report of her injuries as a tactic to negotiate and ask for a divorce.

Divorced or separated women often experience blame and stigma for the break-up of their relationships. Aisha recalled how her mother-in-law criticized her for not enduring the marital problems in order to take care of her diabetic husband. She thus reinforced Aisha's burden and role as a caretaker of the household. The mother-in-law's position lends weight to Anser's (2013) point that 'public sentiment that families should stay together at all costs may also serve to keep abusive fathers/husbands in place' (59). We can clearly see the pressure that Aisha faced from other family members, and the ways in which she was blamed for not complying with her care duties.

The value placed on the family structure might explain the views that the mother-in-law upholds. According to Al Gharaibeh and Bromfield:

> given the emphasis on tradition and family in the Arab world and the stigmatization and limited options available to divorced women in the region, the rising divorce rates are seen by some as a social emergency that needs to be quelled (2012: 437–38).

This echoes exactly the mother-in-law's views that the family structure is vital and should be maintained, despite a context of domestic violence. I asked Aisha whether she worried about what other people thought about her separation:

> Yes, and I still worry. People usually put the blame on the woman; they tend to pressure her to stay in the marriage. If the husband seems OK to them, if he's not a drunk or a murderer, then you have to be patient.

It was clear to Aisha that the stigma or blame is usually imposed upon the woman. It took her years to finally come to the decision to separate because she was 'told constantly by friends and family to wait and to be patient'. Societal opinions and perceptions often affect the decisions of women who wish to separate or divorce. Oftentimes women are pressured into upholding an appearance of the ideal family, which is the result of a combination of familial and societal pressures. 'Considering how significant conjugal life is for family stability, Muslim societies, like others, have always upheld the sanctity of marriage and family', which explains the source of the pressure

GULF WOMEN'S LIVES

that women face when deciding to divorce or separate (Anser 2013: 59). Moreover, Al Gharaibeh and Bromfield state that in the UAE, 'the family is central to social life, and divorce is especially devastating for most couples and even their extended families' (2012: 440). Thus the importance of the family is upheld and enforced through society as well as the state.

Divorce presents Qatari women with multiple challenges that affect their livelihoods. The financial burden of the post-divorce phase often forces women into severe economic strains. In this way violence is not terminated along with the marriage; rather, the violence continues and is maintained by the family (societal pressure) and state (the law).

Conclusions

This chapter centred on the narratives presented by my interviewees while also trying to understand their experiences as part of wider social and legal systems, structures and processes. One of the main insights to emerge from my analysis is the clear continuum of violence which stretches from the family to the state and back again. This reveals a picture of the family unit as an everyday regulator of gender dominance, while the state gets involved when the family's ability to regulate and control women begins to fail.

Given the limited literature on Qatari women's experiences with marriage, divorce and court processes, as well as the decisions behind their divorces, it is essential to examine the Qatari marriage and divorce laws to examine how women are impacted by them. Several studies have explored the topics of divorce, personal status laws and violence in the Gulf states. However, not many studies have employed in-depth interviews to showcase how Qatari women are impacted by the personal status laws, and the detriments of these laws on their livelihoods as well as their children. This chapter aims to fill this knowledge gap, specifically in the context of Qatar, to provide an understanding as to why some women make certain choices regarding divorce. Moreover, the in-depth interviews with my participants provide a more nuanced insight into the lived experiences of Qatari women.

In conducting this research, my aim was to shed light on the hidden and private matters that affect Qatari women on a daily basis. There is a need to take this research further and conduct a similar study on a larger scale in order to showcase how Qatari women are impacted by the legal system and family structures, and the ways in which women navigate and strategize within those systems and structures.

Acknowledgements

I would like to thank Dr Sophie Richter-Devroe: your insightful feedback and support throughout my research journey have been invaluable.

To my wonderful and resilient participants, I cannot begin to express how thankful and grateful I am for your willingness to participate and share your experiences, without you this research would not have been possible.

References

Adra, N., Al-Ali, N., Farhat, S., Joly, D., Larzillière, P. & Pratt, N. (2020). *Women, Violence and Exiting from Violence with a Gendered Approach: MENA Region and Diaspora.* https://hal.archives-ouvertes.fr/hal-02498142

Al-Ghanim, K.A. (2009). Violence Against Women in Qatari Society. *Journal of Middle East Women's Studies*, 59(1), 80–93. https://doi.org/10.2979/mew.2009.5.1.80

Al Gharaibeh, F. & Bromfield, N.F. (2012). An Analysis of Divorce Cases in the United Arab Emirates: A Rising Trend. *Journal of Divorce & Remarriage*, 53(6), 436–52. https://doi.org/10.1080/10502556.2012.682896

Al-Noaimi, H. (2014). *Personal Status Laws in Gulf States: A Comparative Study into Guardianship Laws in Marriage* [unpublished master's thesis]. Sorbonne University, Abu Dhabi.

Aldosari, G.H. (2016). The Personal Is Political: Gender Identity in the Personal Status Laws of the Gulf Arab States. *The Arab Gulf States Institute in Washington*, 8, 1–19.

Allen, M. (2011). Violence and Voice: Using a Feminist Constructivist Grounded Theory to Explore Women's Resistance to Abuse. *Qualitative Research*, 11(1), 23–45. https://doi.org/10.1177%2F1468794110384452

Anser, L. (2013). Divorce in the Arab Gulf Countries. In A. Abela & J. Walker (eds), *Contemporary Issues in Family Studies* (pp. 59–74). John Wiley & Sons. https://doi.org/10.1002/9781118320990.ch5

Cockburn, C. (2004). The Continuum of Violence: A Gender Perspective on War and Peace. In W. Files, & J. Hyndman (eds), *Sites of Violence: Gender and Conflict Zones* (pp. 24–44). University of California Press.

Expatistan (2022). *Cost of Living in Qatar.* https://www.expatistan.com/cost-of-living/country/qatar

GULF WOMEN'S LIVES

Galtung, J. (1996). *Peace by Peaceful Means: Peace and Conflict, Development and Civilization.* SAGE.

Hesse-Biber, S. (2012). Feminist Research: Exploring, Interrogating, and Transforming the Interconnections of Epistemology, Methodology, and Method. In S. Hesse-Biber (ed.), *Handbook of Feminist Research: Theory and Praxis* (pp. 2–26). SAGE.

Joseph, S. (2010). Gender and Citizenship in the Arab World. *Al-Raida Journal*, 1, 8–18. https://doi.org/10.32380/alrj.v0i0.50

Joseph, S. (2018). Introduction: Family in the Arab Region: State of Scholarship. In S. Joseph (ed.), *Arab Family Studies: Critical Reviews* (pp. 1–13). Syracuse University Press.

Kandiyoti, D. (1991). Islam and Patriarchy: A Comparative Perspective. In N.R. Keddie & B. Baron (eds), *Women in Middle Eastern History: Shifting Boundaries of Sex and Gender* (pp. 23–45). Yale University Press.

Kelly, L. (1987). The Continuum of Sexual Violence. In J. Hanmer & M. Maynard (eds), *Women, Violence and Social Control* (pp. 46–60). Palgrave Macmillan.

Law No. 22 of 2006 Promulgating 'The Family Law' (2006, 29 June). https://www.almeezan.qa/LawPage.aspx?id=2558&language=en

McLarney, E. (2010). The Private Is Political: Women and Family in Intellectual Islam. *Feminist Theory*, 11(2), 129–48. https://doi.org/10.1177/1464700110366805

Moghadam, V. (2005). Gender and Social Policy: Family Law and Women's Economic Citizenship in the Middle East. *International Review of Public Administration*, 10(1), 23–44. https://doi.org/10.1080/12294659.2005.10805059

National Human Rights Committee, Doha—Qatar (2018). *The Fourteenth Annual Report: Human Rights Situation in Qatar*. https://nhrc-qa.org/en/annual-reports/

Numbeo (2022). *Western Asia: Cost of Living Index by Country*. https://www.numbeo.com/cost-of-living/rankings_by_country.jsp?title=2022&region=145

Permanent Constitution of the State of Qatar (2004). https://www.almeezan.qa/LawView.aspx?opt&LawID=2284&language=en

Rahman, F.Z. (2012). Gender Equality in Muslim-majority States and Shari'a Family Law: Is There a Link? *Australian Journal of Political Science*, 47(3), 347–62. https://doi.org/10.1080/10361146.2012.704006

Sev'er, A. (1998). Separation, Divorce and Violence Against Women by Male Partners. *Frontiers in Women's Studies: Canadian and German Perspectives*, 167–95.

World Health Organization (2012). *Intimate Partner Violence: Understanding and Addressing Violence Against Women*. https://www.who.int/reproductivehealth/publications/violence/rhr12_36/en/

PART III
Places

Female Socialization in the Omani Oases and the Impacts of Modernization on Women's Identity after 1970

Aminah Khan

Introduction

This chapter focuses on the hitherto unknown experiences of Omani women of the *aflaj*-oases villages before 1970 and how modernization affected them and the oases that they inhabit(ed). Studies about the female element and experience of *aflaj* society before 1970 are not available. The gap between life before 1970 in the *aflaj* and the rapid implementation of modern infrastructure thereafter impacted their lives materially, emotionally and psychologically. The ancient ways of *aflaj* society changed in only a few decades, now only surviving in the memories of elders. Such research informs Omanis and non-Omanis of this unique aspect of Oman's history and validates the pre-1970s generations of women, their stories, their existence and their role in modern Oman.

The word *aflaj* (singular: *falaj*) has two connected but distinct meanings. Firstly, they are ancient channels, possibly dating back to 2000 BCE (Al-Ghafri 2018), used for irrigation and the conveyancing of water. Secondly, the *aflaj* are the symbiosis between their structure and the socialization of the community that lives around them—that is, the oasis village and its inhabitants. A water channel is only an *aflaj* when there is a community to interact with it. Structural and societal *aflaj* work in synergy; in an arid region that receives very little rainfall, people must use water prudently and avoid waste. The *aflaj* structures meant that water could be gathered and used wisely for irrigation,

Aminah Khan, 'Female Socialization in the Omani Oases and the Impacts of Modernization on Women's Identity after 1970' in: *Gulf Women's Lives: Voice, Space, Place*. University of Exeter Press (2024). © Aminah Khan. DOI: 10.47788/IIJD8427

GULF WOMEN'S LIVES

and thus a settled agrarian society emerged. How this *aflaj* society emerged and flourished has been studied by Wilkinson (1977, 2008) and Ghubash (2006), but they have focused on the religious and masculine aspects of the *aflaj* and how they operate. For this chapter, the societal *aflaj* will be investigated—in other words, the world of the elder women in the oases.

Studies by Al-Ghafri (2016, 2018) and Al-Kalbani and Price (2015) on the Omani *aflaj* have focused on agriculture, hydrology, environment, engineering and science. Research pertaining to the individuals of this unique environment deals with the workers, farmers and labourers who work within the *aflaj* structures (Al-Ghafri 2018). There are very few studies focusing on the female aspect of the *aflaj* specifically (Eickelman 1984), or as part of a study about the *aflaj* environment (Limbert 2010), or as a wider investigation of post-traditional and modern Oman (Olson 2011). This chapter employs the narratives of Omani women who were born before 1965 and experienced life in the *aflaj* before 1970 and before modernization known as the Nahḍa or Renaissance. The year 1965 was chosen as a cut-off point. Although Peterson (2021) argues that memories can start as early as two and a half years old, scholars hold differing opinions as to the age when children embed their earliest reliable memories (Akhtar et al. 2018; Bauer et al. 2014; Nicoladis et al. 2022). Women born after 1965 may have had limited reliable memories and experience of the *aflaj*-oases. However, Omani women's social history of the *aflaj* is still within living memory but lacks documentation.

The year 1970 was a momentous one for Oman. Sultan Said was ousted by his son, Qaboos, who engaged in a modernization of the country; medicine, modern education and better standards of living were made available (Jones & Ridout 2015). Data from pre-1970 generations of Omani women provides information about their lives and highlights the disappearing *aflaj* culture, as well as tangible and intangible heritage.

This chapter focuses on female society and socialization—the activity of mixing socially with others and learning social norms of behaviour—in the *aflaj*-oases of Oman before and after the beginning of the Qaboos era (1970–2020). Using semi-structured group interviews with women who have lived in the oases since before 1970, it explores the impact of modernization on traditional Omani society and the identity of the pre-Qaboos generations of women.

134

By employing grounded theory-based data analysis, this chapter argues that the implementation of modern infrastructure had mixed material and psychological benefits for the women of oases. Their lives were eased, but socialization patterns and family and neighbourly relationships were negatively affected, contributing to feelings of isolation, loneliness and solastalgia—distress that is produced by environmental change in the home (Albrecht et al. 2007; Limbert 2010; McNamara & Westoby 2011). The narratives show that the pre-1970 generations of Omani women not only had a social role to play but also worked in and around the oases, which counters the usual narrative of the oppressed Gulf woman.

Most Omanis of the pre-Qaboos era have little to no literacy. The process of narrating their lives orally and sharing their knowledge and experiences of living, working and socializing in and around the *aflaj* before 1970 offered the women self-validation, and an opportunity to reclaim their identity as functioning members of today's local society.

Literature review

The histories of Omani women of the *aflaj* (pre-1970) are predominantly absent from scholarship. Eickelman (1984) documented early changes that were present in the oases—the introduction of soft drinks (11) and tinned, packet and frozen foods (33), and the gradual decline in female socialization (50–51). Eickelman's study was not followed up and her descriptions of life in Al Ḥamra's *aflaj*-oasis remains situated in one point in time. Limbert (2010) shows how modern infrastructure in Baḥla, particularly modern education, has seen psychological shifts in traditional and religious practices between the elder and younger generations. Limbert (2010) cites two situations that occurred during her fieldwork: the first examples the intergenerational tensions between a father and son, the former wanting to provide a drinking point outside his home for use by anyone without charge, to fulfil a well-known and widely practised religious injunction. His adolescent son sets such concerns aside, arguing that there ought to be a monetary charge for its use (126). In the second, a modern-educated granddaughter contends that the pre-1970 social bathing practices of her grandmother were *ḥarām* (forbidden) according to the Islamic precepts that she learned in school; her grandmother, and to some extent her mother, insists that there were no forbidden intentions or actions on the part of the women (Limbert 2010: 128–29). Both examples show disconnects between the old pre-1970s social and religious practices and the post-1970 modern society of Oman, and the generational divide between elders and youth.

Dutton (2016: 5) sought to use and adapt existing agricultural and folkcraft practices. Some aspects of this work included oases women (outside Ad-Dākhilīyah) and the adaptation of their lives 'from the village of al-Khabura in the centre of the Batina coast to Ibri in the Dhahira' (Dutton 2016: 3). Olson's work (2011) recorded the lives of different generations of Omanis in order to chart changes that had occurred in them and the sultanate as a whole. However, his work lacks the nuances of women's oases life pre-Qaboos.

Mentions of the women of the *aflaj* pre-1970 list the usual domestic routines associated with water—collecting potable water, cleaning and washing—while other activities—praying, bathing, socialization and animal husbandry—go unmentioned. Academic works featuring these women are often authored by men, such as Harrison (1943), Wilkinson (1977; 2008), Gwynne-James (2001) and Al-Shaqsi. Al-Shaqsi describes the disappearance of the female *aflaj* culture, lamenting that 'The ladies' washing areas have fallen completely out of use. Women are no longer seen carrying drinking water in large pots on their heads or washing clothes and dishes beside the falaj' (2015: 23).

The psychological impacts of environmental change on the *aflaj* women are not tackled in existing literature. Mellor (1997), a Western ecofeminist, maintains that men and women face different challenges with respect to the environment, and experience dissimilar outcomes from and impressions of the same place. Together with other ecofeminists (Brownhill & Turner 2019; Giacomini et al. 2018), Mellor argues that women and nature share the same subjugation and marginalization from patriarchal social set-ups. Mellor (1997) indicates that environmental change has a greater psychological than physical impact on women. Ostrom et al. (1999) focus on the use of land that is held and looked after by the community, known as 'commons' or 'usufructs'. They argue that when usufructs are abandoned or neglected, the resulting deterioration of the land and its environment impacts biodiversity and human well-being—physical, mental and emotional. This goes some way in backing up Mellor's claims (1997). In Olson's research (2011), one interviewee, Muhammad Al-Araimi, elaborates on the psychological impact that pre-1970s generations experienced, and adaptation strategies that his father's generation went through 'without much suffering' (116). The emotional, psychological and physical impact of such changes on women, their social ties, their responsibilities, their customs and their practices in traditional settings is not explored.

Jokha Alharthi's novel *Celestial Bodies* (2018) centres around a northern *aflaj* settlement, illustrating women's practices before 1970 until the present day. The fictional story revolves around the lives of a family living through the changes brought about by the modernization of the country. The intergenerational aspect emphasizes the changes that have occurred. Alharthi shares that she wrote it to feel connected to her mother tongue, starting off with thoughts 'about the traditional ways, which are rapidly vanishing in Oman' and reflecting on how 'to think about the past [is] to think about history' through prose, reflecting on certain unaddressed historical practices (Edemariam 2019).[1]

Undertaking such research opens up the neglected field of women's contributions to environment, culture and history in Omani *aflaj* studies, and records first-hand narratives of this now vanished facet of Omani society.

Methodology

The study took place in Ad-Dākhilīyah governorate between October 2019 and January 2020. The average age of women participants was seventy-seven. Participants' names and identifying features were anonymized due to cultural sensitivity and to establish a relationship of confidence with the researcher (Limbert 2010).

A research framework was developed that was as close to Omani ways of socialization as possible. The interviews included procedures adapted from Yarning (Bessarab & Ng'andu 2010), an Aboriginal and Torres Strait Islander way of sharing knowledge in a designated space: two or more participants sit in a circle and take turns to speak while the other(s) listen respectfully. Yarning is an indigenous method of research which gives power to the 'other' (Bernardes et al. 2020), namely the elder women, rather than the outsider, the researcher.

---

1. For a comparative social and literary analysis of the novel, please refer to Buscemi's chapter in the present volume (Chapter 3).

For this research, Yarning procedures were adapted to the Omani context. The action of placing a *sufrah* (dining mat) on the floor with refreshments brought back memories of coffee visiting and other traditional socialization patterns that the women undertook frequently before 1970 (Figure 7.1). Moreover, the positional approach of the researcher—interviewing subjects in familiar places such as at home, association gatherings or social centres—enabled the elder women to feel at ease and engendered trust between them and the researcher (Råheim et al. 2016).

This research adopted a qualitative approach based on grounded theory (GT) (Chun Tie et al. 2019). Ecofeminist works were also utilized to further an understanding of the connection between the Omani women's socialization within the *aflaj* and their emotional and psychological experiences of such an environment as women.

Snowball sampling fitted with the Omani way of conducting research. The first contact was the mother of an associate of the UNESCO Chair for Aflaj Studies—Archaeohydrology (UCASA). She was part of a women's group that

Figure 7.1: The *sufrah* during an adapted Yarning interview. © Aminah Khan 2020.

met weekly, and was keen to be interviewed. She told her elder female friends in the group about the research and they invited me to attend their group. Snowball sampling through word of mouth produced a sample size of twenty-five *aflaj* women separated into eight groups. The study was designed to use one-to-one interviews, but the first women to be interviewed decided that they would hold their interviews in a group. Instead of insisting on following the original plan, I decided to comply with their request: the women felt at ease and were able to share memories about their pre-1970s oasis lives. Subsequent interviews were held in a focus group. The participants were Omani women, born before 1965, who had lived in the *aflaj*-oases of Ad-Dākhilīyah (northern interior of Oman) before and during the 1970s.

Results and discussion

The twenty-five women who participated in the interviews highlighted facets of their lives before 1970 that had been overlooked previously. There were recurring themes—the poor state of Oman before 1970; insecurity; the absence of young men from the *aflaj*; the traditional roles of *aflaj* women; women fulfilling the work roles of men; and female oases socialization before 1970. The female perspective presents a more rounded holistic culture than the respective male one.

The reality of the aflaj society before 1970

Before 1970, Oman was in an impoverished and deplorable state (Eickelman 1985). This was the status quo for the majority of Omanis (Allen 2016; Morris 1990). Modern infrastructure was limited to Muscat and Salalah, due to several factors; some had historical roots, long before the reign of Sultan Said bin Taimur (r.1932–1970), while others were exacerbated during his reign (Al-Khalili 2005). However, the majority of Omanis experienced similar aspects to the reality endured by the *aflaj* women:

> There was no employment. The men had to travel abroad to work [...]. There was insufficient wood, no medicines, no hospitals [...]. Life was difficult. You couldn't imagine how difficult. There [was ...] no education, no schools. [F]

GULF WOMEN'S LIVES

[There were] no passports, very few clothes and it was very difficult to travel. [E]

The situation described by the women above is documented in research on Oman (Barth 1983; Eickelman 1984; Jones & Ridout 2013, 2015; Limbert 2010; Morris 1955; Olson 2011; Wikan 1990). Life was difficult and dangerous for the *aflaj* women, partly due to inter-tribal fighting and, from 1954 until 1959, war and its associated threats:

[I]f I wanted to go to another [area], I would have to tell my neighbours so that they would not worry about me being missing. Maybe they would think you had been kidnapped or had run away or were lying injured somewhere. [A]

The tribal leader was responsible for the security and safety of the village. There was a war on Jabal Akhḍar and everyone, man and woman, had a loaded weapon readied […]. It was not allowed for people to travel. [G]

This is verified by Gwynne-James, a British officer stationed in Oman in the early 1960s. He describes a situation in early 1963 where an innocent woman was captured: 'when caught [she] just screamed […], she had been frightened by all the soldiers in the area and was fleeing for her life (kidnapping is still prevalent here)' (2001: 82).

The population profile of the *aflaj* before 1970 included the elderly, children and women of all ages. Many *aflaj* men had left in order to find work or pursue an education, a prevalent phenomenon throughout the reign of Sultan Said bin Taimur. A significant number of them had left without the prior permission of the sultan. This left many *aflaj* women without a *mahram* (male guardian). Before 1970, it was a criminal offence to leave Oman without the permission of the sultan, who was often reluctant to give his assent. Some men returned secretly, but many stayed abroad until after 1970, when Sultan Qaboos issued a general amnesty for all Omanis to return home:

They went to Zanzibar and Saudi Arabia to work […] because there were no jobs in Oman […]. There were no men in the villages, at least no younger men, only elderly men, or small boys. [C]

The men had to travel abroad to work. They sent letters to their families to keep in touch and to send them a little money. My father […] returned

FEMALE SOCIALIZATION IN THE OMANI OASES

Figure 7.2: Old Al Hamra—deserted traditional dwellings but a verdant oasis. © Aminah Khan 2020.

from abroad aged sixty, [he] travelled to Bahrain for work and he sent letters [and some money]. [F]

My husband worked in Saudi Arabia in the Empty Quarter [...]. Only men travelled for jobs in groups, and that too in secret [...], many young and able men had left for work and education abroad [...]. My husband was in the UAE working in the army [...], there was nothing in Oman for them. [G]

The female aflaj-oases

Before the exodus of men from the *aflaj* (Figure 7.2), women followed a life pattern similar to their female ancestors, performing household chores, fetching water from the *falaj*, overseeing animal husbandry, and bringing wood from the *sīḥ*—the barren lands outside the *aflaj*: 'they appear to work hard collecting wood, water and food—and have few perks to life' (Gwynne-James 2001: 80). Daily chores took precedence:

> We would go with our mothers to the *falaj* to bathe, wash clothes, washing utensils, and we brought water for washing our yards and drinking water for our animals also. [A]

141

GULF WOMEN'S LIVES

> We would go in a group to collect wood from the *siḥ* and water from
> the *falaj* which was far away—and always a group of women. [G]
>
> All the women would collect wood from the *siḥ* [barren lands] so we
> could use the wood to fire the hearth and for cooking. [B]
>
> Women balanced the firewood load on their heads; it was extremely
> heavy. Also, we carried water in a jug or two jugs at the same time, and
> that was very heavy work, too. [G]

There were seasonal changes to the women's daily routines:

> In winter we went to the farms to cultivate vegetables [...]. The village had
> one millstone and we ground the wheat for flour on the communal quern
> [...]. We would grind it by hand [...]. When we slaughtered an animal
> [...], we preserved the meat [...]. We collected water for drinking and
> cooking daily [...]. We would do [ablution] here for prayer. Then we would
> go to our small women's [prayer area] to pray. [A]

The feminization of work

All the interviewees mentioned women's traditional work roles, and undertaking
work that the absent men would have done. There were not enough men left
in the *aflaj* to fill the 'male' jobs but the women were not content to hide
away out of a sense of 'shame', or perhaps rely on (distant) male relatives for
support. Therefore, these women began to fulfil the male work roles. They had
no choice, not least because this meant survival for them and their families.
They came together out of comradeship. Every *aflaj* woman was in the same
position as her neighbours. By working together, the sense of community and
solidarity that had always been present in the female environments of the *aflaj*
grew in the male environment. Such actions had not been recorded before—
neither Limbert (2010) nor Eickelman (1984) had noticed this feminization
of male work, and it has not been found in any other scholarly work connected
to the *aflaj* environments.

> We worked in the village; we didn't just sit at home. [B]
>
> We had to work on farms because there were no men to do the jobs. [F]

FEMALE SOCIALIZATION IN THE OMANI OASES

The women undertook strenuous jobs which many assumed they would not be able to bear:

> For wheat cultivation, we planted, tended, harvested, and dried wheat. We used the donkeys to carry the wheat, and we brought the wheat from the gardens [...]. Several *qadf* [the palm leaf sheaf and petiole] were brought, then the women would gather, and they would take the palm stem and use it for threshing the wheat. [A]
>
> Work was done by Omani women and the men that were left in the village. [G]

Ultimately, much of the women's daily routine was taken up by hard work, regardless of it being traditionally feminine or masculine:

> After cooking, we went to weed the onion and garlic fields. We also cut alfalfa [...] and also [ground] the wheat to make bread. There was always work to be done. [D]
>
> Before Sultan Qaboos' era, we went to cut grass from farms located outside the oasis village, from the *sīh*. [E]
>
> Before, I was climbing the date palms to cut and harvest the bunch of dates [...]. We made the mixture for making mudbricks that our houses were built from and we women collected all that was necessary for it to be made [...]. One day, while I was pregnant, I went to bring water [...] to make mudbricks and then I went home and gave birth, all in the same day. [C]

The women saw their roles as aiding their menfolk, speaking with pride and dignity about their complementary position as wives and mothers. None of the twenty-five women interviewed for this study felt subjugated or inferior. Undoubtedly, the women's lives were hard, they lived in poverty, but they had a sense of self-worth:

> We cultivated onions and vegetables [...] to help our husbands, and this was not easy work; it was hard. However, the husband and wife in their separate roles would work together and help each other. [B]
>
> We would go to Jabal Akhḍar and brought weeds for the livestock, for fodder. [C]

GULF WOMEN'S LIVES

Moreover, anything that was *ḥalāl* (permitted) to eat was gathered. The lack of food security meant that starvation and malnutrition were a reality:

> When it rained, little edible leaves were more abundant. We depended on these little leaves, to eat and to live. We had dates [...] and we also ate locusts to supplement our food intake and nutritional requirements [...]. Before, some people in the family would not eat dinner and sleep on an empty belly. We didn't have lunch and malnutrition was rife. [G]

Historically and to this day, certain jobs were male-only, such as weaving blankets. The *aflaj* women, however, learned to weave blankets too, to supplement their meagre living by selling them:

> We took the wool from goats and sheep and made thread with a distaff, and we wove it into the blankets which were the red cloths that you can still see today. [C]

Female socialization

Socialization was an integral part of daily life for the *aflaj* women before 1970, especially around the oases, the *sīḥ* (barren lands) and the village, reiterating the social and communal aspects of the *aflaj* as being central to its people. Socialization strengthened cohesion between neighbours and the wider village and offered material and psychological support (Garcia & Miralles 2017). Though life was difficult, the women always set time aside for socialization, especially in their homes. This was more than just partaking in coffee and hearing the local news and gossip; these coffee gatherings were a psychological and material support for the women. They knew that they shared a similar situation and that they could rely on each other:

> Every day we visited each other. [G]
>
> We had coffee at one lady's house, the next day at another, just to meet up, just to gather, talk, share the news of the village and anything in our families like a new baby or a wedding or engagement. [A]
>
> When a woman had a new baby, we would visit those women who could not come visiting [...]. Also, women who were elderly, sick, infirm—those were the women who were housebound or could not leave their homes—we went and visited them, too. [C]

FEMALE SOCIALIZATION IN THE OMANI OASES

The other women would come to your house, and they would bring fire and Omani bread for you and your [family] and they brought the water from the *aflaj* for you and your animals. The women did your household chores whilst you convalesced. This was done for any woman: one day you and the other women would do this for a sick neighbour-woman [...], and when you were ill or weak, the women would come to you and look after you and your home. [A]

You would have your own chores to do, but you knew that these women would do the same for you if you were in the same situation. It was just something that we did, and we didn't grumble about it. [B]

Moreover, the women of the *aflaj* were generous and selfless, sharing what little they had with others. This seems to have been ingrained personally and socially in the elder women, who would try to meet each other's needs. An Islamic *ḥadīth* (practice) states that water, fire and grass may not be withheld from those who need them (Dawud 2008). Additionally, *aflaj* customs dictate that the very first point where water comes to the surface, often adjacent to the *masjid* (Islamic place of worship; mosque) and at the entrance to the village—the *sharīʿāh*—is designated as a place where drinking water can be collected by any person, villager or stranger, Muslim or otherwise (Khan 2022).

If they had something which we needed and could spare, we could avail ourselves of it [...]. We would go [...] to glean the wheat and we would bring the gleanings back for the poor people of our village [...]. We could take the gleanings back to our homes [...]. When we visited a woman, we took from our homes the coffee beans, sugar, chickpeas, kidney beans [...], and we would cook small meals, more like a snack, and we would make the coffee. Then we would put out the *sufrah* and sit down and have coffee. The woman whose house it was did not have to do anything and we had to provide the necessary coffee and food, even though she may have had these things. It would have been a shame on us—*eeb*—to visit these housebound women without the coffee, spices, and foodstuffs that we used during the coffee visits. [A]

Sharing whatever the women had with others seemed to be intrinsic to their being, even with basic amenities such as wood or food:

When we gathered together for coffee or the visiting, we sewed dresses by hand [...]. We would share the foodstuffs and snacks as well as the coffee. We used to gather for coffee, and we still do, even now. [B]

145

> The women would sit together in a woman's home for a long time in the evening until late [...] and the same in the morning [...]. Each woman would bring some wood to keep the hearth going. [G]

Modernization and its effects

From the ascension of Sultan Qaboos (1970), Oman saw a rapid modernization. The feminization of work in the oases came to an end. The material benefits of modernization were welcomed by all the elder women: better housing, piped water, air conditioning and all other modern amenities within or near to their new homes outside the oasis. However, these new conveniences and dwellings changed relationships in the *aflaj* communities. The women expressed solastalgia for the lost environment, and a real grief for its disappearance which had more to do with emotions and psychology than the material aspects. There had been a physical, emotional and mental dislocation that ran deep. Although many of the older traditional ways of living have been abandoned or replaced, the elder *aflaj* women are still keen to practise their customs and traditions (Figure 7.3).

> I refuse to wear those black things [*abāya*] that the women wear now. It is not my clothing; it is not Omani dress. [...] These black things came in after 1970, but I have never, and I will never wear one! Never! [C]

Figure 7.3: *Aflaj* women preparing for visitors. © Aminah Khan 2020.

FEMALE SOCIALIZATION IN THE OMANI OASES

Figure 7.4: Traditional domestic architecture of closely built houses and narrow lanes. © Aminah Khan 2020.

The solastalgia that an interviewee in group F felt was very real:

> People and neighbours cooperated with each other. Life was not like it is now. The neighbours gathered in the lanes [...]. Because the houses were very close to each other [Figure 7.4], there were no walls surrounding the exterior land of the homes. It is not like this now as people wall off their land and houses; they wall themselves in and wall their neighbours out. [F]

To reiterate, the women's testimonies show that the cost of modernization to the *aflaj* (materially beneficial or not) was the loss and decline of the intangible heritage practised before 1970 (Limbert 2010; Olson 2011):

> Do we miss the life before? Yes, we miss it. Life was simple, we were like one family [...]. There were no pipes, no electricity, so we had to go to the *falaj* several times a day. These are the good things about modern houses. The food was healthier, we used wood for cooking but now people use ovens, and the food is not as tasty [...]. Food [...], it just doesn't taste as good from the oven [...]. We used natural, home-made perfumes and cosmetics. [...] Some of us still maintain this tradition of applying it to our faces and to visitors [Figure 7.5]. [A]

GULF WOMEN'S LIVES

Figure 7.5: Traditional cosmetics applied to a visitor. © Aminah Khan 2020.

Female society post-1970

The women have noticed a shift in the mindsets of the younger generations, echoing Olson (2011) and Limbert (2010). This includes a lack of respect for elders and a shift from the traditional tribal values to the individual, modern outlook (Wilkinson 1977). This change in the younger generation has meant a dislocation of intergenerational relationships and a mutual misunderstanding:

> I miss the life and our lifestyle, but now we are comfortable. [B]
> It is better now of course [...]. Mud houses fell, and people lost their homes [...]. Most of our food [...] came from the *sīh* [barren lands] and a lot of the traditional foods were meals made from the leaves that still can be collected there [...]. Now everything is available in the markets, but today's generation do not know how to bring wood, what work is needed on the farms, how dates are produced, what leaves to collect from the barren

FEMALE SOCIALIZATION IN THE OMANI OASES

lands. In fact, women don't even know how to make bread. Even if we were tired, we would do it! Now, it's a lazy generation! [G]

Neighbours, before Sultan Qaboos, were like one family. There was also a shortage of food, so, if one neighbour cooked meat or fish, they would distribute some of it to their neighbours [...]; we even shared the fire [...]. We shared everything and there was no avarice or selfishness in our village. [A]

Interview H revealed that *aflaj* women's traditions and customs have been somewhat lost in the vast changes that have occurred in Oman:

Now everyone is an individual and no one works together, but still, in some of the villages, they are still connected to their neighbours and visit each other, but in other places [they do not]. My feelings and emotions are indescribable because there is such a huge gap in the changes that came about, a huge, incomprehensible change from the life past and the life now. Villages have become towns; towns have become cities [...]. Old structures were destroyed in the early days of the Renaissance [...]. Women, old women, still gather together and visit each other and other homes, but today's generation do not. That is a shame. [H]

The findings from the interviews are thought-provoking. In certain aspects the changes that occurred after 1970 were not anticipated; the way in which these women negotiated the challenges in both eras is remarkable. As Roberts (2016) states: 'social and cultural change happens slowly, and in a piecemeal fashion' (89), yet women in this study did not have that luxury.

Conclusions

This largely unexplored area of female socialization in the Omani oases and the impacts of modernization after 1970 fills a gap in existing research, providing a starting point and impetus for further studies. The heritage-rich *aflaj* of Ad-Dākhilīyah have been portrayed as a masculine environment, yet during the twentieth century and until 1970, they were female-centric. These women did not hold high political positions, but the oases themselves functioned and survived through the socialization and work of their women.

Mellor (1997) puts forward several interesting arguments: for instance, anything that affects the (natural) environment has an effect on its women.

149

GULF WOMEN'S LIVES

She points out that environmental change often has a greater psychological than physical impact on women (Mellor 1997). This is seen with the solastalgia that the women voiced and their grief over the loss of specific *aflaj* environments and their associated customs. The price paid for the significant material benefits was the disappearance of the traditional, pre-1970 social customs in and around the oases. The *aflaj* structures were the main casualties in terms of a decrease in female socialization due to the appearance of private domestic wells, the introduction of water deliveries by tankers and, later, piped water to individual homes (Limbert 2010). The impact of this on *aflaj* women's socialization as rapid urbanization gained pace in Oman cannot be underestimated; once the 'government water' (Limbert 2010: 127) became the primary source of water for the household, women no longer needed to visit the *aflaj* several times a day.

As men returned from working overseas or from their new employment within the sultanate (Limbert 2010) in the 1970s, an increased disposable income was available to their families. Moreover, men who returned to their home villages came back to a place that was untouched by modern infrastructure. Dissatisfied with the lack of work opportunities, many used their savings and moved their families out to new houses. Newly built houses were clean and had air conditioning, electricity, running water and other modern conveniences. Through residents moving to new neighbourhoods across the main roads from the oases or to other towns (Limbert 2010), the disintegration of the *aflaj* and their community ties and customs which had been built up over centuries commenced.

Having a reliable income allowed the women to hand over their farming and animal husbandry to immigrant workers. Along with a wider availability of food, women no longer engaged in hard work to keep their families fed. Again, the socialization that would have been commonplace through work, whether in the oases or in the *sīh*, gradually disappeared after 1970.

Grounded theory analysis of the data showed that poverty was an unfortunate phenomenon in the women's lives. Poverty itself was a cohesive factor in the *aflaj* women's lives before 1970. It drove women to share their lives and time with each other. Fulfilling *aflaj* social dictates was a source of support and psychological provision for the women. As living conditions improved, men returned from abroad, and food and physical security after 1970 meant

FEMALE SOCIALIZATION IN THE OMANI OASES

that the women from the oases could rely on their primary *maḥram*—father, husband, son—or the government to provide for them. They could now enjoy better material conditions, and poverty was tempered with employment and state welfare. The women's need for support from their social and neighbourhood networks lessened.

Acknowledgements

I am indebted to and wish to thank the following people: Dr Nicola Halenko, Adham Mardini, Karen Smith, the University of Central Lancashire, UK; Dr Abdullah Saif Al-Ghafri, Zahra Saif Zahir Al-Abri, the elder women of the aflaj-oases of Ad-Dākhilīyah, Oman, UNESCO Chair on Aflaj Studies-Archaeohydrology (UCASA), the University of Nizwa, Oman.

References

Akhtar, S., Justice, L.V., Morrison, C.M. & Conway, M.A. (2018). Fictional First Memories. *Psychological Science*, 29(10), 1612–19. https://doi.org/10.1177/0956797618778831

Al-Ghafri, A. (2016). *Sustainability of the Oman Aflaj*. University of Nizwa.

Al-Ghafri, A. (2018, October). *Overview about the Aflaj of Oman*. Retrieved 24 December 2019, from https://www.researchgate.net/publication/328560516_Overview_about_the_Aflaj_of_Oman

Al-Kalbani, M. & Price, M. (2015, June). *Sustainable Aflaj Water Management in Al Jabal Al Akhdar, Sultanate of Oman*. https://www.researchgate.net/publication/300883487_Sustainable_aflaj_water_management_in_Al_Jabal_Al_Akhdar_Sultanate_of_Oman

Al-Khalili, M. (2005). *Oman's Foreign Policy: Foundations and Practice*. https://digitalcommons.fiu.edu/etd/1045/

Al-Shaqsi, S. (2015). *The Changing Environment of Oman's Aflaj: A Study of Falaj Lizugh* (1st edn). Diwan Royal Court & The National Field Research Centre for Environmental Conservation.

Albrecht, G., Sartore, G., Connor, L., Higginbotham, N., Freeman, S., Kelly, B., Stein, H., Tonna, A. & Pollard, G. (2007). Solastalgia: The Distress Caused by Environmental Change. *Australasian Psychiatry: Bulletin of Royal Australian and New Zealand College of Psychiatrists*, 15(1), S95–S98. https://doi.org/10.1080/10398560701701288

Alharthi, J. (2018). *Celestial Bodies* (1st edn). Sandstone Press.

Allen Jr, C. (2016). *Oman: The Modernization of the Sultanate*. Routledge.

GULF WOMEN'S LIVES

Barth, F. (1983). *Sohar: Culture and Society in an Omani Town.* Johns Hopkins University Press.

Bauer, P.J., Tasdemir-Ozdes, A. & Larkina, M. (2014). Adults' Reports of Their Earliest Memories: Consistency in Events, Ages, and Narrative Characteristics over Time. *Consciousness and Cognition*, 27, 76–88. https://doi.org/10.1016/j.concog.2014.04.008

Bernardes, C.M., Valery, P.C., Arley, B., Pratt, G., Medlin, L. & Meiklejohn, J.A. (2020). Empowering Voice Through the Creation of a Safe space: An Experience of Aboriginal Women in Regional Queensland. *International Journal of Environmental Research and Public Health*, 17(5), 1476. https://doi.org/10.3390/ijerph17051476

Bessarab, D. & Ng'andu, B. (2010). Yarning about Yarning as a Legitimate Method in Indigenous Research. *International Journal of Critical Indigenous Studies*, 3(1), 37–50. https://www. researchgate.net/publication/281308868_Yarning_About_Yarning_as_a_Legitimate_Method_ in_Indigenous_Research

Brownhill, L. & Turner, T. (2019). Ecofeminism at the Heart of Ecosocialism. *Capitalism Nature Socialism*, 30(1), 1–10. https://doi.org/10.1080/10455752.2019.1570650

Chun Tie, Y., Birks, M. & Francis, K. (2019, 2 January). Grounded Theory Research: A Design Framework for Novice Researchers. *SAGE Open Medicine*, 7, 1–8. https://doi.org/10.1177/ 2050312118822927

Dawud, S.A. (2008). Chapter 60: Regarding Withholding Water and Chapter 61: Regarding Selling Surplus Water. In Abu-Khaliyl (ed.), *English Translation of Sunan of Abu-Dawud (Imâm Hâfiz Abu Dawud Sulaiman bin Ash'ath* (pp. 128–30). Maktaba Dar-us-Salam. https:// archive.org/stream/SunanAbuDawudVol.111160EnglishArabic/Sunan%20Abu%20Dawud% 20Vol.%204%20-%203242-4350%20English%20Arabic#page/n129/mode/2up

Dutton, R. (2016). *Changing Rural Systems in Oman: The Khabura Project.* Routledge.

Edemariam, A. (2019, 8 July). Books: Jokha Alharthi: 'A lot of women are really strong, even though they are slaves'. *Guardian.* https://www.theguardian.com/books/2019/jul/08/ jokha-alharthi-a-lot-of-women-are-really-strong-even-though-they-are-slaves

Eickelman, C. (1984). *Women and Community in Oman.* New York University Press.

Eickelman, D.F. (1985). From Theocracy to Monarchy: Authority and Legitimacy in Inner Oman, 1935–1957. *International Journal of Middle East Studies*, 17(1), 3–24. https://doi.org/10.1017/ S0020743800028737

Garcia, H., & Miralles, F. (2017). *Ikigai: The Japanese secret to a long and happy life* (1st ed.). London: Hutchinson.

Ghubash, H. (2006). *Oman: The Islamic Democratic Tradition.* Routledge.

Giacomini, T., Turner, T., Isla, A. & Brownhill, L. (2018, 6 March). Ecofeminism Against Capitalism and for the Commons. *Capitalism Nature Socialism*, 29(1), 1–6. https://doi.org/ 10.1080/10455752.2018.1429221

Gwynne-James, D. (2001). *Letters from Oman: A Snapshot of Feudal Times as Oil Signals Change.* Blackwater Books.

Harrison, P. W. (1943). *Doctor in Arabia* (1st ed.). London: Robert Hale Ltd.

FEMALE SOCIALIZATION IN THE OMANI OASES

Jones, J., & Ridout, N. (2015). *A History of Modern Oman.* St. Ives: Cambridge University Press. https://doi.org/10.1017/CBO9780511921070

Khan, A. (2022). The Impacts of Post-1970 Modernization on Women's Socialization: Narratives from the Aflaj-Oases of Ad Dākhilīyah Governorate. *Journal of Oman Studies*, 23, 14–42.

Limbert, M. (2010). *In The Time of Oil: Piety, Memory and Social Life in an Omani Town.* Stanford University Press. https://doi.org/10.1515/9780804774604

McNamara, K.E. & Westoby, R. (2011). Solastalgia and the Gendered Nature of Climate Change: An Example from Erub Island, Torres Strait. *Ecosystem Health*, 8(2), 233–36. https://doi.org/10.1007/s10393-011-0698-6

Mellor, M. (1997). *Feminism and Ecology.* Polity Press.

Morris, J. (1990). *Sultan in Oman.* Arrow Books.

Nicoladis, E., Svob, C. & Smithson, L. (2022). What Is the Source of Preschool Children's Memories of Events from Their Own Lives? *Applied Cognitive Psychology*, 36(2), 445–52 https://doi.org/10.1002/acp.3915

Olson, C. (2011). *Voices of Oman: A Different Mid-East Story.* Stacey International.

Ostrom, E., Burger, I., Norgraad, R. & Policansky, D. (1999). Revisiting the Commons: Local Lessons, Global Challenges. *Science*, 284(5412), 278–82. https://doi.org/10.1126/science.284

Peterson, C. (2021). What Is Your Earliest Memory? It Depends. *Memory*, 29(6), 811–22. https://doi.org/10.1080/09658211.2021.1918174

Råheim, M., Magnussen, L. H., Sekse, R. J. T., Lunde, A., Jacobsen, T., Blystad, A. (2016). Researcher–researched relationship in qualitative research: Shifts in positions and researcher vulnerability. *International Journal of Qualitative Studies on Health and Wellbeing*, 11(1). https://doi.org/10.3402/qhw.v11.30996

Roberts, A. (2016). *The Celts: The Search for a Civilization* (2nd edn). Heron Books.

Wikan, U. (1991). *Behind the Veil in Arabia: Women in Oman.* University of Chicago Press.

Wilkinson, J. (1977). *Water and Tribal Settlement in South-East Arabia: A Study of the Aflaj of Oman.* Clarendon Press.

Wilkinson, J. (2008). *Oman 1965.* Al Roya Press & Publishing House.

Women's Narratives and (Im)mobilities in English: Modern Literature from the Arab Gulf

Alice Königstetter (0009-0002-2597-0639)

Introduction

Cultural production in the Arab Gulf has undergone a dynamic development in recent years. The literary sphere in particular has been flourishing. Book fairs and literary festivals are frequent and popular in all Arab Gulf countries. But it is not only Arabic-language publications that have been thriving. More recently, the Gulf's literary scene has seen a surge in published works written in English. Thus, this chapter will discuss the poignant works of three female writers, each a member of this anglophone literary movement: *The Pact We Made* by Layla AlAmmar, *The Hidden Light of Objects* by Mai Al-Nakib and *That Other Me* by Maha Gargash.

The storylines of the three analysed works touch upon sensitive topics such as agency over the female body, women's psychological trauma and physical abuse. They are stories of female protagonists who achieve freedom and solace in artistic expression. These creative channels enable them to overcome their muteness, caused by systematic silencing fostered by the neopatriarchal societies in which they were raised. The protagonists' scopes of action and agency are analysed through the *new mobilities paradigm* (Pearce 2020), which explores movements of people and their broader social implications. The concept of *neopatriarchy* (Sharabi 1992) serves as a framework for the Gulf's social structure. This chapter deploys an interdisciplinary approach from literary

Alice Königstetter, 'Women's Narratives and (Im)mobilities in English: Modern Literature from the Arab Gulf' in: *Gulf Women's Lives: Voice, Space, Place*. University of Exeter Press (2024). © Alice Königstetter. DOI: 10.47788/LUYI4361

WOMEN'S NARRATIVES AND (IM)MOBILITIES IN ENGLISH

studies, mobility studies and social studies to address anglophone Gulf literature as an instrument to diversify cultural production from the region.

Arab Gulf literature in the past and present

Modern literature in the Arab Gulf dates back to the 1930s (Michalak-Pikulska 2016: 9). Contemporary prose of the small Arab Gulf states Kuwait and the United Arab Emirates (UAE), whose literary production shall be the subject of this study, started with a divergence of almost forty years; while in Kuwait the first short story can be traced back to 1930,[1] literary prose in the UAE has only been recorded since the 1970s.[2] Despite the region's increasing relevance in terms of cultural production, Arab Gulf literature continues to be understudied (Hassan 2017: 7). The reason for this is threefold: first, prose from the region is novel in comparison to that of the Levant and Egypt and stems out of a culture of oral traditions (Noori 2011: 33). Second, book distribution remains fragmented, which often makes acquiring literary works difficult outside their countries of publication (Hassan 2017: 8). Third, censorship continues to be prevalent in the Arab Gulf countries (Al Yousef 2020).

Lately, language has been playing a more dominant factor in the region's prose. While most literary expressions continue to be in Arabic, several Arab Gulf writers have turned to the use of English in their works. This is particularly true for women authors (Alshammari 2022: 314). Shahd Alshammari, a Kuwaiti author and scholar, is one of the few researchers who has published on female anglophone Gulf literature. She explains that 'the choice of writing in English places these women writers outside the margins of the dominant literary culture' (2022: 317), and observes that the female writers publishing in Arabic are favoured in comparison. Alaaeldin Mahmoud (2018) classifies anglophone Kuwaiti literature as minor literature in a Deleuzian–Guattarian sense, introducing a hierarchical order in favour of Arabic. Emanuela Buscemi

---

1. Kuwait was the first Arab Gulf state to publish short stories. The publication of 'Muneera' by Khalid al-Faraj in 1930 constitutes the first literary prose publication in the country (Tijani 2009: 14).
2. Abdallah Saqr Ahmad's story 'Al-Khashaba' ('The Woodblock') is among the first short stories written in the UAE. 'Al-Raheel' ('The Departure') by female writer Shaykha al-Nakhi was written in 1970 (Ramsay 2006: 250; Tijani 2014: 131).

GULF WOMEN'S LIVES

(2020; 2022) discusses identities and belonging in anglophone Kuwaiti literature and literature in translation. Other academic publications cover Arabic
female literature from the Gulf (Ramsay 2006; Tijani 2009) or female Gulf
authors in English translation (Driss 2005; Nash 2017). Analyses of anglophone prose tend to focus on works from Arab-American or Arab-British
diasporas, which in their beginnings bore an element of cultural translation
and were mainly targeted towards a Western audience (Nash 1998, 2017).
Layla Al Maleh's anthology on *Arab Diasporic Literature* (2009) is also worth
noting. Despite its focus on writers in *ghurba* (absence from the homeland)
and its lack of coverage of anglophone Gulf writers altogether—since there
have only been a few—the work represents a significant scholarly contribution
to anglophone Arab literature. Al Maleh notes in the introduction of the
anthology that Arab British writers are 'mostly female, feminist [and] political
in character' (2009: 13), which is also applicable to anglophone Gulf literature.
Tasnim Qutait's publication *Nostalgia in Anglophone Arab Literature: Nationalism, Identity and Diaspora* (2021) discusses memory and identity in Arab
anglophone literature. She innovatively connects Arab anglophone literature
with Arab literary traditions (1). Surprisingly, anglophone Gulf novels did not
make it into the anthology *Oxford Handbook of Arab Novelistic Traditions*
(Hassan 2017), which includes individual chapters on literature from all Arab
Gulf states and comprises a section of over 200 pages on Arabic diasporic
literature covering geographic spheres from Latin America to Europe. Hence,
the study at hand contributes to a much-needed discussion on Arab literary
scholarship and the debate over whether anglophone literature is to be included
in the canon of Arab writership. It aims to advance the recognition of this
flourishing and under-researched literary phenomenon.

Anglophone versus Arabic: the debate over Arab literature in English

As the term suggests, Arabic literature has conventionally been limited to
literature written in Arabic (Hassan 2017: 10). Until recently, anglophone
writers of Arab descent were classified as anglophone writers regardless of
their origin. The same applies to francophone Arab writers. Hassan acknowl-
edges that these two colonial languages 'have produced a body of work that

WOMEN'S NARRATIVES AND (IM)MOBILITIES IN ENGLISH

is difficult to categorize' (2017: 11). In addition, Gana (2013) pinpoints how the question of national or ethnic identity places a burden on Arab writing in English.[3] It is common to classify literary works according to the author's origin and/or language. However, due to globalization, socio-economic changes, and more fluid notions of language use, this no longer seems to be the sole approach. I argue that the contemporary anglophone Gulf writers' *oeuvre* has become an integral part of regional cultural production. The authors rightfully claim their space both in the Arab as well as the international domain.

As we have seen, anglophone Arab literature has repeatedly been categorized as 'diasporic' (Al Maleh 2009; Hassan 2017; Nash 1998). This definition stipulates that the author is an immigrant and foreign to the country they currently live in. While this categorization is historically accurate, contemporary anglophone literature draws a different picture. Authors tend to be highly educated, have lived abroad, and started to take up issues in their countries of origin, channelling them creatively. This is indeed the case for the authors examined in this study—Maha Gargash (from the UAE), Layla AlAmmar and Mai Al-Nakib (both from Kuwait), who publish their prose exclusively in English.

Despite its increasing relevance, anglophone Gulf authorship is still rather sparse. Since self-publishing remains popular, it is also difficult to determine how many anglophone authors are active in the region.[4] Hence, the corpus of works is small. The three selected authors, AlAmmar, Al-Nakib and Gargash, have been successful in and outside the Arab Gulf region. Gargash's first novel *The Sandfish* is promoted as an 'international bestseller' by its publisher (Harper Academic 2022) and was adapted for a screenplay in the UAE. The Emirati newspaper *The National* mentions Gargash as 'one of the rare Emirati authors who was globally published' (Saeed 2021). AlAmmar is a new voice on the Kuwaiti literary scene. Her first novel *The Pact We Made* was published in 2019 and was billed as the 'Kuwaiti #MeToo novel' by British-Sudanese writer

---

3. For further reading on Arab identity and the anglophone language discourse, see Bayeh (2017).
4. An insightful article on anglophone Kuwaiti female writers was published by Shahd Alshammari (2022). Olatunbosun Tijani (2014) notes in a publication on contemporary Emirati writing that the only English novel written by an Emirati writer he was aware of was Maha Gargash's *The Sandfish*.

157

GULF WOMEN'S LIVES

Leila Aboulela (East 2019). However, AlAmmar's work is far more than that: the intimate narrative evolves around a twenty-nine-year-old female heroine 'trapped by societal restrictions and cultural taboos in contemporary Kuwait' (Buscemi 2022: 89). AlAmmar's beautifully crafted novel combines elements of art, poetry and psychology. Al-Nakib's book *The Hidden Light of Objects* was the first short story collection to win the Edinburgh International Book Festival's First Book Award in 2014. It comprises ten stories, interconnected through vignettes, that are all (loosely) tied to Kuwait.

The choice of English for literary expression by an author of Arab origin continues to foster debates and criticism. It also raises the question of adequate representation of their Arab heritage. The writer's audience plays a pivotal role in that debate. AlAmmar stressed during a webinar organized by the Columbia Center in Amman that she was convinced that English-speaking readers could no longer be limited to a certain demographic. She underlined that the matter of audience needed to move beyond the dichotomy of Eastern versus Western audiences (CGC Amman 2021). While Al-Nakib says that she did not consider audience when writing *The Hidden Light of Objects*, during an interview with ArabLit, an online platform for Arab literature in translation, she ponders her choice of language:

> English reflects the reality of many of us living between worlds, even if we happen to live in one place physically. English also reflects a specific reality of the Middle East—its colonial history, its globalized present. It is, therefore, both appropriate and inevitable that English will be utilized by contemporary Arab writers living in the Middle East and not just by those who immigrate to the UK, the US, Canada, or Australia. (Qualey 2014)

Al-Nakib implies what Waïl Hassan expresses more explicitly when he states that 'Arabness today is a pan-ethnicity that is no longer based on language alone' (2017: 12). As in many places of the world, English has become a lingua franca in the Arab Gulf, at least partially because in most Arab Gulf countries—except for Saudi Arabia and Oman—the number of migrants exceeds that of the local population (GLMM 2020). Studies examining language use in the UAE (Dahan 2017) and Kuwait (Dashti 2015) have shown that global English is prevalent. Arabic is no longer the sole marker for an Arab author's identity or their literary production. This circumstance

WOMEN'S NARRATIVES AND (IM)MOBILITIES IN ENGLISH

and its reflection in contemporary literature from the region calls for what Hassan terms a 'redefinition of the category of Arabic literature' (2017: 12). Kilpatrick argues that Arab literature in English 'requires familiarity with both (or all) the literary traditions on which the individual work draws' (2000, as cited in Qutait 2021: 1). Just because English is the author's main language of expression, it does not mean that Arabic has not found a way into the stories of the anglophone Gulf writers. AlAmmar alienates the non-Arabic reader through Arabic and Kuwaiti dialect words that remain untranslated. Her primary concern is the inclusion of the Arab reader (CGC Amman 2021). Al-Nakib and Maha Gargash use similar techniques, inserting short Arabic phrases or words that lack explanation for the monolingual English reader. None of the works include a glossary of Arabic words.

Female anglophone Arab writers face additional obstacles attributed to their gender. As Alshammari highlights, anglophone Kuwaiti women writers are doubly marginalized: first, they need to claim their space in a male-dominated culture and second, make their voices heard in an Arabic-speaking environment (2022: 317). Their topics of choice, such as the female body or psychological trauma, remain sensitive issues in Arab Gulf societies and can be considered a plausible reason for the choice of English over Arabic. Overtly addressing topics like homosexuality, sexual abuse within the family or marital betrayal committed by a woman (AlAmmar) as well as descriptive narratives of sexual practices (Gargash) is more cumbersome in Arabic. Alshammari believes that 'In adopting English to write about Kuwaiti female protagonists, these writers are actively subverting the status quo of Arabic literature' (2022). Female anglophone Gulf literature is transforming the cultural production of the region. It shapes the literary sphere and calls for its own space. Its belonging to the Arab Gulf region has the right to be acknowledged.

Female mobility and immobility in neopatriarchal spheres

This study investigates (im)mobilities of female characters based on two methodological frameworks: Lynne Pearce's interpretation of the *new mobilities paradigm* (NMP) (2020) and Hisham Sharabi's concept of *neopatriarchy* (1992). Pearce grounds her elaborations on Mimi Sheller and John Urry, who initially introduced the notion of the NMP in 2006. The concept of mobility does not only entail the movement of the physical body but also the circulation of ideas and entities in imaginative spaces (Sheller & Urry 2006). The analyses of stories will showcase how the limitations of heroines' tangible movements stand in conjunction with mental restrictions. According to the NMP, all places are tied into networks and connections without isolation from one another. In this context, mobilities are examined within their interdependence rather than in silos. Increased mobility of some people, however, might lead to more restricted mobilities for others; for example, in the sense of neopatriarchy, the claim of male power results in restrictions on female spaces. Furthermore, places are often regarded as fixed, but the NMP argues otherwise, as it sees a relationality between places, people and performed activities. The notion of the tangible space is therefore fluid. The fluidity of spaces and their influence on characters' mobility is part of this study. The influence of their geographic homes that goes beyond any physical space heavily impacts their behaviour and feelings and triggers agitations, which will be explored further in the following section.

Like Pearce, I am convinced that mobility studies are infused with the insights of literature and literary scholars (2020: 77). Even though they complement each other, there seems to be very little interaction between these two academic fields. Pearce highlights the limitations of literary studies, as she argues that they heavily rely on literary criticism (2020: 79), while stressing the benefits of a text-based approach. She suggests approaching literary texts as 'text-as-means' in comparison to 'text-as-end-in-itself' (2020: 76–84). Pearce believes, and I argue likewise, that a sociocultural phenomenon such as mobility or migration can be much better explored through the NMP lens, and that textual practice can locate itself more productively within the field of mobility. Hence, this study uses the NMP lens to explore the female heroines' (im)mobilities.

Complementary to this, Sharabi's concept of neopatriarchy (1992) is linked to the (im)mobilities of the female characters analysed. Sharabi understands neopatriarchy as a modernized form of patriarchy, highly dependent on modernity, which he sees as a 'uniquely European phenomenon' (15). Modern capitalism has played a major role with regards to the formation of a modern society. While Max Weber and Karl Marx (Sharabi 1992: 2) believed that Western capitalism was exportable one-on-one, a dependent form of capitalism was fostered in Arab countries, among others, by the Western-led world

WOMEN'S NARRATIVES AND (IM)MOBILITIES IN ENGLISH

market. This formed a dependent society with a non-modern socio-economic structure. Sharabi calls neopatriarchal society a 'quintessentially underdeveloped society' (6) incapable of performing as an integrated social, political or economic system. The psychosocial features of neopatriarchal societies are characterized by the dominance of the father, the patriarch, around whom the natural family organizes itself. Vertical relations are prevalent, both within and outside family structures. The paternal will is the absolute will, subsequently often executed by female members of the family. This male-oriented ideology privileges the male at the expense of the female. It is evident that this circumstance has influenced the studied works. My analyses of the literary works have shown that women are kept under legal and social constraints. Like Sharabi, I believe it is imperative that social change comes from within Arab society (151) and is not imposed from any outside force. In that context, he stresses the significance of the women's movement, which he sees as a driving force for radical democratic change: 'Even in the short term, the women's movement is the detonator which will explode neopatriarchal society from within' (154). That said, precisely how the heroines in the literary works anticipate challenging the neopatriarchal system in their respective societies will be showcased in this analysis. It will further focus on exploring to what extent creative and intangible spaces can be observed as a means of freedom and increased mobility for the heroines. Finally, a link between the female authors' and the protagonists' mobilities in terms of expression will be established.

To interpret the works, this chapter uses textual analysis from a feminist perspective as outlined by Tijani (2009), who defines a feminist text as follows:

> [Any] female fictional character who thinks, behaves, and acts subjectively—on her own conviction—and in a way that contradicts societal norms, or one who defies patriarchal order and resists her oppression and subjugation in whatever way. A text that depicts women in this manner is considered a 'feminist' text. (3)

This chapter comprehends feminism as *Third World Feminism*, as proposed by Haneen Shafeeq Ghabra (2015: 3). Not only does this approach consider the Middle Eastern patriarchal system, but it also adds race and class to the discussion. Ghabra's intersectional proposition is a regional one and represents a counter-narrative to hegemonic white feminism.

GULF WOMEN'S LIVES

Three works of female anglophone writers from the Arab Gulf: Layla AlAmmar, Mai Al-Nakib and Maha Gargash

This section discusses the intersections of agency, (im)mobilities, trauma and social restrictions in two novels and one short story by female authors from Kuwait and the UAE. The novel *The Pact We Made* (2019) written by Kuwaiti-American author Layla AlAmmar tells the story of Dahlia, an unmarried thirty-year-old Kuwaiti woman, whose life is shaped by voicelessness and unacknowledged trauma. *That Other Me* (2016) by Emirati writer and journalist Maha Gargash narrates the lives of two cousins, Dalal and Mariam, who live in Cairo and are exposed to the control of the patriarch of their family despite the distance from their hometown Dubai. Lastly, 'The Diary', a narration of eighteen pages by Kuwaiti scholar and writer Mai Al-Nakib, published in her short story collection *The Hidden Light of Objects* (2014), presents Mina, who finds solace in writing but is driven by the urge to find her place in a restrictive environment.

Voices and silences in physical and intangible spaces

In the analysed works, the female protagonists are exposed to collective silencing: by their parents, close relatives and societal norms. This leads to restrictions of their physical and intangible spaces, their choices and subsequently, their agency over their lives. According to Spivak (1988), the oppressed can speak and are aware of their condition if given the chance (73). Sharabi (1992) stresses the element of the *monologue* in his elaborations within the neopatriarchal discourse. It is a mode of expression that dominates social interactions, which not only leads to increased authority of the speaker but also to a culture that discourages dialogue and amplifies the notion of absolute truth. Consequently, this fosters a culture of silence and intimidation (92), which is to be observed throughout the three analysed works. In *The Pact We Made*, Dahlia's family opposes the idea of her studying outside Kuwait. The paternal restrictions are expressed in the form of concern about her protection and well-being (AlAmmar 2019: 148–49). However, these seem to be excuses to limit her scope and force her to adhere to societal norms. According to Alshammari (2022), Dahlia is '[struggling] against patriarchal oppression that

WOMEN'S NARRATIVES AND (IM)MOBILITIES IN ENGLISH

renders [her] invisible and would rather have [her] dead'; her '[voice] is muffled, she hesitates, she stutters and stammers' (322) and has great difficulty speaking up against her family members and close friends. Dahlia goes through massive character development in the novel, finds her voice and speaks more openly about the trauma of abuse she had experienced since her childhood. Only when her perpetrator is killed in a car accident can she close that chapter in her life.

The element of muteness caused by patriarchy is also prevalent in *That Other Me*. Despite their physical absence from Dubai, both Dalal and her cousin Mariam are being controlled from afar by Majed, the head of the al-Naseemy family. When he visits Cairo to check on the women of his family, Mariam reflects on how his sudden appearance affects her: 'My voice weakened to a hoarse warble and my tongue felt swollen in my mouth: too large, too dry. An overstuffed parcel of wretchedness no longer able to produce a word' (Gargash 2016: 145). Likewise, Dalal is unable to say or do anything except 'make mousey sounds' (134) when she sees him. The portrayal of Majed is the personification of a patriarch. He uses all his influence and power to control the members of his family, with particular focus on the women. Their obedient behaviour is in line with Emirati family traditions, shaped by a strong respect for elders and men, and is controlled by him. Most importantly, female diso- bedience would be a negative reflection on him, which he wants to avoid at all costs.

Mina, the protagonist in Al-Nakib's story 'The Diary', is unable to articulate herself when her mother finds her writings, a mixture of real-life experiences and fiction, in her room. Over the years, she collected stories in hundreds of notebooks. Her mother reads a few of them and wonders whether her daughter has indeed 'done such reprehensible things' (70) as described in her writings. Mina's immediate reaction is almost non-existent, as she feels unable to explain to her mother what the diaries reflect. Instead, 'she accepted the guilt implied by her silence. She accepted the tears that her words had caused to stream down her mother's face' (70), as her mother realizes that her daughter is not as dutiful as she had believed.

Voicelessness is triggered by a social system arranged in vertical power structures. Parents and relatives inherit a controlling force over the female characters, which leads to uneven communication and acts as a restrictive

163

GULF WOMEN'S LIVES

notion in their lives. Neopatriarchy fosters an ambience of silence and numbing, which the heroines have internalized so deeply that they mute themselves.

Unacknowledged trauma and the abused female body

The literary works of AlAmmar, Al-Nakib and Gargash challenge male social and physical control over the female body. Elizabeth Grosz argues that 'human subjects never simply have a body; rather, the body is always necessarily the object and subject of attitudes and judgments' (1994: 81). Judgement of the body also leads to the question of whom the body belongs to and who has control over it. Dahlia in *The Pact We Made* is the most vocal heroine on the matter: 'I realized a long time ago, in a lot of ways, that my body is not strictly mine. It's a shared entity, something to be criticized, guarded, commented on, and violated' (AlAmmar 2019: 54). She sees a relation between her body and her life, which she feels was never hers either (55). AlAmmar's novel deals with Dahlia's unacknowledged trauma from her experiences of sexual abuse during her teenage years. Her trauma manifests itself in physical sensations, which are personified in the form of a *yathoom*. Here, AlAmmar utilizes a Kuwaiti word that she contextualizes but does not translate. The *yathoom* is described as a demon, which comes to her at night, sits on her chest, and makes breathing hard (2019: 15). The heroine observes her 'loneliness in form and function' reflected in the *yathoom* (16), and despite the stark physical sensations, remains voiceless and unable to scream (58). The *yathoom* is a muting agent and the patriarchal extension of her silence. Alshammari summarizes that Dahlia is 'sexually traumatized and carries the shame and stigma within her body' (Alshammari 2022: 321).

Similarly, Mariam in *That Other Me* is exposed to sexual abuse by her boyfriend, who oversteps his boundaries and touches her without her consent. Immediately after the incident, Mariam states: 'I am numb with shame and a vague sense of loneliness, a physical feeling of emptiness. It's as if some essential part of me—heart, stomach, gut—has been taken away' (Gargash 2016: 241). Like Dahlia, Mariam is numbed by guilt and shame and falls into a depression that makes her unable to sleep or eat (295). Out of hopelessness, she decides to get married to a stranger of whom her family approves. Within a society that silences her, she silences herself further through the unaddressed traumatic experience she does not dare to talk about.

Mina in 'The Diary' equally experiences physical sensations caused by shame and guilt. Hers are not caused by physical abuse but by deliberate self-silencing and shame. When her mother finds her notebooks, she sees no other way but to burn them. She does not give herself time to reflect on the decision. The following day, she is unable to get out of bed:

> Outwardly, her body registered a fever. Inwardly, it felt like her lungs and stomach had been scooped out. The violence of what she had done the night before hit her in full force, and she didn't think she could survive the realization. She felt herself deflating, becoming smaller and smaller, as small as a tadpole in a rotten swimming pool. She whimpered all afternoon. (71)

Guilt and shame trigger the young heroine to destroy her writing. Instead of speaking up, she numbs herself and her creative output. Her voicelessness leads to a physical reaction in her body. Mental health tends to be sidelined by academic studies in the Arab Gulf region (Barbato et al. 2021). Seeking help for mental matters is socially rejected and heavily stigmatized (Al-Khalidi 2022), so silence becomes the accepted way forward. Furthermore, the abused female body, whether through illness or external force, is associated with stigma in Arab Gulf society (Alshammari 2020). Rape is still culturally seen as something a woman has brought upon herself, and '[w]omen are often blamed for their own victimization, which absolves their male assailants of responsibility' (Halim & Meyers 2010). Brownmiller underlines that rape is 'a conscious process of intimidation by which *all* men keep *all* women in a state of fear' (2005: 15). To address such topics literally is, to this day, rather brave and exposes the authors to criticism. Despite this, or rather because of it, it is crucial that such topics are taken up in literary expressions, as they possess the power to shape narratives around taboo issues.

Freedom, choice and female agency

This section examines the impact of freedom of choice and its effects on women's agency and mobility in the selected stories. Mina in 'The Diary' attributes the implications of womanhood to her scope of physical movement.

She feels a 'restless urgency to move, the longingness for travel' (Al-Nakib 2014: 64) like her grandfather. But she is aware that she is 'not an Arab man, but an Arab girl' (64) and that her aspirations most likely would not prove popular within her family structures. In a similar context, Dahlia in *The Pact We Made* envies male freedom, which entails physical freedom, such as 'the freedom to study anywhere in the world [and] the freedom to live life without constant [scrutiny]' (AlAmmar 2019: 30). Women's physical mobility remains restricted and is mainly controlled by the men of the immediate family.

To dismantle the neopatriarchal society around them, the female protagonists claim space and freedom through creative channels. I argue that these open intangible ways to enhance the mobility of the characters. The main characters in the literary works, Dahlia, Dalal and Mina, find solace and freedom through creativity—Dahlia through drawing and painting, Dalal through singing and Mina through writing. However, this comes at a price. The heroines must fight for society's recognition of this type of freedom. Dahlia's father in *The Pact We Made* sees art as 'a hobby' and not a job (AlAmmar 2019: 146), and does not consider it an honourable occupation. Similarly, Dalal's father in *That Other Me* regards her ambition to pursue a career as a singer as despicable. In his view, she brings shame on him and the whole family. A commonality can also be observed in 'The Diary'. The protagonist Mina writes stories. Her father finds her habit 'disconcerting and intriguing', whereas her mother is encouraging at first but becomes 'increasingly uneasy' (Al-Nakib 2014: 60) with her daughter's pastime. However, through internal struggles, time passing and perseverance, the female protagonists in the three stories succeed in claiming mobility and freedom through artistic expressions. Dahlia continues to draw and paint, exhibits in a gallery, and even considers going to art school abroad to continue her passion. Dalal becomes a professional and successful singer who travels the world. After seventeen years of abstinence from creative writing and the agency she gained through it, Mina expresses herself again literally, which can be rendered as a triumph over the restrictions implicitly imposed upon her and a move towards increased agency.

All the female protagonists claim the freedom of choice and agency of which they are being deprived. In *That Other Me*, Dalal is determined to pursue her dreams and deliberately makes choices that do not resonate with her father's wishes. She relocates to Cairo and terminates her formal education to become a singer. Like Dalal, her cousin Mariam leaves her hometown Dubai after receiving a government stipend to study abroad. Dubai is portrayed as a restricting space for the cousins, where a self-determined life does not seem feasible. Their close-knit family back home acts as a constraining and controlling factor with 'stifling rules and proper conduct' (Gargash 2016: 191). Their female family members take over the controlling functions of the patriarch, which is typical for neopatriarchal societies. In a similar manner, Dahlia from *The Pact We Made* explicitly voices her limited decision-making, which runs like a thread through her life, comprising her education, her work, her acquaintances and how her life is conducted overall. Dahlia expresses this very clearly: 'It felt like my life had been just a series of situations that I'd fallen into, like I had no agency or control over anything. I was through living like that' (AlAmmar 2019: 147). In addition, she articulates that she wants to leave Kuwait permanently (208). Her story ends with her making a major life decision by marrying a man who enables her to leave the country. The last lines of the book read: 'I am thirty, and I have made my first decision. I have chosen this. I have chosen him. I have chosen' (274). Dahlia's unanticipated decision can be interpreted by the reader as a self-determined step out of neopatriarchal society. Despite her making that choice, it shall not go unnoticed that a man is the means of her liberation. This closes the circle of neopatriarchy—Dahlia is limited, but also released, through male dominance, even by choice.

Conclusions

This chapter discussed stories from Layla AlAmmar, Mai Al-Nakib and Maha Gargash, to examine female protagonists' physical and intangible mobilities within the wider framework of neopatriarchy. In the analysed works, the authors challenge the prevalent neopatriarchal image of voiceless women. They create alternative narrations of women who go through substantial character development to find their own voice in the Spivakian (1988) sense and (re) claim agency over their own lives. Overcoming neopatriarchy has been treated as intangible mobility. The heroines in the presented stories use their creativity and artistic expression to deal with neopatriarchy. They become vessels for issues such as female agency over their lives and bodies, trauma, as well as abuse. As demonstrated earlier, mental health matters remain marginalized

GULF WOMEN'S LIVES

topics and sometimes even constitute a stigma in the Arab Gulf states. Such topics are less disputed in English. In addition, Buscemi (2022) argues that the writer's linguistic choices contribute to 'decolonizing the Western canon' (102), as AlAmmar, Al-Nakib and Gargash interweave English with unglossed Arabic. This kind of language use estranges the non-Arabic reader, while being inclusive to the reader familiar with Arabic.

Moreover, the collective silencing of women in the stories draws parallels with the authors' lives: two of the three works, namely *The Hidden Light of Objects* and *The Pact We Made*, were subject to governmental censorship. Female anglophone Gulf authors are being marginalized not only for being women but also for their choice of language, which is contrary to societal expectations, as the main language of literary expression by native Arab speakers from the region continues to be Arabic. Despite that, their writing has become a fluid platform for challenging the neopatriarchy experienced both by the authors and their heroines. Through addressing topics that continue to be sidelined in English, AlAmmar, Al-Nakib and Gargash pave the way for a new generation of writers—both male and female—to diversify and mobilize the tenor (and language) of cultural and literary production in the Arab Gulf region.

References

Al-Khalidi, K. (2022, 1 March). Uptick in Suicide Deaths in Kuwait Points to Social Stigma around Mental Illness (trans. R. Chacko). *The New Arab*. https://english.alaraby.co.uk/features/kuwait-shaken-suicide-surge

Al Maleh, L. (ed.) (2009). *Arab Voices in Diaspora: Critical Perspectives on Anglophone Arab Literature*. Rodopi. https://doi.org/10.1163/9789042027190

Al-Nakib, M. (2014). *The Hidden Light of Objects*. Bloomsbury Qatar Foundation Publishing.

Al Yousef, M.J. (2020, 21 September). *Controlling the Narrative: Censorship Laws in the Gulf*. The Arab Gulf States Institute in Washington. https://agsiw.org/controlling-the-narrative-press-and-publication-laws-in-the-gulf/

AlAmmar, L. (2019). *The Pact We Made*. Borough Press.

Alshammari, S. (2020). Writing the Silenced Body: Notes on the flesh. *Journal of Middle East Women's Studies*, 16(1), 79–86. https://doi.org/10.1215/15525864-8016575

Alshammari, S. (2022). Kuwaiti Women Writers and Anglophone Choices: Charting New Territories. *International Journal of Arabic-English Studies*, 22(1), 313–26. https://doi.org/10.33806/ijaes2000.22.1.17

Barbato, M., Al Hemeiri, S., Nafie, S., Dhuhair, B. & Dabbagh, N. (2021). Characterizing Individuals Accessing Mental Health Services in the UAE: A Focus on Youth Living in Dubai. *International Journal of Mental Health Systems*, 15(1), 29. https://ijmhs.biomedcentral.com/articles/10.1186/s13033-021-00452-4

Bayeh, J. (2017). Anglophone Arab or Diasporic? The Arab Novel in Australia, Britain, Canada, the United States of America. *Commonwealth Essays and Studies*, 39(2), 13–26. https://doi.org/10.3316/informit.546907730406149

Brownmiller, S. (1975). *Against Our Will: Men, Women, and Rape*. Simon and Schuster.

Buscemi, E. (2020). Bamboo and Bougainvillea: Literary Perspectives on Identity and Belonging in Contemporary Kuwait. In H.S. Ghabra, F.Z.C. Alaoui, S. Abdi & B.M. Calafell (eds), *Negotiating Identity and Transnationalism: Middle Eastern and North African Communication and Critical Cultural Studies* (pp. 236–59). Peter Lang.

Buscemi, E. (2022). The Pact(s): Identity, Gender and Social Order in Kuwaiti Literature. In S. Hopkyns & W. Zoghbor (eds), *Linguistic Identities in the Arabian Gulf: Waves of Change* (pp. 89–104). Routledge.

Columbia Global Centers (CGC) Amman (2021, 6 April). *Shahd Alshammari in Conversation with Author, Layla AlAmmar* [video]. YouTube. https://www.youtube.com/watch?v=lxd-fkp7uz0

Dahan, L.S. (2017). The Age of Global English: Language Use and Identity Construction in the United Arab Emirates. In A. Gebril (ed.), *Applied Linguistics in the Middle East and North Africa: Current Practices and Future Directions* (pp. 89–113). John Benjamins. https://doi.org/10.1075/aals.15.05dah

Dashti, A. (2015). The Role and Status of the English Language in Kuwait. *English Today*, 31(3), 28–33. https://doi.org/10.1017/S026607841500022X

Driss, H. (2005). Women Narrating the Gulf: The Gulf of Their Own. *Journal of Arabic Literature*, 36(2), 152–71. https://doi.org/10.1163/1570064054909145

East, B. (2019, 5 May). 'The Pact We Made' Is a Complex Novel Championing Feminism in the Arab Qorld. *The National News*. https://www.thenationalnews.com/arts-culture/books/the-pact-we-made-is-a-complex-novel-championing-feminism-in-the-arab-world-1.857473

Gana, N. (2013). *The Edinburgh Companion to the Arab Novel in English: The Politics of Anglo Arab and Arab American Literature and Culture*. Edinburgh University Press. https://doi.org/10.1515/9780748685554

Gargash, M. (2016). *That Other Me*. Harper Perennial.

Ghabra, H.S. (2015). Through My Own Gaze: An Arab Feminist Struggling with Patriarchal Arabness Through Western Hegemony. *Liminalities*, 11(5), 1–16.

Grosz, E. (1994). *Volatile Bodies: Toward a Corporeal Feminism*. Routledge.

Gulf Labour Markets, Migration, and Population (GLMM) Programme (2020). *Percentage of Nationals and Non-nationals in Gulf Populations*. https://gulfmigration.grc.net/media/graphs/Figure1percentageofnationals%20non-nationals2020v2.pdf

GULF WOMEN'S LIVES

Halim, S. & Meyers, M. (2010). News Coverage of Violence Against Muslim Women: A View from the Arabian Gulf. *Communication, Culture & Critique*, 3(1), 85–104. https://doi.org/10.1111/j.1753-9137.2009.01059.x

Harper Academic (2022). *That Other Me: A Novel.* https://www.harperacademic.com/book/9780062391384/that-other-me/

Hassan, W.S. (ed.) (2017). *The Oxford Handbook of Arab Novelistic Traditions.* Oxford University Press. https://doi.org/10.1093/oxfordhb/9780199349791.001.0001

Mahmoud, A. (2018). Of Majors and Minors: Reflections on Kuwaiti Literature in English. *1616: Anuario de Literatura Comparada*, 8, 107–20.

Michalak-Pikulska, B. (ed.) (2016). *Modern Literature of the Gulf.* Peter Lang. https://doi.org/10.3726/978-3-653-05961-8

Nash, G. (1998). *The Arab Writer in English: Arab Themes in a Metropolitan Language, 1908–1958.* Sussex Academic Press.

Nash, G. (2017). Arab Voices in Western Writing: The Politics of the Arabic Novel in English and the Anglophone Arab Novel. *Commonwealth Essays and Studies*, 39(2), 27–37. https://doi.org/10.4000/ces.4603

Noori, S. (2011). Looking at the Emirati Novel. In S. Shimon (ed.), *Banipal*, 42, 32–35.

Pearce, L. (2020). 'Text-as-Means' versus 'Text-as-End-in-Itself'. *Transfers*, 10(1), 76–84. https://doi.org/10.3167/TRANS.2020.100109

Qualey, M.L. (2014, 25 July). Mai Al-Nakib and Writing Histories: 'That's not our version of things. How dare she?' *Arab Lit & Arablit Quarterly.* https://arablit.org/2014/07/25/mai-al-nakib-and-writing-histories-thats-not-our-version-of-things-how-dare-she/

Qutait, T. (2021). *Nostalgia in Anglophone Arab Literature: Nationalism, Identity and Diaspora.* I.B.Tauris. https://doi.org/10.5040/9780755617623

Ramsay, G. (2006). Globalisation and Cross-cultural Writing in the United Arab Emirates and the Sultanate of Oman. In S. Helgesson & G. Lindberg-Wada (eds), *Literary History: Towards a Global Perspective* (pp. 241–77). De Gruyter. https://doi.org/10.1515/9783110894110.4.241

Saeed, S. (2021, 3 March). 10 Emirati Authors You Need to Know About: From Maha Gargash to Omar Ghobash. *The National.* https://www.thenationalnews.com/arts-culture/books/10-emirati-authors-you-need-to-know-about-from-maha-gargash-to-omar-ghobash-1.1176585

Sharabi, H. (1992). *Neopatriarchy: A Theory of Distorted Change in Arab Society.* Oxford University Press. https://doi.org/10.1093/oso/9780195079135.001.0001

Sheller, M. & Urry, J. (2006). The New Mobilities Paradigm. *Environment and Planning A*, 38(2), 207–26. https://doi.org/ 10.1068/a37268

Spivak, G.C. (1988). Can the Subaltern Speak? In P. Williams & L. Chrisman (eds), *Colonial Discourse and Post-colonial Theory: A Reader* (pp. 66–111). Routledge. https://doi-org.uaccess.univie.ac.at/10.4324/9781315656496

Tijani, I. (2009). *Male Domination, Female Revolt: Race, Class, and Gender in Kuwaiti Women's Fiction.* Brill. https://doi.org/10.1163/ej.9789004167797.i-165.2

WOMEN'S NARRATIVES AND (IM)MOBILITIES IN ENGLISH

Tijani, O.I. (2014). Contemporary Emirati Literature: Its Historical Development and Forms. *Journal of Arabic and Islamic Studies*, 14, 121–36. https://doi.org/10.5617/jais.4641

Tijani, O.I. (2019). Raising Feminist Consciousness Through Literature: Two Women's Texts from the Arabian Gulf. *Journal of Arabian Studies*, 9(2), 145–63. https://doi.org/10.1080/21534764.2019.1738034

9 Palestinian Women in the Gulf: Gender, Sexuality and Alienation in Selma Dabbagh's Fiction

Nadeen Dakkak (0000-0002-7514-6747)

Introduction

Any understanding of women's lives in the Gulf is incomplete without encompassing the stories of migrant women, expatriate women or, for lack of a better umbrella term, non-citizen women who have resided there permanently or temporarily. In the realm of Arab literature, the stories of non-citizen women in the Gulf are rarely acknowledged. Even if gender, sexuality and women's experiences have a large presence in works of fiction by Arab male authors, these do not adequately convey the voices of women and they often narrate personal journeys of migration for work in the Gulf. Unlike male migrants, Arab women, many of whom migrate as dependants rather than on work visas, additionally occupy the roles of housewives and mothers who build the families and communities that have become part and parcel of Gulf societies. They are also there as daughters and granddaughters in multigenerational migrant families for whom the Gulf is both a semi-permanent home and a temporary space in which non-citizens ultimately do not belong. With increasing scholarship on Gulf migration in recent years, the urgency of tackling marginalization amongst migrant workers from lower socio-economic groups, including female domestic workers, may have inadvertently diverted our attention away from the experiences of these multigenerational communities (Ahmad 2012; Babar 2017), which makes it all the more important to look at how they appear in works of fiction.

Nadeen Dakkak, CC BY-NC-ND, 'Palestinian Women in the Gulf: Gender, Sexuality and Alienation in Selma Dabbagh's Fiction' in: *Gulf Women's Lives: Voice, Space, Place*. University of Exeter Press (2024).
© Nadeen Dakkak. DOI: 10.47788/NZQW3091

PALESTINIAN WOMEN IN THE GULF

I focus in this chapter on the work of British-Palestinian writer Selma Dabbagh, namely her short story 'Me (the Bitch) and Bustanji' (2006) and one section of her novel *Out of It* (2011). The former is set in Kuwait during the period of the Iraqi invasion in 1990, and the latter is partially set in an unnamed Gulf city. A human rights lawyer before becoming a writer, London-based Dabbagh grew up and lived in different Gulf countries, hence her interest in the region and particularly in the space it offered to Palestinians since the 1948 *nakba* (catastrophe) and later on, the 1967 *naksa* (setback), both of which saw the dispossession of thousands from their homeland after the establishment of Israel, their displacement in neighbouring Arab countries and their subsequent migration to the Gulf.[1] In an interview with Lindsey Moore, Dabbagh comments on the familiarity of the diasporic Palestine–Gulf trajectory and on why the Gulf 'intrigues her':

> I have spent almost half of my life, nearly 20 years, living in the Gulf (Saudi Arabia, Kuwait, Bahrain) and I have experienced these places as non-places to the foreigner: impersonal, featureless public spaces that you pass through, but are not expected or encouraged to impact upon in any way. It's an alienation from one's environment and an increasing sense of only being valued as a producer and consumer of wealth that is heightened in the Gulf but is increasingly found globally. (Moore 2015: 328–29)

Dabbagh here pinpoints the temporariness of life for foreigners in the Gulf. In one sense, the alienation she describes is a by-product of modern urbanization, which transformed Gulf cities into transient non-places that hinder feelings of attachment and are designed to accommodate temporary residents (Elsheshtawy 2019; Khalaf 2006). We see this Gulf city in *Out of It* (2011) where skyscrapers, shopping malls and huge billboards overwhelm Iman, the Palestinian protagonist, but simultaneously urge her to look beneath this façade and observe how it was made possible through excessive exploitation of depletable energy sources and migrant labour. Dabbagh's condemnation of the capitalist logic that underpins global cities in the Gulf and elsewhere thus corresponds to frequent critiques of the economic and

---

1. As Shafeeq Ghabra notes, the Palestinian presence in Kuwait and the Gulf is the result of voluntary migration and needs to be differentiated from the displacement Palestinians experienced in countries bordering Palestine (2018: 16).

173

GULF WOMEN'S LIVES

environmental unsustainability of a profit-oriented urbanization that alienates Gulf inhabitants and ultimately produces fragile cities (AlShehabi 2015;
Elsheshtawy 2019).

In another sense, the alienation that Dabbagh describes is an outcome of
structural exclusion and the inevitable temporariness of non-citizens in the
Gulf, no matter how integral their contributions are to the functioning of the
host states. Nowhere did the inherent precarity of living in the Gulf become
more manifest than in the experiences of Palestinians in Kuwait, who had
built the country since the 1950s and taken it as a second home, only for
thousands of them to be expelled in the aftermath of the 1990 Iraqi invasion
because of the Palestine Liberation Organization's decision to support Iraq
(Lesch 1991). This uprootedness and the hostility to which Palestinians were
subjected in Kuwait for what was perceived as their betrayal of a long-standing
political ally and generous host are central to the Palestinian protagonist's
attempt to retrieve her memory and construct an alternative narrative of the
invasion in 'Me (the Bitch) and Bustanji'. Contrary to migrants from other
countries, Palestinians established a more entrenched presence in Kuwait and
the Gulf because the prospect of return was contingent on the liberation of
Palestine, and the formation of solid communities in the diaspora was essential
to the survival of Palestinian identity and culture (Ghabra 2018). Their vulnerability at a time of political crisis shows how migrants generally become victims
due to political alliances and disputes between states, but it also reflects the
precarity of life in a place that has both offered Palestinians a safe haven and
threatened to take away so much in return.

For Palestinians, the Gulf was simultaneously an alienating space of dislocation and further displacement, and an empowering place offering economic
opportunities, as we see in earlier Palestinian narratives of migration to Kuwait
and Saudi Arabia, such as Ghassan Kanafani's *Rijal fil Shams* (1999 [1962],
translated as *Men in the Sun*) and Jamal Naji's *al-Tariq ila Balharith* (*The Road
to Balharith* 2016 [1982]). From the writings of Palestinian-Kuwaiti scholar
Shafeeq Ghabra, we also know that Kuwait in particular was a primary location of Palestinian diaspora formation and thus promised political and social
mobilization towards liberation before the Palestinian presence in the country
was shattered in 1990–91 (2018: 53). Dabbagh evokes this history and, in a
way, treads in the footsteps of these earlier Palestinian writers through the

174

PALESTINIAN WOMEN IN THE GULF

dual image she depicts of the Gulf as a refuge and a site of alienation. However, she writes from the perspective of young Palestinian women whose unique experiences and observations allow her to centre gender and sexuality in how alienation is articulated. In 'Me (the Bitch) and Bustanji' and *Out of It*, the two female protagonists feel out of place because of the way in which their bodies are perceived by others and, in turn, because of their discomfort with their own bodies. Even though their feelings of alienation can be attributed to family circumstances and their sense of otherness as outsiders, it is in the sexualization and objectification of their bodies that alienation is most manifest. Dabbagh's fiction thus offers a much-needed reflection on how non-citizen women from middle-class and/or privileged backgrounds encounter the Gulf. Writing from within this positionality raises questions on intersections between gender, sexuality, citizenship and class in a context where the citizen/non-citizen dichotomy and the marginalization of workers dominate discussions on migration and power dynamics in society (Vora & Koch 2015), and where non-citizen women are often excluded from, if not further subjugated by, feminist discourses that are concerned with the struggles of citizen women (Kareem 2016).

At the same time, Dabbagh goes beyond the subjective lens that emerges from the particular positionality of her female protagonists. Whether through first-person narration in 'Me (the Bitch) and Bustanji' or the third-person subjective narrative tone that alternates between different characters in *Out of It*, there is a clear investment in pointing out other positionalities and subjectivities that fall outside the protagonists' own feelings and experiences, or even outside the scope of Dabbagh's representation of the Gulf. The reader is constantly pulled away from the main narrative and urged to observe other unexplored realities, including the struggles of migrant workers, of Palestinians from lower socio-economic backgrounds, or even of economically privileged but socially confined Gulf women. I understand this self-reflexive recognition of the limits of the subjective and of literary constructions of place as an important attempt to acknowledge the multiplicity of ways in which the Gulf is experienced, and the extent to which positionality shapes the narratives that could emerge from it. We therefore see different forms of marginalization and alienation intersect within the same geographic and/or temporal space in the two narratives. However, this emphasis on intersectionality is not without

175

GULF WOMEN'S LIVES

limitations. I argue that Dabbagh's fiction demonstrates how critical engagement with social realities in the Gulf often faces the challenge of moving away from the essentialist terms with which the region has tended to be constructed in scholarly and literary writings (Kanna et al. 2020).

The Gulf as refuge and loss

Out of It moves between Gaza, the Gulf and London where members of the Palestinian middle-class Mujahed family attempt to live away from the oppressive Israeli occupation and its constant bombardment of Gaza. Divided into five parts, 'Gazan Skies', 'London Views', 'Gulf Interiors', 'London Crowds' and 'The Gazan Sea', the novel is focused on the twenty-seven-year-old twins Rashid and Iman, who each escape Gaza temporarily and pursue education in London, but it also brings in the stories and perspectives of their mother and elder brother in Gaza, and their father, a former PLO member who resides in an unnamed Gulf country. 'Gulf Interiors' zooms in on the day of Iman's arrival to the Gulf for a short visit she is forced to make by her father after nearly becoming involved with radical Islamic resistance fighters in Gaza a few days earlier, and before leaving for London shortly after. *Out of It* is 'a self-consciously spatial text that questions the interrelationship between the contrasting spaces of London and Palestine's urban areas', as Elleke Boehmer and Dominic Davies (2015: 404) note in their postcolonial reading of Dabbagh's depiction of the former imperial metropolis. Here the seeming absence of political consciousness about the situation in Palestine both alienates Iman and allures Rashid with the possibility of really getting out of it, of being detached from the politics of Palestine. Although the Gulf is mostly left out of this reading of the novel, similar observations can be made about the clearly delineated contrast between Palestinian and Gulf spaces, the latter overwhelming Iman with their unrealness in comparison to the real events she had witnessed in Gaza and to which her mind keeps returning. As she is dragged by Suzi, her father's girlfriend (or wife), into shopping malls and beauty salons, her detachment from the place even leads her to imagine its destruction: 'Iman found the mall overwhelming. The amount of glass for a start. Even a weeny little bomb, Iman thought, would lead to carnage in there. She saw large jagged panes of it dropping down on the croissant eaters, the

PALESTINIAN WOMEN IN THE GULF

lipsticked smokers, and the backs of adults bent over children' (Dabbagh 2011: 176). A violent scene from Gaza is spatially transported into a Gulf mall where the superficiality of consumption is complicit in, if not punishable for, continued atrocities elsewhere.

Unlike London, though, where we similarly see these 'geographical super-impositions' that reveal 'the banality of the apparently depoliticized everyday life of London's citizens' and connect it with life in Gaza (Boehmer & Davies 2015: 405), Iman's 'condemnatory perspective' on the Gulf, as Dabbagh describes it (Moore 2015: 328), harks back to earlier literary representations of it as a place that nurtures materialism and self-interest. These themes reflect the way in which the Gulf for Arab migrants and for Palestinians in particular, especially in early waves of migration in the 1960s and 1970s, was associated with betrayal of the homeland and symbolized further displacement, alienation and detachment from the Palestinian cause—as we see, for example, in the aforementioned Palestinian texts. 'Gulf Interiors' is as much about Iman's observations of a new landscape as it is a window, for her and the reader, into the seemingly materialistic life her father and other Palestinians lead in the Gulf and, accordingly, their distance from the reality in Palestine. Her father, Jibril, talks about Palestinian suffering while he wears branded clothes and indulges in a consumerist lifestyle that makes him buy unnecessary gadgets and think of shopping as a way to get his daughter out of politics (2011: 170, 172). The Palestinian waiter he meets at the airport while waiting for Iman, and whom he tries to introduce to her as a potential suitor, does not seem to mind working at a café that is known to support Israel and has been singled out for boycott, nor does her father mind getting coffee there (164).

Iman's own privileged background and the European schooling she received abroad was in the first instance made possible by Jibril's past work with the PLO, which often led to accusations of corruption (161). While she condemns the materialism she encounters during her visit, the middle-class life the Mujahed family has managed to maintain in Gaza is clearly dependent on Jibril's work in the Gulf. To this he 'offered a prayer of gratitude' (161) for taking him in despite his political background, and for allowing him to leave politics: 'He thanked the glittering forest of duty-free shops around him [...] *I'm so glad to be here. I'm so glad to be out of it*' (161). The Gulf with its glittering buildings and shops seems to be an escape for Jibril from political impasse,

GULF WOMEN'S LIVES

although we find out at the end that he was actually forced to leave politics for other reasons. It is an escape as well for his girlfriend, Suzi, from the traumatic memories of Palestinian refugee camps in Lebanon (177). The Gulf has indeed been a refuge for displaced Palestinians who were betrayed by politicians and political organizations. Alienating though it may be, it is an everyday space of survival for them, as well as for Palestinians in Palestine and in refugee camps who have for decades relied on the financial support of those who migrated to the Gulf. Iman has a simplistic, if not reductive, image of the Gulf, hence her harsh perspective on what she sees as the complete dissonance between materialism and political commitment. At the same time, she is shown to be rightly exasperated at Jibril and Suzi's attempt to make the Gulf her escape too by immersing her in the superficiality of a consumerist lifestyle, precisely because this attempt takes the form of her feminization, settling down through marriage, and distancing from politics.

Dabbagh in 'Gulf Interiors' centres the Palestine–Gulf connection and raises questions about the possibilities and the losses that ensued from it, which can be understood as part of her desire to 'find a linkage between Palestinians everywhere' through the focus on 'political consciousness as the connector' (Moore 2015: 331). 'Me (the Bitch) and Bustanji' is an earlier reflection on this connection, but here loss is at the heart of the Palestinian experience in Kuwait, counteracting decades in which both Kuwait and the Palestinian community thrived through the former's support of the latter, and the latter's dedication and investment in their host country's development (Ghabra 2018: 16, 70, 83). The half-Palestinian first-person narrator retrospectively recalls the first few days of August 1990 when the Iraqi army invaded Kuwait during an otherwise boring summer which she, a teenager at the time, spent noting down unremarkable detective observations in her diary. With British passports and the financial means to live elsewhere, the narrator and her father manage to travel to Jordan a few days later, leaving behind a less privileged extended family who were later expelled from the country they considered home and refused to leave during the invasion. They also leave behind Bustanji, the Palestinian gardener at the centre of the narrator's diary, whose fate symbolizes the status of Palestinians as scapegoats at times of crisis. Bustanji's son, into whom 'he puts everything' (Dabbagh 2006: 64)—as is typical of Palestinian parents' dedication to building future generations who will work towards liberation—is kidnapped and never reappears. Here Dabbagh refers to the hundreds of revengeful attacks Kuwaitis carried out against Palestinians, who became scapegoats for the PLO's support of Iraq after liberation in 1991 (Lesch 1991: 47–50). A former PLO member, Bustanji too dies after being held by the police upon reporting the disappearance of his son, suggesting another deliberate act of killing. As if anticipating this fate, the narrator's diary makes it possible to retell the story of the invasion. Years later, she writes, 'A whole occupation had occurred, but I have no note of it, as when I heard the bangs I had not logged them, as I kept forgetting to look at my watch when they happened' (2006: 63). Instead, the diary records the regular visits of Bustanji who refused to neglect the garden even after the invasion, making it a testimonial to his dedication to the land and the plants he nurtured (63). As in *Out of It*, Kuwait in this story is a refuge, a second home to Palestinians, but it is also a place where it seems that decades of hard work do not pay off or put them in a less precarious situation. They are welcomed as workers and consumers, but are not offered belonging and stability in return, hence the heightened sense of alienation that Dabbagh's story conveys.

Gendered experiences of alienation

Despite being centred on the Palestine–Gulf connection, Dabbagh's representation of the Gulf in *Out of It* and 'Me (the Bitch) and Bustanji' is entwined with the subjective experiences of the two female protagonists. The teenage narrator's foreign appearance and background in 'Me (the Bitch) and Bustanji' arguably determines how her body is perceived in public spaces in Kuwait, while Iman's already-existing feelings of insecurity about her body and sexuality in *Out of It* are heightened in the Gulf mainly due to her family's perception of her as in need of feminization. In both narratives, the alienation that ensues from the protagonists' evident discomfort with their bodies necessitates recognizing how gendered and sexual relations shape Gulf spaces and women's experiences of them.

In *Out of It*, Iman's vulnerability, or seeming readiness, to being recruited by Islamic resistance in Gaza is a sign prompting Jibril to decide that his daughter needs feminization and a husband—'the girl really should be thinking of settling down' (2011: 163). He gives Suzi the mission of 'sorting her out'

GULF WOMEN'S LIVES

through shopping mall trips, what he happily thinks of as Suzi's 'adoption of Iman's upbringing' (163). Iman momentarily feels secure in the ability to be little again in her father's embrace (164), but the disconnection between them becomes immediately clear and she is struck, perhaps not for the first time, by his insensitivity to her actual feelings and needs, and his seemingly traditional thinking of a woman's body as a symbol of family honour and of menstrual blood as shameful. When she asks for some time to get changed in the airport bathroom after she arrives, he does not have the intuition to connect her period to this request which he immediately dismisses, even if he does find the time to introduce her to the Palestinian waiter he met earlier (164–65). Later in the car when he finds out that she had bled through her trousers because the Israelis at the Gaza border did not allow her to go to the bathroom, he has a fit of anger at the humiliation of being denied this need as a Palestinian, despite his insensitivity to Iman's same request shortly before that. When she tells him about worse kinds of humiliation other girls have gone through at the border, including being strip-searched, 'Jibril's eyes were wild and demanded one answer only' to his question of whether they searched her like that, a comforting no that would allow him to rest in the knowledge that his own daughter's honour, and hence his own, was not violated (167). Jibril's fury at Iman's half-satisfying answer of 'not this time, but before', an experience he does not even bear to hear about, suddenly but not surprisingly shifts the blame on her for allowing this to happen, and even for allowing her body to bleed, before he quickly realizes how nonsensical his anger is and explains that he is just upset at 'the situation' (167). This scene between father and daughter—interspersed with interjections from the radio playing in the car and with Iman's window observations of the foreign world around her—encapsulates the distance and tension in their relationship. Iman is frustrated at her father because, as Dabbagh explains, he 'has deserted the family for reasons she does not know or understand' (Moore 2015: 328)—hence her alienation in the Gulf. We do not know much else about this relationship before we find out at the end of the novel that Jibril's decision to move to the Gulf was a direct consequence of his wife's political activities that went against his own political work and caused his embarrassment in the party, which could explain his attitude towards his daughter's political engagement.

PALESTINIAN WOMEN IN THE GULF

Iman is surrounded by expectations of marriage and femininity ever since returning to Gaza from education abroad with the hope of finding a new meaningful political role for herself, only to 'find that there was no role offered to her at all, except for that of wife and mother' (2011: 18). However, it is during her temporary passage through the Gulf that expectations of femininity become central to the narrative and to her perception of herself, heightening her self-consciousness of her body and her lack of sexual experience. As befits a place that is depicted as superficial, materialistic and detached from the reality of Palestine and political commitment, these expectations take the shape of compulsory visits to malls and beauty salons with Suzi, who is at home in these places. After a day of waxing and shopping in which each woman grudgingly tries to appease the other for Jibril's sake, Suzi decides that it is 'far better to just be rude' with a girl of Iman's 'type' and to spell it out for her when the latter objects to whatever her father and Suzi want her to become: 'if you take my advice you will start to work on developing yourself as a *woman* rather than [...] whatever it is that you are trying to do. You want to be a *politician* of some kind? Or an *activist*? Is that it?' (178). Iman is determined to get herself out of her father's place and of the Gulf, 'out of all this frippery' which Suzi has made her wear, but these words still trigger her insecurities (180). They make her self-conscious of her unexpressed sexuality, which she begins to think of as visible in how her own body appears to others: 'What had Suzi picked up on? Suzi knew, she was sure of it, of her inexperience and ineptitude in *that* way, in the sexual way; women like Suzi could sniff these things out' (181). Iman continues to be haunted by Suzi's judgement of her body after she moves to London and until she finally has her first sexual experience, with someone she immediately contrasts with the men Suzi had set her up with in the Gulf when she finds out that he does not have a car (206). These men, for whom fancy cars seemed to be an extension of their masculinity that needed her praise and recognition, are like her father and Suzi, an outgrowth of the same materialistic and alienating space that could not accommodate her political subjectivity, and in which she was expected to acquire and perform a superficial feminine one that thrives through a consumerist lifestyle. Her father is the one who eventually sends her off to London after a date in which Iman's vocal opinions, interpreted by the Palestinian-American man she meets as the 'dangerous beliefs' of a 'militant communist',

GULF WOMEN'S LIVES

reach Jibril and appear to threaten his reputation and her own (195). As she laughingly tells her brother later in reference to the inevitable trouble she would have caused her father and herself by living in a place that does not tolerate her political opinions, 'there was no place for me in the Gulf', a sentiment she reciprocated by refusing to change and conform with how she was expected to behave as a woman and as a non-citizen (195).

The Gulf in Iman's experience is alienating because it appears to be completely disconnected from possibilities of meaningful political action. Yet her out-of-placeness derives in the first place from the gendered social expectations that surround her and make political commitment seem incompatible with being a woman, particularly when womanhood is equated with a set of predetermined feminine qualities as well as marriage and motherhood. Because of her confusion at her political role and insecurity about her sexuality, Iman struggles to reconcile her desires and feelings as a woman with her abhorrence of these expectations and resistance to being subjected to them. As she reflects later in London, 'It bugged her immensely that despite the disrespect she felt for every aspect of Suzi, the judgement had resonated and caused so much self-doubt' (205). She is only able to gradually move beyond this self-doubt after her sexual experience in London and after she finds out about her mother's past political activism, 'a discovery of a legacy that she deserved' and that goes against the 'woman' that Jibril and Suzi wanted her to become (208). In Iman's eyes, the Gulf embodies a life that is irreconcilable with both her political aspirations and understanding of herself as a woman.

While Iman's temporary passage through the Gulf reveals how already-existing gendered social expectations become amplified in materialistic and consumerist spaces, Dabbagh depicts a different kind of alienation in 'Me (the Bitch) and Bustanji', one which ensues from the sexualization of the protagonist's body, particularly in gendered public spaces. The title of the story is itself a reference by the narrator to the hostile gazes and sexual harassment she received as a teenager in Kuwait, such as in the space between her house and the neighbourhood's grocery:

> My bitch status was normally confirmed to me at least twice on the way back from Hajji's shop and more than that if I stopped for a cigarette [...]. Sometimes they were a joke, the lines coming out of the guys in the cars [...], 'Hey sexy,' weighed down with accent, sometimes the words were a

blur of consonants, sometimes it was just a horn, but it was always there, as an undertone, as an overtone, ever since I was a kid, even if there was no skin showing at all, it was always there, *Bitch, hey Bitch, yeah Bitch, I can see you. Bitch.* (2006: 60)

The suggestion here and elsewhere is that the narrator's foreign appearance, her fair skin and blonde hair, lead to her sexualization in a place where whiteness is fetishized and associated with promiscuity, hence the perceived sexual availability that is projected onto her body. The narrator's mother is Hungarian, although others casually refer to her as Romanian before correcting themselves in a sarcastic slip of the tongue that perhaps seeks to bring to the mind of the reader associations with sex trafficking. Her status as an outsider becomes most visible in contradistinction to the anonymity and easy mobility of Kuwaiti women in spaces where her body is marked not only for its foreignness, but for being dressed differently. When she finds the fancy lingerie store where her mysterious Kuwaiti neighbour shops—part of the detective investigation occupying her boring summer—she 'did not want to go inside because a crowd was gathering: *Bitch! Hey Bitch! We can see you. Bitch!* The black *abaya*-clad ladies had glided in and out like medieval princesses' (70). Evident here is the adolescent protagonist's increasing self-consciousness of her body, but also the retrospective narrator's recognition of how her foreignness and secular background intersected with her female positionality in gendered spaces and made her feel out of place. Even though Bustanji and the fate of Palestinians after 1990 are at the heart of the narrative and define the image of Kuwait that has remained in her memory, her perspective is dominated by subjective recollections of how she felt about her body as a teenager in Kuwait. Dabbagh weaves the political marginalization of Palestinians with the protagonist's gendered experiences to construct a subjective image of Kuwait as an alienating place.

The Gulf beyond the subjective

With their non-linear narrative structure and their reliance on the voices of protagonists, their impressions and memories of the spaces they encounter and inhabit in the Gulf, *Out of It* and 'Me (the Bitch) and Bustanji' do not exhibit a traditional realist mode of writing. *Out of It* in particular refuses to

GULF WOMEN'S LIVES

pinpoint the geographic location of Iman's encounter with the Gulf, which allows it to construct a place that is a mixture of reality and fiction and whose petro-modernity is on the brink of collapse, almost anticipating its demise. At the same time, we see in both narratives a commitment to reflect on the Palestine–Gulf connection and to represent the reality of Palestinians and others in the Gulf. In this way, Dabbagh's texts share with other literary works on Gulf migration the urge to reveal and criticize political and socio-economic marginalization through subjective narratives. Yet we also see in her represen-tation of the subjective encounter with the Gulf a similar urge to go beyond the stories of her protagonists and remind the reader of their limited capacity to adequately represent how a place is experienced by different people. In the same way in which literary realism as a mode of writing has the ability to examine its formal limitations and actively experiment with writing techniques that communicate to readers the challenges of representation, even while being committed to the necessity of representing the world (Beaumont 2007: 4), the narrative voice in both of Dabbagh's texts repeatedly directs the reader's attention towards other realities, and hence other possible stories, that intersect spatially and temporally with the protagonists' own experiences in the Gulf, but that remain outside the scope of representation.

In 'Me (the Bitch) and Bustanji', the narrator's self-consciousness of her sexuality and otherness is entwined with her interest in the Kuwaiti woman who lives across the road and whose movements in and out of the 'space station house' are recorded in her diary (2006: 59). The Sheikha, as the narrator calls her—a title symbolizing power, especially when preceded by the definite article that differentiates it from the more common first name Sheikha—embodies a juxtaposition that is stereotypical of the Gulf and often marks its perceived inauthentic modernity where conservative religious and cultural values, seen as backward, persist alongside material modernization: 'Her *abaya* was always black. Her face was always covered. Her bags were always full of high-class shopping' (58). The narrator is particularly interested in investigating the brands she sees on those shopping bags. When viewed in contrast to the black *abaya*, the lingerie items she finds in the fancy stores suggest the extent to which she is especially intrigued by the Sheikha's sexual life, a reflection of her own new adolescent concerns, but also of the seeming disparity between her own life as a young woman in Kuwait and that of the Sheikha. They are

PALESTINIAN WOMEN IN THE GULF

two women who share the same neighbourhood but who come from different socio-economic and cultural backgrounds. Indeed, if it weren't for the narrator's privileged economic status as the daughter of two doctors, she would not be living in this neighbourhood at all but in Hawalli, a non-Kuwaiti area where Bustanji and her Palestinian relatives live. Even if the narrator has access to a life not available to other Palestinians and migrants and she lives in the same neighbourhood as the Sheikha, their bodies do not inhabit the same social space, nor are they perceived in the same way in public spaces. References to the Sheikha are interspersed throughout the text, offering a distraction to the reader from the narrator's recollections of the invasion, just as the Sheikha herself offered a distraction to the bored protagonist and became the figure of the 'other' upon whom she could project fantasies of a mysterious and exotic life not available to her.

Dabbagh hints at the possibility that the Sheikha's life is not as mysterious and enviable as it appears in the eyes of her naïve protagonist. The brief detective notes in the diary build in the reader's imagination a set of stereotypical assumptions about what a Kuwaiti woman's life must be like in a patriarchal and oppressive society. These assumptions are solidified in a moment of epiphany for the protagonist, who realizes upon her departure from Kuwait that her gaze at the house across the road was reciprocated and that she may have similarly been the object of the Sheikha's envy. As they leave the neighbourhood, she writes,

> my eye caught her moving behind the vent-shaped windows of her top floor. The Sheikha. The lights were on and her face was so close to the window, her hands pressed flat on it [...]. She looked so much younger than I had thought she was and I found myself thinking for some reason that maybe she had been watching me as much as I had been watching her. (72–73)

The Sheikha's unexpected young age and apparent longing for freedom suggest her marriage and subjugation to a life in which she lacks the protagonist's independence. Dabbagh makes room for another unwritten story that intersects with that of her Palestinian protagonist. It is a conscious and important literary attempt to recognize wider issues of gender and patriarchy that cut across citizenship and class but that manifest differently according to every woman's positionality in Kuwait. However, Dabbagh here falls into the trap of

185

GULF WOMEN'S LIVES

reproducing the image of the oppressed and silenced Gulf woman who enjoys the comforts of material modernization and a consumerist culture but remains the victim of a conservative and backward society.

This depiction of material modernization as a façade behind which lurks a dark social reality is central to the image Dabbagh paints of the Gulf in *Out of It* as well, and which we particularly see in the chapter on Iman's first impressions after her arrival. Here, the father–daughter conversation that takes place in the car is interrupted a number of times by the characters themselves or the third-person subjective narrator to make room for observations about this dark reality. As the radio transports to them news from Gaza, Jibril speculates that the traffic must be due to construction worker riots. Venting off his frustration at the news, he unsympathetically calls them idiots when Iman asks for details. 'They'll all get deported in the morning, the lot of them' (165–66). As Iman observes the passengers of other cars stuck in traffic, her eyes immediately register a snapshot that captures both the cosmopolitanism and socio-economic inequality that mark this modern Gulf space, where

> middle-aged Western men stared hard at the stationary traffic [...], women in black headscarves chewed gum with open mouths, East Asian women in the safari uniforms of the Chinese proletariat held toddlers in backseats, their foreheads slumped against the windows [...], two bearded men gesticulated to each other from either side of a suspended cardboard disc imprinted with the image of a Lebanese cleric. (166)

As in 'Me (the Bitch) and Bustanji' where the diary's record of Pakistani and Afghan migrants walking in the neighbourhood actively inserts them into the geographic landscape of Kuwait, references to the marginalization of migrant workers in 'Gulf Interiors' are central to Dabbagh's sketch of the alienating geographic and social landscape that Iman encounters. Unlike Jibril, for whom the plight of migrants seems like a taken-for-granted reality, even an insignificant detail of everyday life—he read and sought sections of the newspaper and only 'skimmed the runaway housemaids and discontented manual labourers section' (157–58)—the reader gets the sense that Iman's observations of this reality are part of her overall condemnatory perspective on the Gulf. Notwithstanding her own alienation in a place that seems to offer fertile soil for the negation of her political subjectivity as a woman, Iman experiences the Gulf from a particularly privileged position. Dabbagh's investment in drawing the reader's attention to the realities of marginalized migrants thus reflects her attempt to go beyond the perspective that can emerge from her protagonist's positionality.

However, like in 'Me (the Bitch) and Bustanji', this attempt to condense what we can call the Gulf's 'problems'—migrant worker exploitation, but also alienating modernization, and economically and environmentally unsustainable urbanization—in a brief encounter has the effect of producing a reductive image in which the Gulf, a heterogenous and complex place like any other, loses its complexity and becomes only possible to conceive of through the extreme binaries of modernity/tradition, privilege/marginalization, amongst other apparent paradoxical features. Dabbagh's representation of the Gulf rightly sheds light on these urgent social realities in the same way in which it self-reflexively recognizes the different position the Kuwaiti Sheikha occupies in relation to the teenage Palestinian protagonist. Nonetheless, what we see in both texts is the difficulty of critically engaging with such realities in the Gulf without resorting to tropes and images that do not adequately convey their complex dynamics. Dabbagh's fiction demonstrates the challenge of writing about and representing a place that has so often been, and remains, the subject of essentializing narratives (Kanna et al. 2020).

Conclusions

Considering the scarcity of writings on the Gulf from the perspective of non-citizen women, Dabbagh offers an important gendered insight into the alienation that tends to be associated with the region. Her representation of the Gulf in *Out of It* and 'Me (the Bitch) and Bustanji' evokes the feelings of ambivalence that we see in earlier Palestinian writings, and in which the Gulf is both a refuge and a site of alienation. At the same time, alienation here is most clearly articulated through the subjective experiences of her female protagonists from whose perspective an even more alienating Gulf is narrated, one where their bodies are subjected to sexual and gendered expectations. The narratives demonstrate that the Gulf is perceived and experienced in various ways that cannot be reduced to the status of non-citizens as outsiders, and that inevitably emerge from one's particular positionality; but I also argued

GULF WOMEN'S LIVES

in this chapter that Dabbagh makes room in her narratives for other possible stories, other experiences of alienation. Even if this self-reflexive technique does not adequately capture the nuance needed when approaching the marginalization of women and migrant workers in the Gulf and even uncritically reproduces stereotypical images of the region, it highlights the limits of representation and the challenge of critical literary engagement when writing on the Gulf. This challenge is not unique to literary representation and can be examined within other kinds of writing, including scholarly knowledge production on the region. Yet it is in works of fiction like Dabbagh's, where the narrative form is just as central as the narrative itself, that the challenges and limits of representation are laid bare to the reader—thus inviting a broader discussion beyond literary writing on how contentious issues on the rights and freedoms of women, migrants and other marginalized groups can be tackled in the Gulf.

References

Ahmad, A. (2012). Beyond Labor: Foreign Residents in the Persian Gulf States. In M. Kamrava & Z. Babar (eds), *Migrant Labor in the Persian Gulf* (pp. 21–40). Hurst.

AlShehabi, O. (2015). Rootless Hubs: Migration, Urban Commodification and the 'Right to the City' in the GCC. In A. Khalaf, O. AlShehabi & A. Hanieh (eds), *Transit States: Labour, Migration and Citizenship in the Gulf* (pp. 101–32). Pluto.

Babar, Z. (ed.) (2017). *Arab Migrant Communities in the GCC*. Oxford University Press. https://doi.org/10.1093/oso/9780190608873.001.0001

Beaumont, M. (2007). Introduction: Reclaiming Realism. In M. Beaumont (ed.), *Adventures in Realism* (pp. 1–12). Blackwell. https://doi.org/10.1002/9780470692035.ch

Boehmer, E. & D. Davies. (2015). Literature, Planning and Infrastructure: Investigating the Southern City Through Postcolonial Texts. *Journal of Postcolonial Writing*, 51(4), 395–409. https://doi.org/10.1080/17449855.2015.1033813

Dabbagh, S. (2006). Me (the Bitch) and Bustanji. In J. Glanville (ed.), *Qissat: Short Stories by Palestinian Women* (pp. 58–77). Telegram.

Dabbagh, S. (2011). *Out of It*. Bloomsbury.

Elsheshtawy, Y. (2019). *Temporary Cities: Resisting Transience in Arabia*. Routledge. https://doi.org/10.4324/9780429457838

Ghabra, S. (2018). *Al-Nakba wa Nushu' al-Shatat al-Filastini fil Kuwayt* [The Nakba and the Emergence of the Palestinian Diaspora in Kuwait]. Arab Center for Research and Policy Studies.

Kanafani, G. (1999). *Men in the Sun and Other Palestinian Stories* (trans. Hilary Kilpatrick). Lynne Rienner.

Kanna, A., A. Le Renard & N. Vora. (2020). *Beyond Exception: New Interpretations of the Arabian Peninsula.* Cornell University Press. https://doi.org/10.7591/cornell/9781501750298.001.0001

Kareem, M. (2016, 14 January). 'Manifesto Against the Woman.' *Jadaliyya.* www.jadaliyya.com/Details/32849/Manifesto-Against-the-Woman

Khalaf, S. (2006). The Evolution of the Gulf City Type, Oil, and Globalization. In J.W. Fox, N. Mourtada-Sabbah & M. al-Mutawa (eds), *Globalization and the Gulf* (pp. 244–65). Routledge.

Lesch, A.M. (1991). Palestinians in Kuwait. *Journal of Palestine Studies*, 20(4), 42–54. https://doi.org/10.2307/2537434

Moore, L. (2015). A Conversation with Selma Dabbagh. *Journal of Postcolonial Writing*, 51(3), 324–39. https://doi.org/10.1080/17449855.2014.954755

Naji, J. (2016). *Al-Tariq ila Balharith* [The Road to Balharith]. Amman, al-Shuruq.

Vora, N. & N. Koch. (2015). Everyday Inclusions: Rethinking Ethnocracy, *Kafala*, and Belonging in the Arabian Peninsula. *Studies in Ethnicity and Nationalism*, 15(3), 540–52. https://doi.org/10.1111/sena.12158

Index

#MeToo 157
11 September 2001 102, 103 *see also* 9/11
9/11 102 *see also* 11 September 2001

Abaya 183, 184
absence 15, 21, 61, 69, 91, 97, 101, 139, 156, 163, 176
ableism 28
able-bodied 24, 26, 31, 33
Aboulela, Leila 158
abuse: 64, 106, 116, 119, 122, 163, 167; physical abuse 119, 120, 122, 123, 155, 165; emotional abuse 199; sexual abuse 159, 164
activism 3, 7, 91, 104, 108; political activism 182; embodied activism 34; disobedience as 163; online campaigns 98; street demonstrations 98 *see also* women's activism; feminist activism
agency 2, 4, 8, 10, 15, 23, 34, 55–59, 62, 67, 68, 69, 96, 154, 162, 165, 166, 167; embodied agency 9
Aghal (black cord used by Arab men to keep a *ghutrah* or *keffiyeh* in place) 88
Ahmed, Sara 9, 32
Aib (shame) 39 *see also* shame
AlAmmar, Layla 4, 52, 154, 157–59, 162, 164, 166–68
Al-Bishr, Badriya 58
Al-Essa, Bothayna 58
Alem, Raja 58

Alharthi, Jokha 3, 12, 54, 58–60, 62–64, 67–68, 70, 137
Alhinai, Manar 38, 39
Alhinai, Sharifa 11, 38
alienation 172–75, 177, 179, 180, 182, 186, 187, 188
Aljohani, Laila 12, 54, 58, 62–65, 67, 68, 70
Al Maleh, Layla 156, 157
al-Maqtari, Bushra 58
Al-Maria, Sophia 1, 2, 4
Al-Nakib, Mai 3, 10, 22, 154, 157–59, 162–64, 166–68
Al Oraimi, Suaad 76
Al Qadiri, Fatima 1, 2
Alsanousi, Saud 3
Alshammari, Shahd 4, 11, 12, 22, 25, 26, 54, 58, 61, 62, 65–70, 155, 157, 159, 162, 164, 165
Al-Sharif, Manal 104
al-Shidi, Fatma 58
al Othman, Laila 58
Al-Yousef, Aziza 108
Alvar, Mia 3
Anglophone Arab literature 156 *see also* Anglophone Gulf writers *see also* Anglophone Gulf authors *see also* Anglophone Gulf literature
Anglophone Gulf authors 157, 168 *see also* Anglophone Arab literature *see also* Anglophone Gulf literature *see also* Anglophone Gulf writers

INDEX

Anglophone Gulf literature 155, 156, 159 *see also* Anglophone Arab literature *see also* Anglophone Gulf authors *see also* Anglophone Gulf writers

Anglophone Gulf writers 156, 157, 159, 162 *see also* Anglophone Gulf authors *see also* Anglophone Arab literature *see also* Anglophone Gulf literature

animal husbandry 136, 141, 150

Anthias, Floya 55

Anzaldúa, Gloria 56–57, 59, 66

Arab diasporic literature 156–57

Arab feminism 39; Islamic feminism 91, 105, 106, 110

Arabian Gulf 2–6, 8, 11, 15, 58, 59, 88; Arabian Peninsula 80; the Gulf 2, 12–15, 22, 27, 32, 38, 39, 47, 53, 155, 156, 162, 172–76, 178–84, 186–88; Gulf countries 2, 3, 55, 125, 173; Gulf cities 173; *hadar* (city dwellers) 22; Arab Gulf States 47, 128, 168; Gulf societies 13, 63, 159, 165, 172; Arab Gulf region 10, 14, 116, 156, 157, 165, 168 *see also* Gulf Cooperation Council (GCC)

Arab media corporations 78, 81, 83, 85: Egyptian Radio and Television Union 88; Egyptian Radio Networks 81; Egyptian State Television 88; Sout Al Sahel Radio Station 82

Arab Spring 8 *see also* Arab Uprisings

Arab Uprisings 104 *see also* Arab Spring

Arab women 9, 10, 14, 50, 51, 61, 62, 86, 172, *Khaleeji* women 1, 6, 58; stereotypes on Arab women: passivity 95, 61; subjugation 14, 136, 161, 185; submissiveness 61; submission 7, 68, 90, 96

Arab world 26, 38, 42, 44, 45, 47, 49, 50, 52, 90, 127; Islamic world 110

archetypes: feminine archetypes 56

art 3, 39, 48, 49, 51, 83, 90, 154, 158, 166, 167: arts 38, 43, 45, 48, 49, 81; artistic expression 154, 166, 167; artist 2, 4, 8, 48, 50, 52, 87; creative work 85; museum 39; the Khaleeji Art Museum 39

autoethnography 11, 21–23, 29, 31, 34, 35 *see also* ethnography

Bahrain 4, 7, 8, 141, 173

Bedouin 6, 11, 21, 22, 28, 66; Bedouin culture 21, 23, 30; Bedouin tribe 31; Bedouin women 23, 24, 25, 31, 32, 34, 35

belonging 3, 5, 6, 27, 56, 62, 66, 68, 91, 156, 159, 179; loyalty 6, 100

betrayal 174, 177; marital betrayal 159

Bhabha, Homi 6

blame 77, 127, 165, 180

Bidūn (stateless people) 4

bread 125, 143, 145, 149; breadwinner 80

borders 56–58, 60, 62, 65, 67–69, 180: border control 106; border crossing 15, 59, 64; border thinking 56, 66, 69; Borderlands 6, 59; in-betweenness 3, 28, 56, 65, 68, 69; liminality 4, 6, 31, 57, 60–62, 66, 67

capitalism 1, 160

censorship 76, 78, 79, 82, 84, 90, 168; self-censorship 78, 82, 84, 89

citizenship 5, 7, 8, 14, 109, 116, 175, 185; gendered citizenship 115, 116; citizenship laws 7; 'impossible citizenship' 3; citizens 2, 5, 39, 97, 107, 109, 110, 116, 172, 175, 177; non-citizen women 172; women citizens 107, 108, 175, 187

civil society 8, 97, 114

colonialism as colonial experience 56; coloniality 60; coloniality of gender 56; colonial discourse 60, 64; colonial gaze 5; colonial history 101, 158; colonial languages 156; neo-imperialist gaze 5; postcolonial theory 54, 176; decolonial theory 54, 56

Committee to Protect Journalists 90

191

GULF WOMEN'S LIVES

community 45, 50, 64, 68, 69, 133, 136; patriarchal community 121; community ties 150; communities 55, 58, 146, 174; 'commons' 136; national communities 7; Bedouin communities 21, 24; multigenerational communities 14, 172; ethnosexual communities 62; sense of community 142; community-building 27

conservatism 101; conservative society 186; conservative values 184

corruption 77

creative economy 42

cultural diplomacy 40

culture 4, 8, 14, 15, 31, 32, 35, 38, 39, 43, 45, 48, 49, 53, 55, 64, 67, 68, 78, 83, 86, 90, 120, 134, 136, 137, 139, 155, 162, 174; cultural hybridity 67; cultural norms 15, 58, 90, 115; cultural production 6, 154, 155, 157, 159, 168; cultural taboos 158; cultural translation 156; consumerist culture 186; digital culture 47; male-dominated culture 159; sexist culture 85; Western culture 31 *see also* Bedouin culture

Dabbagh, Selma 14, 172–80, 182–88

death 30, 67, 125: quasi-death 68

diaspora 63, 66, 156, 174; Palestinian diaspora 4, 174; *ghurba* (absence from the homeland); displacement as diaspora 63, 77, 173, 177 *see also* Palestine

disability 11, 21, 23–28, 30–32, 34, 35, 61, 63, 66: disability studies 30; Multiple Sclerosis (MS) 24–26, 32, 34, 54, 61; disabled heroines 30; disabled body/bodies 9, 31, 33, 61; disabled characters 30; disabled women 21, 23–35, 39; disability as othering 61

discrimination 25–28, 84, 85, 89, 91, 98, 108

divorce 6, 13, 89, 114, 116–28; divorce laws; divorced women 13, 125, 127; *khul* (annulment upon compensation) 124;

judicial divorce 117, 124; custody of children 7, 120, 122, 123, 125; "I divorce you" 123; reconciliation 120, 124; separation 118, 124, 125, 127; separated women 125, 127; financial burden of divorce 106, 127, 128

diwaniyya 8

duty 6, 59, 66

education 26, 40, 63, 64, 75, 78, 91, 116, 119, 134, 135, 139, 167; education abroad 81, 140, 141, 166, 176, 181; public education 97; education as emancipation 75, 91

Egypt 78, 81–83, 88, 155; Cairo 162, 163, 166

El-Azhary Sonbol, Amira 6, 7

elites 79, 99

El Sadat, Muhammad Anwar 83

Emirates Writers Union (EWW) 82

Emirati journalists: Abdullah Lootah, Hessa 81, 82; Al Ossaili, Hessa 82; Al Qassimi, Amal Khalid 81; Al Qassimi, Nama 81; Al Sayegh, Habib 90; Al Suwaidi, Thani 77; Al Suwaidi, Ousha bint Khalifa (Bint Al Arab) 81; Ghubash, Hussein 77; Ghubash, Mohamed Obaid 82; Gubash, Rafia Obaid 82; Khamis, Dhabiya 77; Khamis, Mouzah 81, 82; Rabei, Khairiyah 82

Emirati media regulators: Media Regulatory Office 84; Ministry of Culture and Youth 84; Ministry of Information and Culture 84; Ministry of Interior 84; National Media Council 84; Security Media Department 84

Emirati print and broadcast: Abu Dhabi Media Company 78; Abu Dhabi News Centre 87; Dubai Channel 2 82; Abu Dhabi Television Channel One 78; *Akhbar Al Emarat* 88; *Al Azminah Al Arabiya* Magazine 78, 81–83, 90; *Al Bayan* Newspaper 78; *Al Khaleeji* Newspaper 82; *Al Ittihad*

INDEX

Newspaper 78, 81; *Al Roeya* Newspaper 78; *Awraq* Magazine 78, 90; Dubai Media Incorporated 78; Dubai News Centre 78; Emirates News Agency (WAM) 78; Kuwait Television 81, 82; *Zahrat Al Khaleeji* Magazine 78, 81; Abu Dhabi News Centre 78, 87; *The National* 157

English: English language 30, 52, 104, 154–59, 168,

environmental change 135, 136, 150; environmental unsustainability 174

ethnography 3, 10, 21, 23 *see also* autoethnography

fame: fame in the media 87; glamour 87

family 12, 13, 25–27, 29, 30, 34, 54, 58–61, 63, 67, 68, 69, 80, 84, 85, 105–7, 114, 115, 117, 119, 121–29, 135, 137, 144, 145, 147, 149, 159, 161–64, 166, 167, 175–77, 179, 180: extended family 59, 178; as genealogy; family as gatekeeper 58, 92, 116, 126–28; family honour 180; family law 10, 91, 116, 123–25; ruling family 103; personal status law 116, 124, 128

fashion 51, 52, 85; modelling 52

femininity 26, 100, 181; Islamic femininity 100

feminism 75, 76, 106, 161; alternative communities 68, 69; communities of solidarity 15, 57; community of choice 69; Black feminism 4; embodied feminism 21, 28; solidarity; Gulf feminism 3, 10, 106; ecofeminism 136, 138; Gulf feminism 10; positionality 9, 13, 23, 54, 175, 183, 185, 187 *see also* intersectionality; postcolonial feminism 5; sisterhood; state 89; Third World feminism 5, 14, 28, 95, 161; transnational feminism 97; family feminism 105, 107; inclusive feminism 97; white feminism 5, 161; hegemonic feminism 5; state feminism 8, 89; feminist discourse 95,

175; feminist text 161; feminist research 11, 23, 114; feminist movement 80, 92; feminist politics of survival 29; feminist allyship 28; feminist ethics of care 24; feminist politics 10; feminist theory 9; 'world making' as feminist theory 9

Feminist Critical Discourse Analysis (FCDA) 99, 100, 109, 111

feminist media studies 75

film 51; filmmaking 92

fire 65, 142, 145, 149; firewood 142

folkcraft 136

freedom 14, 59, 62, 68, 89, 90, 126, 154, 161, 166, 185, 188; freedom of choice 165, 166

freedom of expression 82, 89 *see also* freedom of speech *see also* freedom of the press

freedom of speech 82 *see also* freedom of expression *see also* freedom of the press

freedom of the press 82 *see also* freedom of speech *see also* freedom of expression

future 1, 2, 33, 64, 68

futurism 1, 2; Gulf futurism 1, 2

Gargash, Maha 59, 154, 157, 159, 162, 167

gender 3, 4, 8, 13, 14, 15, 24, 55, 54, 88, 99, 115, 159, 173, 175, 185, 187; gender biases 91, 116, 124, 126; gender norms 98, 99, 106, 122; gender order 98, 100, 101; gender politics 84, 98, 111; gender roles 86, 91, 105, 126; gendered spaces 183; gendered public spaces 182; gendered social expectations 182; gender as identity marker 54; gender as standpoint 15

gender (in)equality 84, 90, 102, 116; Gender Inequality Index (GII) 75; Global Gender Gap Report 76; gender hierarchies 13, 97, 100

Ghabra, Shafeeq 161, 174

ghutra (traditional Emirati headdress) 88

193

GULF WOMEN'S LIVES

globalization 3, 38, 157: globalization as global economy 66; globalization as Global North 6; globalization as Global South 56; globalization as global cities 173

Grosz, Elizabeth 164

grounded theory 135, 138, 150

guilt 163–65

Gulf Cooperation Council (GCC) 116

Gulf women 3, 5–12, 14, 58, 69, 70, 106, 116, 128, 135, 155, 168, 175, 179 *see also* Women in the Gulf *see also Khaleeji* women

Gulf landscape 15, 62, 177, 186: *aflaj* (oasis) 13, 133–42, 144–47, 149, 150; *falaj* (oases) 3, 133, 136, 141, 142, 147; desert 21, 67, 68; nature 40, 64, 68, 136; oases 13, 133–36, 139, 141, 144, 146, 149–51; oases culture 6; urban landscape 15; palm 77, 143; dates 143, 144, 148

Gulf newsroom 12, 75, 76, 78, 79, 83–85, 87–89

Gulf societies: consumerism 2, 4, 65; cosmopolitanism Gulf societies 186; essentialism 15, 16, 59; exceptionalism 14, 15; foundational myths of Gulf societies 7; materialism in Gulf societies 177, 178; residents in Gulf societies 2, 3, 39, 64, 150, 173; slavery in Gulf societies 3, 59, 60, 63, 64; youth in Gulf societies 2, 53, 136; wealth of Gulf societies 2, 15, 55, 63, 65, 80, 173

Gulf women writers 58, 69, 70, 80, 155, 159

Hamdar, Abir 30

heritage 22, 25, 63, 82, 89; Arab heritage 149, 158; intangible heritage 134, 147

hijab (veil) 44 *see also* veil

home 5, 7, 13, 27, 59, 66, 75, 80, 81, 105, 117, 119, 121, 123, 135, 138, 143–49, 150, 160, 167, 172, 174, 178, 179, 181; homeland 156, 173, 177;

household 67, 125, 127, 141, 145, 150; chores 141, 145

homosexuality 159

human rights 63, 107, 108, 123, 173; human rights violations 8, 15; human rights defenders 7; Human Rights Watch 90, 108

hydrocarbons 1

Jayawardena, Kumari 56

Jordan 78, 178, 110

Joseph, Suad 7, 115

journalism 39, 41, 49, 76–79, 81–83, 89, 90: journalism as method 11; investigative journalism 79, 82, 84; Arab journalism 78; Emirati journalism 77, 81, 83, 89; journalism as watchdog 89; patriotic journalism 89; media writing 39, 77

Kanafani, Ghassan 174

Kandiyoti, Deniz 126

Kareem, Mona 4, 5, 59 *see also* Manifesto Against the Woman

keffiyeh (traditional Arab men's headdress) 88

Khalaf, Amal 4

Khalfan, Bushra 3

Khaleeji: Khaleeji women 6, 58; *Khaleeji* identity 1, 4, 55

kin 7, 120; kinship 60, 92

Kuwait 4, 7, 8, 22, 30, 58, 81, 82, 86, 155–59, 162, 164, 167, 173, 174, 178, 179, 182–87; Hawalli 185; invasion of Kuwait 173, 174, 178, 179, 185; suffrage extension to women 7

identity 11, 22, 25, 27, 30, 52, 59, 60, 61, 67, 76, 84, 89, 91, 103, 106, 133–35, 156, 158; Arab identity 120, 157; naming 55, 57, 59–61; hybridity 3, 4, 57, 66, 67; collective identity 66; diasporic identity 66; ethnic identity 157; *Khaleeji* identity 4, 55; Islamic identity 107; Muslim identity 44 *see also* Palestinian identity

194

INDEX

illness 4, 21, 26, 30–34, 54, 61, 66, 69, 165; chronic illness 116; illness narrative 11, 22, 29, 30, 32–35, 61, 62

imagined community(ies) 2 *see also* nationality *see also* nation

(im)mobilities 3, 14, 59, 159, 160, 162; mobilities 160, 161, 167; mobility studies 155, 160

international organizations; United Nations Entity for Gender Equality and the Empowerment of Women 90; World Health Organization 119

intersectionality 4, 5, 12, 58, 175; class 4, 5, 14, 69, 84, 91, 92, 99, 104, 106, 111, 161, 175–77, 184, 185; race 4, 5, 14, 55, 60, 64, 104, 111, 161; sexuality 14, 15, 58, 172, 175, 179, 181, 182, 184 *see also* feminism

intimidation 119, 162, 165

Iraq 63, 78, 173, 174, 178, 179

Islam 80, 100, 101, 103, 107, 110; Islamic authenticity 100; Islamism 102; Islamic piety 102; Islamic resistance 176; political Islam 101; Islamist groups 101; *fatwa* (edict recognized by religious authorities) 102; moderate Islam 103; religious establishment 100, 102; *masjid* (place of worship) 145; prayer; *hadith* (practice) 145

Israel 21, 83, 173, 177, 180; boycott 177; Israeli occupation (of Palestine) 176

language 14, 22, 29–32, 38, 52, 60, 76, 85, 86, 99, 104, 107, 109, 154–59, 168

Latin America 156

Lebanon 81, 178

life writing 33, 34, 35

literature: Gulf literature, 30, 58, 59, 155, 156, 159; novel 52, 54, 58, 67, 69, 77, 81, 137, 155–58, 162–64, 173, 176, 180; short story; coffee table book 43; book fairs 154; literary prize; Nobel prize 58; International Booker Prize 54; Gulf writers 3, 4, 58, 69,

70; Gulf narratives 35; female protagonists 154, 159, 162, 166, 167, 175, 179, 187

lived experiences 10, 11, 13, 24, 28, 34, 56, 100, 110, 114, 115, 117, 128

locusts 144

loss 15, 22, 23, 28, 29, 31, 34, 59, 77, 88, 147, 150, 176, 178

Lugones, María 56, 68

magazine 11, 12, 38–48, 53, 78, 81, 82, 83, 90: *Vogue* 44; *L'Officiel* 44; GQ 44; *Girl Zone* 41; Iconic Magazines 45; women's magazine 39

Mahdavi, Pardis 3

Mahram (male guardian) 125, 126, 140; Male Guardianship System (MGS) 96, 108

majlis 8

make up or make-up 86, 87

malnutrition 144

Manifesto Against the Woman 5 *see also* Kareem, Mona

marriage 24, 54, 60, 62, 68, 80, 91, 115–18, 121, 122, 124–28, 178, 181, 182, 185; *mahr* 117 (dowry money); wedding 65 87, 144

Marx, Karl 160

media 38, 41, 42, 46–48, 50, 52, 76, 78, 81, 84, 85, 86, 87, 89, 90, 95; media brand 43; media companies 40–42, 46, 47, 49, 51; media outlet 12, 46, 88, 89; media hub 39; media infrastructure 81; media industry 75, 76; media law 82, 83; news anchors 85–89; media corporations 12, 78, 81–83, 85; media studies 10, 75; media surveillance 77

memory 23, 24, 63, 70, 134, 156, 174, 183; memories 23, 62, 63, 67, 77, 133, 134, 138, 139, 178, 183; public memory 70; remembrance 70

mental health 85, 165, 167

mestiza consciousness 56, 66, 68, 69

Middle East 76, 88, 115, 116, 158, 161

GULF WOMEN'S LIVES

migration 3, 4, 10, 14, 160, 172–75, 177, 184; migrant workers 106, 172, 175, 186, 188; expatriates 1; non-citizen(s) 3, 14, 55, 172, 174, 175, 182, 187; *kafila* (sponsorship) 5, 106; impermanence 3; labourers 3, 8, 134, 186; temporariness 3, 173, 174; second-generation migrants 5; migration to the Gulf/Gulf migration 14, 172, 184 *see also* 'impossible citizenship'

Min-ha, Trinh 57

modernity 14, 54, 56, 92, 184, 187; cosmopolitan modernity 96; inauthentic modernity 184; modernization 13, 15, 59, 60–65, 76, 103, 133, 134, 137, 146, 147, 149, 184, 186, 187; petro-modernity 184; secular modernity 96; progress as modernity 104; modern infrastructure 1, 133, 135, 139; electricity as modernity 147, 150; air conditioning as modernity 150

Mohanty, Chandra Talpade 5, 56, 95

Moraga, Cherríe 57, 61, 69

Morrison, Toni 58

Morocco 78

Naga, Noor 3

nakba (catastrophe) 173

naksa (setback) 173

narratives 1–10, 13–15, 22, 23, 29, 31–35, 38, 40, 42, 45, 49, 54, 55, 59, 62, 63, 99, 100, 102, 105, 114, 118, 134, 135, 154, 165, 174, 175, 179, 181, 183, 184, 187, 188; autobiography 23, 33, 54, 61, 69; counter-stories 9; counter-narrative 161; literary production 4, 8, 77, 79, 82, 155, 158, 68; literary works 58, 59, 62, 63, 70, 77, 155, 157, 161, 164, 166; narration 6, 22, 69, 162, 167, 175 *see also* illness narratives; state narratives 12, 13, 97–99, 103, 104, 107, 109–11; official narratives 70

nation 3, 6, 7, 38, 55, 56, 62, 68, 81, 89, 91, 101, 102, 106–8, 110; 'nationness' 6; nation-building 7, 15, 58, 64, 65, 75, 91; nationality 3–5, 104, 111; national identity 96, 157; nationalism 4, 7, 101–3; exclusionary nationalism 100, 107; king as father 107 *see also* Imagined community(ies) 2; national communities 7; patriarchal nation 76; paternalism 107

neopatriarchy 14, 154, 159, 160, 164, 167, 168

Netherlands 45

New Mobilities Paradigm 14, 154, 159 *see also* mobility *see also* mobility studies

norms 4, 24, 58, 64, 75, 106, 115, 122; societal norms 1, 15, 56, 68, 83, 91, 100, 115, 121, 134, 161, 162; double standards 4, 68

nostalgia 81, 156

Obaid, Salha 58

oil 1, 24, 55, 59, 63, 79, 80, 96

Oman 3, 13, 14, 47, 54, 58, 59, 63, 64, 80, 133, 134, 136–41, 145, 149, 150, 158; Sultan Qaboos 140, 143, 146, 149; Sultan Said 134, 139, 140; Omani women 13, 134, 135, 138, 139, 143, 146; Al Hamra 141; Muscat 139; Salalah 139

orientalism 95 *see also* orientalization *see also* Said, Edward

other 5, 11, 57, 59, 61, 89, 137, 154, 156, 162–66, 185: othering 2, 69, 70; otherness 2, 175, 184; discrimination against others 24–27, 84, 85, 89, 91, 98, 108; othering as structural exclusion 6, 101, 174; citizenship as exclusion 8; privilege 6, 26, 69, 161, 187

Pakistan 186

Palestine 78, 173, 174, 176–79, 181, 184; betrayal of the homeland 177; destruction of Palestine 176;

196

INDEX

dispossession 173; displacement 63, 77, 173, 174, 177; Gaza 176, 177, 179, 180, 181, 186; Islamic resistance 176, 179; Palestine Liberation Organization (PLO) 174, 179; Palestinian migration 14; Palestinian identity 174; refugee camps 178; Palestinian diaspora 4, 174

patriarchy 7, 12, 14, 57, 62, 75, 92, 115, 126, 160, 163, 185; paternal patriarchy 126 *see also* neopatriarchy; state patriarchy 116; patriarchal bargain 126

past 1, 2, 10, 33, 34, 58–60, 63, 64, 66–68, 77, 92, 137, 149, 155, 177, 182; past as roots 22, 31, 55, 56, 60, 66, 107, 139

paternalism 107

performance 28, 67, 68, 83; dance as performance 67

petitions 13, 95–100, 104–10; petitioning 6, 12, 97, 98, 111; petitioners 98, 99, 105–11; discursive boundaries in petitions 57, 99, 111; signatories 99

political participation 7; political commitment 178, 181, 182; *see also* petitioning, *see also* activism

political consciousness 176, 178; self-consciousness 181, 183, 184

poverty 143, 150, 151

power 2, 5–7, 12, 23, 29, 39, 40, 56, 59, 60, 62, 67, 84, 87, 97, 99, 100, 118, 121, 124, 126, 137, 160, 163, 165, 184; power dynamics 24, 98, 175; power relations 15, 55, 58, 99

public space 10, 173, 179, 182, 185; public space as public sphere 4, 7, 11–13, 58, 91, 97, 115; gendered public spaces 182, 183

Qatar 4, 7, 10, 13, 38, 114–16, 119, 120, 123, 125, 128, 129; Doha 124

racism: structural racism 64; systemic racism 4; hate 24; hate crime 54, 68

redemption 15, 58, 67, 69

reforms 80, 102, 116: social reforms 103; political reforms 96; gender reforms 96, 102, 108

resistance 4, 7, 10, 57, 59, 62, 64, 69, 86, 90, 97, 115, 126, 182; 'talking back' as resistance 10, 29, 30, 39; 'making space' as resistance 8

Said, Edward 11, 32, 38

salfah (Bedouin oral narrative) 22, 29, 30, 34; oral narratives 10, 13, 22, 29; Bedouin oral narrative 22; oral poetry 29

Saudi Arabia 7, 47, 54, 58, 64, 86, 95–98, 100, 101, 106, 107, 108, 110, 140, 141, 158, 173, 174; Al Saud 100, 101, 103; Vision 2030 96, 100, 103, 108, 109; ban on driving or driving ban 96, 98, 104–7, 109–11; 'Daughters of the Nation' 107; King Fahd 103; King Abdalla 103; King Salman 103, 108; Land of the Two Holy Mosques 110; Mohammed Bin Salman 103, 108; religious clerics 100; religious nationalism 100–2; Riyadh; *Wahhabi* doctrine 102; 'Saudi First' campaign 103; *shura* council 103

sekka (narrow street connecting neighbourhoods) 38

Sekka magazine 11, 12, 38–49, 51, 52; *Sekka* community 42, 44, 48; investors 41, 46; internship 48, 81; retailers 39, 42, 43; revenue streams 46; subscriptions 46

self-publishing 157

sexuality 14, 15, 58, 159, 172, 175, 179, 181, 182, 184

shame 11, 24–26, 35, 61, 62, 76, 142, 145, 149, 164–66

Sharabi, Hisham 92, 154, 159, 160–62

sharaf (honour) 80; honour 24, 76, 80, 180; honour as reputation 76, 88, 102, 103, 182

Sharia (Islamic law) 75, 107, 145

sih (barren lands) 141, 142, 144, 148

silencing 7, 89, 154, 162, 168; self-silencing 165; silence 21, 28, 29, 58, 68, 95, 162–65; silenced bodies 31; muteness 154, 163; voicelessness 5, 162, 163

sleep 27, 68, 144, 164

snowball sampling 138, 139

social change 6, 91, 92, 115, 149, 161

social media 42, 44, 46–48, 51, 88, 98: social media influencers 47; Instagram 45, 48, 88; Twitter 77, 98, 108

Spivak, Gayatri 56, 162, 167

socialization 13, 64, 133–39, 144, 149, 150; female socialization 133, 135, 138, 149, 150; neighbours 101, 140, 142, 144, 147, 149; coffee as socialization 43, 138, 144, 145, 177

society 8, 13, 15, 22, 25–27, 30, 33, 53–57, 60, 61, 64, 66–70, 75, 76, 77, 79, 80, 92, 96, 97, 98, 101, 103–6, 114, 115, 119–21, 124, 126, 128, 133–39, 148, 160, 165–67, 175, 185, 186

solastalgia 135, 146, 147, 150

space 2, 3, 8–15, 26, 28, 31, 32, 49, 52, 57, 58, 59, 61–64, 68, 69, 97, 100, 110, 117, 126, 137, 157, 159–62, 166, 167, 172–76, 178, 179, 181–86; tangible space 14, 101, 134, 160; intangible space 14, 134, 147, 161, 162, 166, 167; fluidity of spaces 160

status quo 7, 13, 90, 139, 159

stereotypes 14, 40, 41, 45, 51, 52, 61, 77, 86, 106

stigma 21, 24, 25, 26, 29, 61–63, 124, 125, 127, 164, 165, 168; stigmatization *see also* taboo

storytelling 11, 13, 15, 29, 34, 59, 69, 70 *see also suwalif*

subjugation 12, 14, 136, 161, 185

sufrah (dining mat) 138, 145

suwalif (oral stories) 11, 22–24, 27–32, 34

Syria 78

taboo 4, 12, 39, 61, 69, 70, 89, 158, 165 *see also* stigma *see also* stigmatization

talent 48, 49, 52, 87, 109

technology 2

temporalities 2, 4, 33; alternative temporalities 1

terrorism 63, 102; radicalization 102

textual analysis 161

theory in the flesh 34, 57, 69, 70

third space 68; third space of disability 26

tradition 3, 4, 7, 25, 33, 54, 57, 59, 60, 62–64, 67, 76, 84, 103, 127, 146, 147, 149, 155, 156, 159, 163, 183, 187; invented traditions 4, 63

trauma 4, 28, 29, 31, 34, 59, 63, 162, 163, 164, 167; psychological trauma 154, 159

tribe 22–26, 29, 31, 54, 62, 80, 84, 91, 106; tribal affiliation 66; tribal patriarchalism 76, 91

Trucial States 80 *see also* United Arab Emirates (UAE)

truth 34, 63, 162

United Arab Emirates (UAE) 47, 58, 75–77, 83, 155: Abu Dhabi 78, 81, 82, 84, 87–89; Dubai 3, 27, 78, 81, 82, 87, 88, 162, 163, 167; *see also* Trucial States

United Kingdom (UK) 39, 45, 47, 151, 158; London 39, 60, 64, 83, 173, 176, 177, 181, 182; Covent Garden 39

United States 44, 47, 63; New York City 45, 102

Unnikrishnan, Deepak 3, 8

urbanization 63, 150, 174, 187; airport 126, 177, 180; beauty salon 176, 181; skyscrapers 173; shopping malls 173, 176, 180, 181

veil 81, 95; veiling 86 *see also hijab*

violence against women 114, 116, 121, 123; rape 60, 165; structural violence 65, 114–16, 120; 122; domestic violence 4, 65, 116, 127; cultural violence 114, 120, 122; physical abuse 119, 120, 122, 123, 154, 165; assault 119; indirect violence 120; continuum of

INDEX

violence 115, 120, 122, 128; intimate partner violence 121, 123; sexual harassment 182; violence against women and children 123

Vora, Neha 3

water 133, 136, 141–43, 145, 146, 150; irrigation 133

Weber, Max 160

wheat 142, 143, 145

women 1–15, 21–30, 31–35, 38–39, 44, 50–52, 54–70, 75–92, 95, 97–100, 102–8, 110, 111, 114–19, 121–29, 133–51, 154, 155, 159, 161, 163, 165–68, 172, 175, 179, 181, 183, 185–87; women as mothers 27–30, 60–67, 80, 101, 106, 119 -27, 135, 137, 138, 141, 143, 163, 165, 166, 172, 176, 181, 182; infantilization of women 60, 101; Third World women 5, 56, 95; women's oppression 4, 6, 25, 56–59, 62, 65, 95, 161, 162; women's subordination; compliance of women; women in the Gulf 2, 11, 12, 14, 15, 32, 172, 186, 187, 188

women's activism 8, 104 *see also* activism *see also* women's agency; Women2Drive campaign 104; 'Ladies of November' 105; 'I Am My Own Guardian' campaign 108; feminist activism 7 *see also* women's movement

women's body; body as border 57, 58, 65–67; containment of the body 57, 58, 67; disabled bodies 9, 31, 33, 35, 56; docility; embodiment 57, 61, 70, 101; feminization 142, 146, 178, 179; healing 11, 27, 30, 31, 69; menstrual blood 39, 180; non conformity 4, 54, 55, 59, 62, 67, 70; obedience 59; objectification of women 95, 175; self-consciousness 181, 183, 184; sexualization 175, 182, 183; social expectations 168, 182; vulnerability 27, 28, 69, 179; womanhood 39, 50, 52, 165, 182; women as reproducers 55; masculine protection 107

women's empowerment 81, 83, 84, 89, 96, 105, 108; liberation as empowerment 80, 167

women's movement 80, 92, 161 *see also* activism *see also* women's activism

women's rights activists 98, 107, 110

women's writing 58; audiences 39, 47, 88, 98, 156, 158

yarning (methodology and space) 137–38

yathoom (demon) 164

youth 2, 53, 136 *see also* Gulf youth

Yuval-Davis, Nira 55

Zanzibar 140

zar exorcism 67